ATLANTIC OCEAN

★ STATESBORO (1)

★ PINEORA (1)

MELDRIM (1) ★
POOLER (1) ★

★ SAVANNAH (5)

BURROUGHS (2) ★

BELFAST (1) ★

★ DARIEN (3)

★ FREDERICA (3)

★ JESUP (1)

★ SATILLA (1)
PENNICK (1) ★
★ BLACKSHEAR (1)

★ WAYCROSS (1)

BRUNS
JEKYLL
TARBORO (1) ★ W
OWENS FERRY (1) ★

2 OTHERS IN C
ST

★ BAXLEY (1)

★ LUMBER CITY (1)

★ MARSHALLVILLE (1)

★ McRAE (1)

★ HAWKINSVILLE (1)

★ MONTEZUMA (1)

★ VIENNA (1)

★ ABBEVILLE (1)

★ AMERICUS (1)

★ CORDELE (1)

★ FITZGERALD (1)

★ OCILLA (1)

★ DOUGLAS (1)

★ ALBANY (2)

★ TIFTON (1)

★ CUTHBERT (1)

★ VALDOSTA (1)

FLORIDA

★ THOMASVILLE (2)

★ QUITMAN (1)

BAINBRIDGE (1)
★

Randolph R. Claiborne Jr.

THE
EPISCOPAL CHURCH
IN GEORGIA
1733-1957

To: Philip F. L'Engle
With best wishes
Henry Thompson Malone

The Rt. Rev. Stephen Elliott, D. D.
Bishop of Georgia 1841-1866

THE
EPISCOPAL CHURCH
IN GEORGIA
1733-1957

❧ · ❧ · ❧ · ❧ · ❧ · ❧ · ❧ · ❧ · ❧ · ❧

HENRY THOMPSON MALONE

Associate Professor of History

GEORGIA STATE COLLEGE

❧ · ❧ · ❧

Published by

THE PROTESTANT EPISCOPAL CHURCH
IN THE DIOCESE OF ATLANTA

Atlanta, Georgia

CONTENTS

• 🕮 •

PART FOUR

THE DIOCESE OF ATLANTA, 1907-1957

ILLUSTRATIONS

· ❦ ·

PREFACE

· ✻ ·

What? Know ye not that . . . ye are not your own? For ye are
bought with a price . . . —I Corinthians 6:19-20

STUDENTS of history may find in these words of St. Paul
an estimate of our debt to the past which is applicable to the
history of the Episcopal Church in Georgia. It is my hope that
readers who trace in these pages the development of the Church
from its settlement in Savannah to the wide expansion of the
present time will obtain some appreciation of the "price" paid
by earlier Churchmen.

In 1957 the Diocese of Atlanta celebrated its Golden Anniversary. As a phase of the observance, the writing of an historical
survey was commissioned to acquaint laymen with the principal
developments in the growth of the Episcopal Church in Georgia.

While the Diocesan committee which arranged for the writing
did not specify as to content and method, other than a proscrip-
tion against footnoting, the writer has chosen to build his story
around key persons. From the individual clergymen of colonial
and post-Revolutionary times through the pioneer Bishops of one
Diocese to the era of Bishops of two Dioceses in Georgia, these
figures have been charged with, and have caused, the important
developments in this history.

The writing is based primarily upon the following sources:
The Colonial Records of Georgia; the Fulham Palace Records of
the Bishop of London pertaining to colonial Georgia (a manuscript collection used by permission of the Library of Congress);
the annual *Journals* and other publications of the Diocese of
Georgia and the Diocese of Atlanta; and individual church histories furnished by many of the parishes and missions throughout

the state. (Exact citations to these and other sources used will be furnished to scholars upon request.)

The writer is also indebted to the following for help as indicated: to Mrs. Doris Kirk Collins, Marietta, Georgia, for the use of her unpublished master's thesis, "The Episcopal Church in Georgia from the Revolutionary War to 1860" (Emory University, 1957); to Mr. Alex M. Hitz, Atlanta, formerly Registrar of the Diocese of Atlanta, for considerable assistance in making church records available, including a large collection of clippings and other memorabilia of the Diocese of Atlanta; to the Wesleyan College Library, Macon, Georgia, for the use of a collection of Bishop Stephen Elliott's correspondence and certain materials pertaining to the Montpelier Institute; to my wife, Mrs. Perrillah A. Malone, for help with research and suggestions for the writing; to Mr. Samuel C. Waller, Augusta, for preparation of the appendix pertaining to the Diocese of Georgia; to the members of the anniversary committee of the Diocese of Atlanta, particularly the Rev. Austin Ford, Mrs. Irwin T. Hyatt, and Mr. Rutherford L. Ellis, for criticisms of the manuscript, preparation of other appendices, compilation of maps and pictures, and assistance with typing, microfilm use, and printing arrangements; and to the Bishops of Georgia and of Atlanta.

The Rt. Rev. Albert Rhett Stuart, Bishop of Georgia, made records of his Diocese available on microfilm and offered pertinent suggestions on Chapters X and XI, particularly for the period within his own memory.

The Rt. Rev. Randolph Royall Claiborne, Jr., Bishop of Atlanta, has been a continual source of inspiration and suggestion to the author, and, throughout an overly long period of this writing, has displayed considerable charity, patience, and understanding.

HENRY THOMPSON MALONE

FOREWORD

• 🌿 •

THE EPISCOPAL CHURCH IN GEORGIA was originally
planned to appear during the celebration of the Golden Anniversary of the Diocese of Atlanta in 1957. For many reasons its publication at that time was not possible. We are happy to present it
now, and I think you will like it.

Our faithful and efficient Golden Anniversary Chairman, Mr.
Rutherford L. Ellis, was most fortunate in being able to persuade
Dr. Henry T. Malone to undertake the task of writing the book.
Dr. Malone has worked arduously and fruitfully, despite many
obstacles. The author's narrative comes to an appropriate conclusion with the Golden Anniversary Festival Service, but the contents of the book have been brought up to date by the addition of
two Appendices written to tell subsequent developments of interest and importance in each Diocese.

This volume testifies to the spiritual vigor of countless souls
who have borne witness to our Faith during the two and one
quarter centuries of the life of the Episcopal Church in the State
of Georgia. It attests the determination of Episcopalians in each
succeeding generation to carry forward the work of our Lord and
His Church. It challenges each one of us to noble achievements as
we build on the foundations laid by our predecessors.

I wish to express my gratitude to the many Church people in
both the Diocese of Atlanta and the Diocese of Georgia who have
helped to make this history possible by furnishing us with records,
information, and pictures. From these sources we have built up a
valuable collection of Memorabilia which is now in the safe-
keeping of the Registrar of the Diocese of Atlanta.

Acknowledgement of assistance has been made by the author
in his Preface but I wish to add my appreciation to Mrs. Irwin T.

Hyatt and the Rev. Austin M. Ford, our Committee on the publication of the book, for their indefatigable efforts.

It is also my privilege and pleasure to express appreciation for myself and the Diocese, and to pay tribute to my secretary, Mrs. Alvin E. Foster, for her unseen part in this complicated and sometimes frustrating undertaking. She has helped a great deal by poring over records and verifying data, with wise counsel in matters of planning and decision, and with much practical help in assembling material for this History.

The Episcopal Church in Georgia is a book which I am sure every family in the two Dioceses will wish to own. I commend it to you.

RANDOLPH ROYALL CLAIBORNE, JR.
Bishop of Atlanta

September, 1960

PART ONE

· ✥ ·

The Anglican Church in Colonial Georgia

CHAPTER

❧ · I · ❧

THE ANGLICAN CHURCH IS PLANTED IN GEORGIA

ON DECEMBER 8, 1957, the Protestant Episcopal Church in the Diocese of Atlanta celebrated its Golden Anniversary. The Bishop of Georgia preached the sermon at the great Festival Service in the Cathedral in Atlanta and the President of the Standing Committee, as the official representative of the Diocese of Georgia, brought greetings. Taking part in this service were twenty-two Bishops from the other Dioceses in the Province of Sewanee. Fifty years earlier, proud of their Church's growth in the state and anxious to continue this expansion by the most practicable means, Georgia Episcopalians had divided the old Diocese of Georgia into two parts, creating the Diocese of Atlanta in northern Georgia.

This event in 1907 was symbolic of the steady growth which the Episcopal Church in Georgia had enjoyed during most of 174 years. A minister of the Church of England stepped ashore with Georgia's first colonists in 1733, and this church has served the people of Georgia ever since. Anglicanism in this country survived the challenge of the American Revolution to become the Protestant Episcopal Church. The Georgia Episcopal structure, very weak after the Revolutionary era, flickered and sputtered but emerged as a small Diocese of three parishes in 1823. Seventeen years later there were six churches, and these half-dozen parishes elected the first Georgia Bishop.

The second great challenge to the Episcopal Church in Georgia came with the events of the 1860's. By that time the Diocese had grown to more than twenty-five parishes, and the number of its members gave them fifth rank amongst Georgia religious groups. The state's Episcopalians had much to do with the organization of a Confederate Church, and the Diocese itself, while ardently supporting the Confederate cause, was able to create at least two more parishes among the state's Episcopalians.

Following these dramatic developments during the first century and a quarter of its existence in Georgia, the Episcopal Church has enjoyed a steady growth in parishes, membership, and community influence. The separation into two Dioceses in 1907 is but symptomatic of this progress. Telling the story of this progress from the 1730's to the 1950's is the purpose of this study.

As surely as the State of Georgia owes its origin to the energy of Dr. Thomas Bray, the Episcopal Church in Georgia also traces its beginnings to this remarkable man. For Dr. Bray's purpose in founding a haven for unfortunates carried with it the desire to colonize the Church of England into this haven. He had already demonstrated an interest in such activity with his own projects in behalf of the colonial Church and in the subscription of funds and books for church libraries. Indeed, the "Associates of Dr. Bray," from whom came the impetus for the founding of Georgia, dated their founding as a group from 1724, when Dr. Bray became the trustee of an estate whose funds were to be used in spreading Christianity among Negro slaves in the various British colonies. The men who joined him, at his invitation, as trustees of the fund were Viscount Percival, Robert Hales, the Reverend Stephen Hales, and William Belitha. Dr. Bray and his "Associates" became well-known in humanitarian and church circles in England for their activities in connection with the missionary field of Christian endeavor.

In 1701 Dr. Thomas Bray had been instrumental in the founding of an organization which played a key role in the transplanting of the Anglican Church to Georgia. This was the Society for the Propagation of the Gospel in Foreign Parts. It is difficult to imagine how the Church could have succeeded in America had it not been for an organization such as this; for while the original purposes of the Society were to supply missionaries for Indian communities and for settlements lacking in formal Protestant worship facilities, by the time Georgia was founded the Society was vigorously interested in supplying and maintaining Anglican clergy in the English colonies.

Another name well associated with the movement which led to the founding of Georgia was that of James Edward Oglethorpe. He also demonstrated an interest in humanitarian activities which put him into contact and cooperation with Dr. Bray. In 1729 Oglethorpe was active in Parliament in a move to change the policy on debtor's prison, and this brought him into the group of "Associates."

It would be over-stating the case to say that Georgia was founded primarily for humanitarian and evangelical purposes. The policy-makers in England foresaw a definite need for such a colony for military and commercial purposes; had not these viewpoints existed, the money to finance a new colony might not have been so readily available. But it is certainly true that the founding of the Anglican Church in Georgia owes much to the humane and Christian purposes of men like Bray and his Associates; for the establishment and maintenance of a church in Georgia would be a *sine qua non* for the success of any humanitarianism or evangelism in the new colony. Oddly enough, the charter which established the Colony of Georgia omitted any mention of the conversion of Indians as a motive for founding the new settlement.

Georgia was legalized as a colony with the issuance of a Charter in 1732. By terms of the Charter, twenty-one Trustees were named to guide the destiny of England's thirteenth American colony. Of the original twenty-one, nearly one-fourth were clergymen, as were many of those who served later. Most of these were probably Anglicans, although this is difficult to prove. Of all the Trustees, James Edward Oglethorpe, James Vernon, and the Earl of Egmont were probably most concerned about the Anglican Church in Georgia.

An early fight developed among the Trustees over the question of whether or not the Anglican Church should be an "Established" religion in Georgia; that is, should the Church of England be supported by the Georgia government. A dissenter named John White led the anti-Establishment movement among the

Trustees; and he was supported by Robert Moore, Robert Hucks, John LaRoche, Alderman George Heathcote, and the Earl of Shaftesbury. In order to understand the background of this controversy, it will be necessary to review briefly the status of the Established Church of England at this particular time. When the Stuart dynasty ended with the death of Queen Anne in 1714 and George of Hanover became king, the position of the "High Church" group was considerably weakened. George's German background favored a liberal church policy, and with this the "Liberal Anglicans" concurred. This development in English ecclesiastical history blocked an early movement on the part of the Society for the Propagation of the Gospel to establish more firmly the Anglican Church in the American Colonies by sending Bishops to America. As far as Georgia is concerned, the ultimate decision by the Trustees was along the lines of those liberal Anglicans known as Latitudinarians, for freedom of worship was granted to all Protestants in Georgia.

In a series of meetings in late 1732 and early 1733, the first Trustees of Georgia made decisions, appointments, and rulings which would largely cast the mold of Georgia church operations during the twenty years of the Trusteeship. For example, glebe lands (church lands) were established for the first Anglican church in Georgia on November 8, 1732. The Common Council of the Trustees ordered Oglethorpe to "set out three hundred Acres of Land in Georgia in America to be appropriated for the Use of the Church of the Town of Savannah, and a Site for the Church, and the Minister's House in the Town and likewise a Burial Place at a proper distance from the town."

On the same day, a minister appeared before the Trustees and "charitably offer'd to go without any allowance, and assist in settling the Colony of Georgia, by performing all Religious and Ecclesiastical Offices." This generous Christian volunteer was Dr. Henry Herbert, son of Lord Herbert of Cherbury. The Trustees lost no time in accepting his offer, and Henry Herbert became, by appointment of the Trustees, the first Anglican minister for the new Colony of Georgia.

In an effort to obtain a donated salary for Dr. Herbert until the Trustees could be in a position to pay it or until the Georgia community could support him, the Trustees passed a motion on November 23 which actually states the role which the Society for the Propagation of the Gospel would carry throughout the Trusteeship. The Trustees ordered "that a Memorial be drawn up to be presented to the Incorporated Society for propagating the Gospel in Foreign Parts, setting forth, that the Trustees have sent forth a Number of his Majesty's Subjects to be settled in Georgia, and appointed a Site for the Church, and a sufficient Glebe for the Minister, and desiring the Society to make the usual Allowance for the Minister in Georgia, as is given to their Missionaries in the other Colonies, till such time as the Glebe shall be sufficiently improved for a Minister; and Desiring the usual Benefaction of Books and Furniture."

Meanwhile Dr. Herbert sailed to America with Oglethorpe and the shipload of Georgia's colonists aboard the *Anne.* He conducted services on board during the voyage. When the travellers landed at Yamacraw Bluff on February 12, 1733, Dr. Herbert led them in a prayer of thanksgiving. He was thus the first English priest in Georgia. He also baptized the first white child born in the colony; and he founded its first parish, Christ Church of Savannah. Dr. Herbert departed for England in 1733 after serving but a few months in Georgia. Sickness during the crossing was fatal; and Dr. Henry Herbert died at sea on June 15, 1733.

Georgia was not long without an Anglican minister. Fortunately, the Trustees had already approved the appointment of the Reverend Samuel Quincy, A.M., as Missionary to Georgia. Quincy was a native of Boston and a graduate of Harvard who came to England seeking Holy Orders. His appointment illustrates the process by which ministers were secured for Georgia, and at the same time the Trustees' approach to this problem. Whereas in other times and other areas the Society for the Propagation of the Gospel had sent clergy to America, the Trustees of Georgia kept rein on those who went, by the process of requiring that those going to Georgia appear before the Trustees for official appointment. Such was the case with Samuel Quincy. Following his ordination in 1730 by the Bishop of London, Quincy worked for a year as assistant to the Reverend Thomas Page of Beccles. When this appointment ended, he applied to the Society for a missionary post, but they responded that they had no vacancy at that time. Next Quincy appeared before the Trustees of Georgia on December 21, 1732, and they named him Missionary to Savannah, presumably to assist Dr. Herbert and to work among the Indians. Then the Trustees called upon the Society to furnish subsistence and salary for the new appointee. After some discussion, the Society responded favorably, naming Quincy as their missionary in Georgia and awarding to him an annual salary of fifty pounds.

Until 1750 this practice was generally followed in finding clergymen to go to Georgia. The Trustees guarded closely their preference for naming their own ministers; yet in each case the Society was called upon for financial assistance.

In the meantime, the Trustees notified Oglethorpe of Quincy's appointment, and that they had "reason to believe, the Society for propagating the Gospel in Foreign Parts will give him as good a Salary as they allow to Any of their Other Missionaries. And as he will be sent over very soon, they recommend to Mr. Oglethorpe the getting what Conveniences he can for the Minister, the laying out a Site for the Church, and making Preparations for building it, and the Minister's house as soon as possible." Because of the continuous insistence by the Society that the colony be made to support the minister as soon as possible, the Trustees seem to have made a genuine effort to bring this about. Oglethorpe was frequently encouraged—as in the above memorandum—to render all possible service to the local minister; especial emphasis was laid on the hope that glebe lands might prove suitable for the minister's support. However, the Society for the Propagation of the Gospel in Foreign Parts proved to be the chief source of ministerial income throughout the Trusteeship and the period as royal colony which followed, although the English Parliament granted some support during the latter era.

Aside from the government's grant of twenty pounds for each clergyman sent to Georgia, the salary given by the Society, and the expected help from glebe land income, the Trustees utilized donations to supplement the church's support in Georgia. The records of Trustees' Meetings show donations of various amounts of money, clothing, books, and other items for the use of the church in the new colony. During the nearly twenty years of the Trusteeship, the cash donations totalled over two thousand pounds. Many ministers throughout England applied for, and quickly received, permission to solicit donations and gifts in their parishes. In addition, leading church officials like the Archbishop of Canterbury, Bishops, Archdeacons, Deans, etc., as well as Cathedral Chapters, Collegiate and Parochial clergy made substantial contributions.

Unhappily, the glebe lands never produced the income for the church which the Trustees had anticipated. It developed that most of the clergymen knew little of agricultural methods and, because of their church duties, could give but little time to supervision. Furthermore, the nature of the land around Savannah made it difficult to find good glebe land for farming purposes. Also, because the original Charter for Georgia forbade the importation of slaves, indentured servants were utilized to work the glebe land; however, most of these also were inexperienced in farming, and often by the time they were well broken-in their indentures had expired. (Indeed, the records reveal that even after slavery was permitted in colonial Georgia only the Savannah glebe was able to support the minister's needs.)

A prime need in Savannah, and one for which financial appeals were almost endless, was for a suitable church building for the Christ Church Parish. When the colonists landed in February, they soon constructed a crude wooden hut "made of split boards, thirty feet long and twelve wide" for worship purposes. This was the church building which Quincy found when he arrived in Georgia in May, 1733. A few years later services were changed to a local townhouse (courthouse) and sometimes other public buildings were used. But Christ Church would not have a church building proper until 1750.

The Reverend Mr. Quincy earnestly desired to erect a suitable church in Savannah, and was encouraged in this purpose by the Trustees and by the donations which they forwarded to him. On December 4, 1734, meeting in Council, the Trustees resolved "that James Oglethorpe Esquire Robert Hucks Esquire and Dr. Bundy be desired to procure an Estimate of the Expences of building a handsome Church for the People of Georgia." A few months earlier, a Mr. John Tuckwell had visited the Trustees and "promised to give a Clock for the first Church at Savannah as his Benefaction." Later, on March 26, 1735, the Trustees recorded the receipt from Tuckwell of a "large Church Clock and Dyal Plate for Savannah . . . and Clock Weights" all valued at twenty-one pounds. Because of such actual and proffered contributions toward a Savannah church, the Trustees ordered on March 20, 1735, "that a Roll be prepared for a Subscription for building a Church in Savannah." Largely through the efforts of Dr. Bray's associates, the Trustees secured a parochial library for Savannah consisting of 437 books and several thousand Bibles, Testaments, and Prayer Books. Other religious reading matter was sent over from time to time.

But despite these and similar contributions for his church, Quincy was unsuccessful in his hope of seeing a church building in Georgia. His principal stumbling block seems to have been the Commercial Agent of the Trustees in Savannah, Thomas Causton. The latter was custodian of the funds received from England. He and Quincy did not get along well, and Causton refused to grant the vicar the necessary money or materials for the building of a Church. Causton was eventually recalled by the Trustees for mismanagement, but not before Quincy left his position as Missionary to Savannah.

While Causton may not have been typical of the Trustees' civil authorities in Georgia, nevertheless it was usually very difficult for the Anglican clergymen to obtain much help from them. The fact was that the Trustees granted very little power to these men, beyond an admonition to support the priests and their religious effort. For example, in October, 1734, the Bailiffs and Recorder received word from London that the Board hoped Georgians would "set a just value on it [the free enjoyment of religion] and be constant in their Attendance on Divine Worship, and duly consider to Whom they are indebted for their Preservation, and from Whom they must expect a Blessing for their Labours." Presumably the Trustees expected this lofty but vaguely specified injunction to guide their agents in supporting religion in the colony.

The most important supporter of religious activity in the early days of the colony, of course, was the principal civil official, James Edward Oglethorpe. But even Oglethorpe could not devote much effort to the cause of the Anglican Church in Georgia. His military and civil duties required too much time. Further, in spite of his membership in the Society for the Propagation of the Gospel and his loyalty to the Church of England, Oglethorpe respected the rights and positions of the various denominations who peopled his colony, and did not attempt to force them into conformity with the English Church.

Mr. Quincy had other difficulties to plague his work at Savannah. During Oglethorpe's first return to England, the surveyor appointed to lay out the glebe lands seems to have surveyed other lands than the area Oglethorpe had had in mind. Of several lots laid out at the time, the poorest one turned out to be the parish glebe, and Quincy refused to make any effort to fence or otherwise utilize it until an adjustment could be made. Furthermore, the Trustees complained to him several times, and with some justice, that they were without knowledge from him of the "State of his Parish," and they desired at least to receive "Duplicates of the Accounts . . . which he is obliged to send to the Society for propagating the Gospel."

Finally Mr. Quincy was removed by the Trustees "for good and sufficient Reasons" in October, 1735. Presumably part of the "good and sufficient Reasons" for revoking Quincy's authority stemmed out of criticism resulting from Quincy's having performed a marriage ceremony for an Englishman and an unbaptized Indian squaw; although this action was later justified after an investigation by Oglethorpe.

One development arising out of Quincy's complaint concerning the glebe lands would profoundly affect the status of the Church in Georgia during the remainder of the Trusteeship. This was the matter of official action pertaining to the glebe, which would have the effect of making the church an "Established" one in Georgia. Further, if the glebe proved sufficiently remunerative, it might make the rector's situation almost impervious to Trustee control. The Trustees argued considerably on this point, with the dissenters and liberal Anglicans generally opposing any designation that the income from the land should be applied to "religious uses." Finally a compromise was reached on March 31, 1736, when the following royal land grant was obtained:

That a Grant be forthwith made under the Seal of the Corporation of three hundred Acres of Land to certain Trustees to be appointed and from time to time to be changed and alter'd as the Common Council . . . shall think fit and proper; And that all such Monies as has been or shall be receiv'd for the Religious Uses of the Colony shall be applied with all convenient speed towards the cultivating and improving the said three hundred Acres; And that the net Proceed arising from the Produce and Profits of the said Lands shall be from time to time applied to the Religious uses of the said Colony in general only, in such manner, as the Common Council . . . shall think fit and proper.

The Trustees' Journal for October 29, 1735 shows that they "Seal'd an Authority to the Revd Mr. John MacLeod to perform Ecclesiastical Offices in Georgia." MacLeod was designated as "Minister to the Scotch Settlement at New Darien" on the Altamaha River. This appointment is an excellent indication of the generous policy which the Trustees maintained in regard to the non-Anglicans in Georgia. This lenient attitude can be explained in part by the presence of a number of dissenters and liberals on the Board. Also, it appears to be a realistic approach in view of the large population of non-Anglicans in Georgia. The colonists included groups of Scotch Presbyterians, French Huguenots, Swiss Calvinists, Lutherans, Moravians, and Jews. Very few Roman Catholics came to early Georgia; as late as 1747, there were only four members of the Roman Church in the colony.

An additional indication of the Trustees' liberality in regard to non-Anglicans in Georgia is seen in the establishment of charity schools similar to such schools in England. These schools were taught usually by schoolmasters who were under the supervision of ministers; sometimes ministers did the teaching, and often the school teachers also gave religious instruction. Essentially the educational purpose was schooling in the Anglican catechism; other simple teaching was given so that the students could more readily understand the Anglican doctrine. However, the school doors were opened to pupils of any faith, and frequently the non-English in Georgia attended so that they could learn the official language of the colony.

So many persons who were objects of humanitarian interest came to Georgia that the Colony's Anglicans were out-numbered. Some, like the Moravians and the Presbyterians, settled in special groups and kept to themselves for the most part. This heterogeneity of religious affiliation broadened the base of the colony of Georgia; but it did little to strengthen the position of the Anglican Church as it tried to gain a foothold in the colony.

As a successor to Mr. Quincy, the Board named one of the most famous priests ever to serve in the American colonies, the Reverend John Wesley. Wesley's name is a familiar one in the annals of the new religious movement which came to be known as Methodism. However, during the term of his service in Georgia, he was still considered as an Anglican clergyman.

John Wesley sailed from England in December, 1735. With him was his brother Charles, who was enroute to become Secretary to General Oglethorpe. An associate of the Wesleys who accompanied them to Georgia was the Reverend Benjamin Ingham, who was "full of missionary zeal for the conversion of the Indians." John Wesley seems to have been well-received in Georgia, according to his own writings. At services in the Courthouse the congregations were numerous; on one occasion when a dance was scheduled to begin at the same hour as public prayer, Wesley wrote that "the Church was full while the ball-room was so empty that the entertainment could not go forward." He found seven hundred communicants in Christ Church; and he remarked that Savannah was "pleasant beyond expectation."

As rector of Christ Church, John Wesley displayed a passion for strict interpretation of the liturgy that often ran him into conflict with some of the more liberal Anglicans in Georgia. His program for Sundays illustrates this tendency: 5 A.M., Morning Prayer; 11 A.M., Litany, Communion, and sermon; 3 P.M., Evening Prayer. He accepted no excuses for absence from worship. No dissenters could receive communion unless they had been re-baptized. Infants were baptized by total immersion. Once, in a fit of emotion, he lifted his arms out and cried to the congregation, "My poor friends, you are the scum of the earth!" Yet Wesley himself later recorded that in his extra-curricular work at Savannah lay some of the germs of Methodism. The first stage of this movement, he wrote, "was in 1729, when four of us met together in Oxford. The second was at Savannah in 1736, when twenty or thirty persons met at my house." He also remarked that the last stage occurred in London in May, 1738, "when forty or fifty of us agreed to meet together every Wednesday evening." Wesley seemed to enjoy working with other religious groups in Georgia. He frequently preached in their languages to Germans, French, and Italians; and he began a study of Spanish "in order," to quote his words, "to converse with my Jewish parishioners."

One of the most lasting contributions of John Wesley to Anglicanism in Georgia was the Christ Church Sunday School which he established. Apparently the first such religious training unit ever founded, Wesley was justly proud of this work. It was his custom to meet with the Anglican children of his parish each Sunday afternoon to hear them "recite the Catechism, question them as to what they had heard from the pulpit in the morning, instruct them still further in the Bible, endeavoring to fix the truth in their understandings as well as their memories."

The critics of John Wesley found a richer fruit for critical devouring when his affair with Sophie Hopkey occurred. He fell in love with her but apparently could not make up his mind to ask her to marry him. Soon she moved to South Carolina and while there she married William Williamson. Then she returned to Savannah to live. In 1737 Sophie Williamson failed to tell Wesley that she intended to receive Communion despite the fact that she was guilty of a minor offense. Evidently in a display of regrettably human emotions, Wesley publicly denounced and excommunicated her. In turn, he was charged with slander by her husband and faced trial on a further charge of illegal actions. This was the signal for his opponents to see that additional charges, some of them ridiculous, were lodged against him. Wesley sent a statement to Mrs. Williamson explaining why he had taken steps against her: "So many as intend to be partakers of the Holy Communion, shall signify their names to the Curate, at least, some time the day before. This you did not do.

"And if any of these . . . have done any wrong to his neighbour by word or deed, so that the congregation be thereby offended, the Curate shall advertise him, that in any wise he presume not to come to the Lord's Table, until he hath openly declared himself to have truly repented." Wesley was found guilty on some of the counts, but managed late in 1737 to slip away to England, arriving there in January, 1738.

Perhaps the judgment of the Reverend William B. Stevens, writing in the next century his history of the Episcopal Church in colonial Georgia, gives an apt, if a bit charitable, summary of John Wesley's Georgia ministry: "As to John Wesley's earnestness, honesty, and self-sacrificing zeal as a Minister, there can be no doubt; but he lacked judgment and prudence. He knew not then how to combine flexibility with firmness, and to mingle the sweet sympathies of his heart with the discipline needed for such a flock."

In the meantime another Anglican parish had been formed in the Georgia colony. This was at Frederica, on St. Simon's Island. The Trustees granted three hundred acres there for support of a minister and a schoolmaster "and other religious uses." Charles Wesley went to Frederica with Oglethorpe and served as the founding minister of what became known as Christ Church, St. Simon's. He also served as Chaplain for Oglethorpe's army. On February 15, 1736, Oglethorpe laid the first foundation of what would become the settlement-fort of Frederica. At that time Anglican religious activity began in the community when Chaplain Wesley conducted an Evening Prayer service.

Unfortunately both Wesleys seemed destined for difficulties in Georgia. Charles' troubles stemmed out of arguments with Oglethorpe. The parishioners at Frederica, mostly soldier members, seemed to echo Oglethorpe's opinions about Wesley. "I could not be more trampled upon," Charles Wesley wrote of this period, "were I a fallen Minister of State. My few well wishers are afraid to speak to me; the servant that used to wash my linen sent it back unwashed." Wesley finally determined to return to England; before he did so, however, he and Oglethorpe had a reconciliation.

As for Charles' brother, on April 26, 1738, the Journal of the Trustees notes that "the Revd. Mr. John Wesley attended and left the Appointment of him by the Trustees to perform Ecclesiastical offices in Georgia." Obligingly, the Board then accepted his resignation and thus officially terminated John Wesley's authority as missionary in Georgia.

Two weeks later the Trustees named a successor to John Wesley. Here again they sent a man destined for religious fame as a leader of Methodism; further, this clergyman would become known especially in America as a champion of the "Great Awakening," a revivalist movement which would sweep the Atlantic seaboard colonies. The new minister was George Whitefield. The Trustees' Journal of December 21, 1737, noted that Whitefield was licensed to do ecclesiastical work in Georgia as a "Deacon of the Church of England." Later, on May 10, 1738, Whitefield was named to minister to the parishes at both Savannah and Frederica until successors to the Wesleys could be chosen.

Whitefield landed in Savannah on May 7, 1738. A former student at Oxford, he was then but twenty-two years old, and had been in the Diaconate for about two years. This youth must have been regarded with some skepticism by the majority of his communicants, but any doubt as to his ability to preach was quickly dispelled when they heard his first sermon. George Whitefield was a powerful and eloquent speaker, as many Americans outside of Georgia would discover in the next few years.

He seems to have been a somewhat restless and energetic pastor. Not long after arrival, he wrote: "We have an excellent Christian School, and near a hundred constantly attend at evening prayers. The people receive me gladly as yet, and seem to be most kindly affected toward me. . . . I visit from house to house, catechize, read prayers twice and expound the two lessons every day; read to a housefull of people three times a week; expound the two lessons at five in the morning; read prayers and preach twice and expound the catechism to servants, &c., at seven in the evening, every Sunday."

Whitefield quickly launched a project which appeared to him as needing immediate attention: that of providing an orphanage at Savannah. Deciding that he could best raise the money in England, and also determined to be advanced to the Priesthood, Whitefield returned to England late in 1738. On the 12th of June, 1739, he was ordained Priest. Meanwhile he had been busy soliciting aid for the proposed orphanage and apparently his eloquence was in good form, for he secured a grant of five hundred acres and contributions totalling more than five hundred pounds.

Back in Georgia by January of 1740, he saw the cornerstone for his beloved orphanage laid on March 25 of that year. He named the institution Bethesda, meaning "house of mercy," and when it began operations forty children were housed there. Whitefield's orphanage was situated near the Isle of Hope, about ten miles from Savannah. The five hundred acres soon had several imposing buildings, so that Bethesda could make an important contribution to both humanitarian and educational purposes.

Whitefield's two main interests kept him busier than many of his parishioners liked. The orphanage was time-consuming; and Whitefield enjoyed travelling about preaching to large audiences. Realizing something of his problems, and desiring also to have a resident minister in Georgia, the Trustees dispatched a clergyman named William Norris whom they had already approved to go to Georgia as a missionary. Norris preached his first sermon in Georgia on October 22, 1738.

The Secretary of the Colony of Georgia was William Stephens, a man of strong opinions frequently expressed in his Journal. In an entry dated October 30, 1738, he gives an interesting comparison of Whitefield and Norris as preachers:

Mr. Whitefield being a Man of peculiar Eloquence in the Pulpit, had captivated his Hearers very much; and withal after reading the second Lesson, was wont generally to expound on the whole Chapter *extempore,* with great Volubility; to make room for which, he laid aside the Use of the first Lesson, and the Psalms, which undoubtedly carry in them the Highest Spirit of Devotion: On the contrary, Mr. Norris did not assume Confidence enough, in that Manner off-hand, to be an Expositor of whole Chapters at a Time in the Bible; but contented himself with going through the Whole Office appointed for Prayer, Mornings & Evenings constantly with great Decency, and was punctual in catechising the Children, baptizing of Infants, visiting the Sick . . . .

As Stephens saw it, Norris deserved to be treated with respect and attention. The implication was, of course, that Whitefield did not. Apparently William Stephens had "High Church" inclinations. Besides, there is evidence that he and Whitefield did not get along very well in non-doctrinal matters.

This animosity deepened in connection with the matter of building a church in Savannah, long eagerly awaited by parish-

ioners and ministers alike. The Town House (Court House) was
still being used for services when Whitefield arrived, and he became impatient for a real church structure. Whitefield therefore
wrote to the Trustees asking that they appropriate what money
they had on hand for church building so that the project could
get underway. Whitefield could not get the support of Oglethorpe or Stephens at this particular time, however, nor could
he persuade any other colonial official in Georgia to take decisive
action. During this period of frustration, he wrote, "I shall wait
a little longer to see what amendments will be made in the
Affairs of Religion. If there's no alteration for the better and the
Church be not built, I shall think it my duty to inform the pious
people in a publick manner, how little good has been done with
their Charitable Contributions." Apparently the threatening tone
of these remarks did not please the Trustees, for they still refused to appropriate church-building money to Whitefield.

Finally by 1740 definite action toward the building of a church
for Savannah was underway. Oglethorpe appropriated £150 to
Whitefield for this purpose, and so notified the Trustees. In his
message Oglethorpe included information that he "had agreed
for building a Church or Chappel of 60 foot long, and 20 foot
wide. It was already framed, the bricks burnt, & they would very
soon go on with the building." Then the Trustees gave another
£150 for the church, but sent the money to a committee consisting of William Stephens, Henry Parker, and Thomas Jones,
any two of whom were authorized to make decisions about spending of this money. Whitefield was told by the Trustees not to
expend more than the total of £300 which represented the two
payments.

Now the building for Christ Church seemed assured. Whitefield began the building with enthusiasm, but also with rather
grandiose plans. Before the end of the year, however, the work
was abandoned, and only a pile of building materials was left to
indicate where a church was supposed to be. Then followed some
rather acrimonious correspondence between Whitefield and the
Trustees over what had happened to the £150 which they had
sent him. Eventually legal procedures were instituted to force
an accounting of this money. Meanwhile, what of Savannah's

church building? Nothing more was done for several years, and it would not be until 1750 that the parishioners of Christ Church could realize their ambitions in this respect.

Part of Whitefield's duties lay at Frederica, where he succeeded the Wesleys in responsibility for that community's Christ Church Parish. When Charles Wesley returned to England, John's jurisdiction was extended to include Frederica. The records indicate that John visited Frederica often to minister to the congregation and conduct services. However, there seems to be no indication that Whitefield went to Frederica.

Shortly after Whitefield's orphanage was launched, he began a series of trips in-and-out of Savannah which largely characterized the remainder of his activities in America. He visited in the other colonies north of Georgia, and he made preaching journeys to England as well. Altogether Whitefield left and returned to Georgia ten times, the last visit to Savannah being in 1770. His primary purpose was in preaching, but the beloved Bethesda remained a lifelong interest. William W. Manross, a leading historian of the Episcopal Church in America, sums up Whitefield in this manner: "This brilliant and earnest, but somewhat undisciplined personality . . . set the colonies in ferment [with his preaching], every province being in some measure affected." Whitefield usually found the Anglican ministers opposed to him, often because of orders from England; but he preached on in spite of this. Generally the converts he made went to other churches, while some of those who were distressed at the emotionalism engendered by Whitefield's eloquence became Anglican converts.

During the period of Whitefield's early ministry in Georgia the Trustees were engaged in a controversy with the Bishop of London on jurisdictional questions which would help shape the course of the Anglican Church in Georgia. In 1728 the Right Reverend Edmund Gibson, Bishop of London, had been granted by the monarch full jurisdiction over certain of the ecclesiastical affairs of the Church of England. These included "inquiry into the morals and conduct of all the priests and deacons in the orders of the Church of England, and the correction and punishment of any offenses by suspension, excommunication or the like." The broad powers thus included affairs of the Church of England in the British Colonies in America, who never had a Bishop or diocese of their own. Bishop Gibson had his hands full supervising church business in England and the colonial Church suffered accordingly. However the Bishop insisted on the right to appoint and remove the colonial ministers; and this point brought conflict with the Trustees of Georgia.

Lord Egmont reported some of this difficulty in his Journal July 5, 1738:

. . . The Bishop [of London] is very angry with the Trustees, for not yielding that those we send to Georgia to preach should take a lycence from him and threatens to try his right with us at law.

We always opposed his Lordship lycensing our Ministers, because in that case we should not be able to remove a bad one without expense & loss of time, unless his Lordship consented thereto, which the least prejudice or misinformation concerning such person might possibly prevail on his Lordship to refuse: And we think it better for the Souls of our people that a good man should by our mistake be removed . . . than that a bad one should be continued by the Bishop.

Egmont reported that the Trustees considered the Bishop's right to control the Church of England in Georgia invalid since his authority to do so for America was issued before Georgia was established. In their view, the logical Diocesan for Georgia was the Archbishop of Canterbury. Eventually, by 1745, relations between Trustees and the Bishop of London became amicable and cooperative—but it is interesting to note that throughout the Trusteeship the Board clung to its right to issue licenses to the clergy assigned to Georgia, although would-be ministers who wanted to serve in Georgia were usually sent to the Bishop for ordination.

During George Whitefield's early absences from Savannah, William Norris served as Rector of Christ Church. When Whitefield returned, Norris shifted to Frederica, where a small chapel now served as the church. Apparently Norris was not happy in Georgia. He had disputes with Whitefield in Savannah who accused him of preaching false doctrine, and with Oglethorpe in Frederica. In the latter instance, Oglethorpe replaced Norris with one of his own army chaplains. Finally, late in 1740, Norris returned to England and resigned. He reported to the Trustees that during his stay in Georgia he had had 142 baptisms, including 71 soldiers.

On June 6, 1740, the Trustees appointed the Reverend William Metcalfe to go to Georgia to assist Whitefield, but Metcalfe died before leaving England. Another appointment a year later (July 25, 1741) named Christopher Orton to preach in Georgia as soon as he could be ordained. There seems to be very little record of Orton's work in Georgia, other than that he arrived late in 1741 and died in Savannah in 1742. When the Trustees learned of Orton's death, they resolved to utilize the services of a Mr. Mariton who had applied, provided he were "found acceptable." Evidently Mr. Mariton was not acceptable, for there is no record of his being sent to Georgia. Instead, on July 4, 1743, the Trustees authorized the appointment of the Reverend Thomas Bosomworth for "religious work in Georgia." He landed in Savannah on December 21, 1743.

Thomas Bosomworth is one of the colorful characters in early Georgia history, but hardly one who brought credit on the ministry. He had first come to Georgia in the 1730's as an "adventurer." Securing Oglethorpe's confidence, he had been named "Agent of Indian Affairs." While agent he came into contact with a mixed-breed woman of the Uchee Tribe, Mary Musgrove. Originally named Consaponakeso, the Indian girl was educated by her father in Charleston. She married trader John Musgrove of Georgia and acquired the name by which she was first known to the early colonists of Georgia. After Musgrove died she married again, this time to Captain Jacob Matthews. With an eye to the future, Mary and Jacob attempted in vain to secure a land grant from the Trustees. In 1742 Jacob died.

Meanwhile Bosomworth had gone back to England to seek Holy Orders. When he returned to Georgia as the Reverend Thomas Bosomworth in 1743, he again sought out the company of Mary "Musgrove," by now widowed a second time. Thomas and Mary were married on July 8, 1744. There may not have been much objection to this marriage in the colony, for Mary was generally well-liked as a person and for her contributions in maintaining good relations with the Indians; and she had already had two white husbands. In a letter to the Society for the Propagation of the Gospel, dated September 3, 1745, Bosomworth gave this explanation for marrying Mary: "the better to enable me to carry on the great work of promoting Christian knowledge among the natives of America." If this reason were true at the time of the marriage, it soon disappeared in a series of adventures rather peculiar to the function of "promoting Christian knowledge" among any persons. To the surprise of the Trustees and the Society, Bosomworth turned up in England in 1745. On October 12 he notified the Trustees of his presence in England without giving any indication of an intention to return to Georgia. The Board thereupon took steps to locate another minister for Anglicans in the colony. Back in Georgia again the following year, Bosomworth seemed to have abandoned completely any clerical function; for he and Mary launched a bitter and violent campaign to assert their rights to three islands and a large land grant near Savannah, claiming that these rightfully belonged to Mary for her good services to Georgia in its early years. These petitions were buttressed by threats of calling in Mary's Indian relatives and friends, and the colony was thrust into a state of considerable tension. The President and Assistants of the Colony resolved to keep a "Watchfull Eye" on the proceedings; and their journals of the late 1740's and early 1750's show frequent awareness of parties of Indians engaging in such threatening tactics as "Fireing their Guns" on the river "in menacing and insulting Manner."

After nearly a decade of this remarkable conduct, the Bosomworths apologized to the colony for the disturbances! They were then given a grant of over two thousand pounds and St. Catherine's Island, on which they had been living for some time. Here they quietly lived out the rest of their days. The difficulties caused by the Reverend and Mrs. Thomas Bosomworth have been termed by a leading Georgia historian, "the most persistent and longest drawn out of the troubles that beset colonial Georgia."

During the brief periods in which he aided the cause of Anglican Christianity in Georgia, Bosomworth served mostly at Frederica. He wrote of the situation there that more than a thousand people needed Christian help, and remarked, "the people had been too long as sheep without a shepherd, and driven to and fro with every wind of doctrine," and he was using his best efforts

"to lay a foundation of the true faith by catechising the children."
On March 28, 1744, Bosomworth performed a special service in
Savannah which must have been extremely pleasing to the parishioners—the foundations of the long-awaited church building
were consecrated.

One reason why there seemed to be definite progress on
Savannah's church at long last was the greater efficiency of the
colonial government. In 1743 the Trustees had instituted a sensible step in Georgia's local government by creating a President
of the Colony and naming the local magistrates as a form of
council called the Assistants. William Stephens was appointed
the first President of Georgia by the Trustees, who told him "to
take Care that God Almighty be Devoutly and duly honoured
and served in the Province according to the Rites of the Church
of England." He and the Assistants were further charged to call
down any minister or school teacher who set poor example and
to report any repeated infractions to the Trustees. Other ecclesiastical duties were to see that good glebe land was properly surveyed, cleared, and planted; to supervise the vicarage; and to
get the church building completed.

The Bethesda Orphanage was thriving at this time. The Rev.
Mr. Whitefield dropped in on the colony every now and then
with fresh donations for the school; and met with continuous ac-
cusations from his opponents. Some accused him of operating a
school for dissenters. Bosomworth said that the school showed
evidences of "popery" and "Jesuitical methods." But Whitefield
brushed aside these criticisms with the claim that his intention
"was to build up Souls for God, . . . But that they may be able
to give a Reason of the Hope that is in them, I constantly instruct them out of the Church of England's Articles, which I
turn into catechical questions."

Actually Whitefield conducted the school with a strict regimen.
From the rising time of five o'clock until bed-time, the children
were kept busy with a variety of activities. There were religious
services every morning before breakfast; the morning's routine
called for two hours of work at learning a trade, such as weaving,
tailoring, carpentry, etc. In the two hours before lunch several
schoolmasters and school-mistresses gave them schooling which

was primarily religious in nature. After the noon meal there were chores to be done, for Whitefield gave them no time "for Idleness or Play, which are Satan's darling Hours to tempt Children to all Manner of Wickedness, as Lying, Cursing, Swearing, Uncleanness, &c. So that tho' we are about seventy in Family, yet we hear no more Noise than if it was a private House." But presumably the children must have regarded these two hours of chores as their recreation, for they spent the time from two to four again in the schoolrooms, and from four to six in their work apprenticeships. After supper the entire evening before bedtime was devoted to worship services.

The least controversial and the most successful of Georgia's Anglican ministers was the native Swiss whom the Trustees named to replace Bosomworth. This was the Reverend Bartholomew Zouberbuhler, a former resident of South Carolina Colony who had been ordained by the Bishop of London. Prior to his ordination, Zouberbuhler served the Swiss Protestants at Purysburg, South Carolina, where his father had been assigned as minister. On November 1, 1745, the Trustees voted to approve Mr. Zouberbuhler's appointment as minister in Savannah.

Lacking the emotional eloquence of Whitefield and the worldliness of Bosomworth, Bartholomew Zouberbuhler soon captured the warm support and admiration of the Savannah parishioners. On one occasion a siege of illness prompted him to write the Trustees asking permission to return to England. This was granted, and the Society for the Propagation of the Gospel named the Rev. William Duncanson to succeed him. The members of Christ Church in Savannah objected strenuously. In the first place, they had heard some gossip about Duncanson which made him appear quite undesirable to them. But also they wanted to keep their Mr. Zouberbuhler, even though he was in ill health. So the Trustees did not send Duncanson; and Zouberbuhler stayed on in Savannah for the rest of his life.

After the difficulties of the early colonial period and problems caused by worldly clergymen, the Anglican Church in Georgia was now to enjoy a period of steady progress. Bartholomew Zouberbuhler would provide the impetus for this development during the next two decades.

CHAPTER

✳ · II · ✳

THE GEORGIA CHURCH BEFORE
THE REVOLUTION

THE MOST notable development in Christ Church Parish in the late 1740's was the renewal of efforts to complete the church building. The foundations which had been laid in 1744 and consecrated by the Rev. Mr. Bosomworth were about as far as the building had progressed, owing to the slowness of income for construction purposes. But the President and Assistants kept hammering at the Trustees about it. President Stephens wrote in 1746 that "the roof of it is covered with shingles, but as to the sides and ends of it, it remains a skeleton." In 1747 enough money was received so that Zouberbuhler felt the structure seemed finally destined for successful completion. The Trustees ordered the President and Assistants "that whatever Plank may be necessary for compleating the Church at Savannah . . . be purchas'd of the Saltzburghers at Ebenezer; And that the Outside of the Church be with the utmost dispatch feather boarded, then tarr'd and Sanded; And that the Inside Walls be boarded and painted."

The Rev. Mr. Zouberbuhler proved to be very acceptable throughout his ministry. He used broken English with a strong German accent; but his gentle manner, sincerity, and hard work endeared him to parishioners. He reported to the Trustees in 1748 that in Savannah there were 388 Dissenters and 63 Anglicans. During his period of service the membership rose considerably. That the Trustees heartily approved of his work is evidenced by the somewhat negative fact that they made no effort to remove him (except the instance of his own request which was refused by his parishioners), and by the more positive fact that they supplemented by fifty pounds his annual allowances from the Society for the Propagation of the Gospel, they granted large land acreages to him and his two brothers, they ordered the President and Assistants to put two good servants to work on Zouberbuhler's glebe lands, and on July 4, 1749, they appropriated one hundred pounds for the rebuilding of the Savannah vicarage.

Perhaps the best evidence of Zouberbuhler's success in dealing with the Trustees and the people of Savannah is shown by the fact that the long-awaited church building for Christ Church Parish was finally completed in 1750. On July 7 of that year Zouberbuhler dedicated the building as a church. A letter from him to the Trustees dated December 20, 1750, describes this event: "The 7th of last July was spent in dedicating our New Church to God's solomn worship & the offices of religion; in praising & adoring the most High God. . . . The Church is large & when finished will be both beautiful & commodious, I wish I could say as lasting. My Parishioners are constant in their attendance & I have the pleasure to see many Negroes decently join our Service. . . ."

As the above excerpt suggests, the letter discusses the state of Zouberbuhler's parish. Further, it reflects his methods and his operations as minister. Feeling that many of the inhabitants of Georgia were in "deplorable Circumstances" regarding spiritual affairs, Zouberbuhler "visited as many adjacent Towns & Villages as my Constitution & the Cure of my Parish would admit." He sought to instruct "in the saving Truths of the Gospel & endeavoured to bring them to a Sense of true Religion." He reported that his visits were kindly received, and that he had had numerous invitations to return and to visit other places as well. Concerning the need for more ministers in Georgia (he was the only Anglican clergyman there), he remarked, "The Harvest would truly be great, if there was more labourers." He indicated his intention to push Christian educational projects, and observed that "Our (Sunday) School in Savannah at present consists of 41 Children, & might encrease to many more, if Masters of Slaves would shew a greater concern to have their young Negroes instructed & brought up in the knowledge & fear of God.—In expectation of which, as well as for the greater Benefit & Improvement of the white I have desired the Society to send me a Quantity of Bibles Testaments, Psalters, Primars Lord Bishop of Man's Essay toward an Instruction of the Indians & some other useful & Pious Tracts. . . ."

After Georgia became a Royal Colony (1752), it was necessary for the minister of Christ Church to petition to the Governor and Council of the colony on certain church matters. One such petition in 1755 reflected Zouberbuhler's continuing interest in education. He asked that they set aside a "Publick Lott" in Savannah for a "Publick School." The Governor and Council resolved "that the Publick Lott (known by Letter R) containing Sixty feet in front and one hundred and eighty feet in Depth in Reynolds Ward, be appropriated for a Publick School."

Zouberbuhler became concerned about the status of the church building which he had helped to bring into reality. On April 28, 1755, he appeared before the Council and complained of the "Ruinous condition" of the Church, asserting that it needed immediate attention. He asked them to launch a drive for subscriptions to rebuild the structure. The Council resolved to have three carpenters examine the building and report back on its needs.

Meanwhile a new parish had been created, the third one in colonial Georgia in addition to Savannah and Frederica. This was St. Paul's in Augusta, a frontier town on the upper Savannah. On July 26, 1749, James Fraser of Augusta presented a petition to the President and Assistants stating that he and other inhabitants of Augusta "had subscribed and gathered a considerable Sum of Money, for the Building of a Church there; that they intended to Build the same adjoining to the Fort, but as many Inconveniences might arise from such a Situation, they now desire that the same be built on some part of the Common belonging to the Town." The Augusta petition was acceded to, the Board granting them authority to use land in the Town Common "not exceeding two Acres, to Build the said Church and for the Burial Place of the Dead."

On April 12, 1750, George Cadogan, John Ral, James Fraser, James Campbell, and David Douglass of Augusta petitioned the

Trustees as follows: "The principal Inhabitants at a General Meeting here, having taken into consideration the Number of Settlers, and the daily Increase of them, together with the many Traders and Servants by them employed in the Indian Countries round us (who twice a year reside two months each Time in this Place) the Necessity of a Place of Divine Worship was too evident not to be taken notice of by them, more especially as those People for many Years had quite been Strangers to the Church Service. . . ." The letter explained that for this and other reasons, they were at work building a church, of which they thought that there was none "so far advanced in the Indian Country as this, and as soon finished." They requested a minister, whom they intended to put "on a good footing," and asked for land grants and furnishings for the church.

On May 24, 1751, the Common Council of the Trustees resolved "that a proper Conveyance be made of the Ground upon Which the Church is built at Augusta, and of the Church Yard to belong thereto, and that three hundred Acres of Land be granted in order to be cultivated for the Support of a Minister there." They further agreed that "some Glass be sent over for the Windows of the said Church, as also a Pulpit Cloth and Furniture for the Communion Table under the Care of the Missionary."

On August 8, 1750, the Augusta Anglicans had petitioned the Trustees to send a minister. The Board passed the request on to the Society for the Propagation of the Gospel. Concerned about the financing and real need for such a missionary, the Society withheld approval for a time. Then in 1751 the men of Augusta notified the Society that they would subsidize the minister's salary by twenty pounds a year. With this in mind, the Society then appointed the Reverend Jonathan Copp as Missionary to Augusta. Copp, a native of Connecticut, was a Yale graduate who had taught school and then studied for the ministry. He was ordained in 1750 in England.

Jonathan Copp arrived in Augusta to establish what was then the Church of England's fartherest penetration into the Old Southeast. He found the church situation far less promising than it had been pictured in the various communications which had been sent to England. No glebe or vicarage yet existed; and the promised twenty pounds annual salary had dwindled considerably. The strongest support for his church came from seven merchant tradesmen who seemed pitiably few to the new missionary. But Copp continued on in Augusta until 1756, at which time he left Georgia for Colleton, South Carolina. He died there in 1761.

One phase of religious effort in which Zouberbuhler showed considerable interest was the Christian instruction of Negro slaves. Although slavery had been banned in colonial Georgia under the original Charter, the Trustees had been under ever increasing pressure to permit this type of labor. Finally in 1749, three years before the Trusteeship ended, the Board authorized slavery in Georgia. Included in the instructions of authorization were certain conditions which should exist for the benefit of the Negroes. For example, masters were to see that their slaves attended religious instruction every Sunday and no work could be required of slaves on that day. When slaves married, they were to have Christian ceremonies; responsibility for this was placed on the ministers, who were also to attempt to prevent or reduce profanity among the Negroes.

Bartholomew Zouberbuhler was anxious to rear young Negroes "in the knowledge and fear of God." He found response to this interest among the Trustees, especially James Vernon, a member of the Bray Associates. With Vernon's support, the Associates pushed the idea; and Vernon also appealed to the Society for the Propagation of the Gospel and to the Archbishop of Canterbury. The first real result of this activity appeared in the assignment of Joseph Ottolenghe to Georgia. The Trustees wanted to utilize his knowledge of the raising and processing of silk, the production of which in the colony of Georgia was one of their pet projects almost throughout the Trusteeship. Also, however, he was told to instruct Georgia Negroes in Christianity.

Ottolenghe arrived in Georgia in July, 1751. Zouberbuhler cooperated with his new helper in Christian education by arranging services for the Negroes that would not conflict with regular worship. The slaves were to meet three times a week, on Sunday, Tuesday, and Thursday evenings. Each meeting began with a prayer. This was followed by a Scripture reading so "that they may be able in Time to come to comfort themselves in reading the Book of God." Exercises in the catechism, and recitations of the Lord's Prayer and the Creed followed. Then Ottolenghe talked to them, telling Bible stories in a simple form. This method seemed to prove successful, or so Ottolenghe reported to the Trustees and to the Society.

Despite the associations with the English Government which the Anglican Church enjoyed at home, the Church of England in Georgia had never become the colony's "Established Church." Dissenting opinion among the Trustees had prevented this, as well as the realization on the part of Georgia's leaders that Anglicans in Georgia were a distinct minority, and further that immigration to the colony might suffer if the Anglican Church became official. However, the question of financial support for the Church of England's operations in Georgia frequently came up for discussion. Generally, the ministers were paid by the Society for the Propagation of the Gospel; and this long-range procedure sometimes increased the difficulties. Also, there was some desire for Church Establishment among Georgia Anglicans; some wanted the colony to support the church directly; and some wanted the act of Establishment to include dividing the colony into parishes for local governmental reasons.

Whatever were the reasons, the issue came to a head in the 1750's. In 1755 and again in 1757 bills were introduced in the Georgia Commons, first to create the parishes, and second to Establish the Church. In each case, the Royal Council used its veto to block such legislation. However, in February, 1758, both houses passed the following measure: "An Act for constituting and dividing the several Districts and Divisions of this Province into Parishes, and for establishing of Religious Worship therein according to the Rites and Ceremonies of the Church of England; and also for impowering the Church Wardens and Vestrymen of the Respective Parishes to assess Rates for the Repair of Churches, the Relief of the Poor, and other Parochial Services."

Although the contents of this act did not specifically state that the Church of England would be *the* church in Georgia, it was nevertheless legislation which was highly significant for the future history of the Church in Georgia. For the next two decades, the operation of this act would strengthen the position of the Anglican Church in the colony. When the Revolution occurred, however, the Church, which in all likelihood would have suffered considerably anyhow, was in an even more vulnerable position because of the act of 1758.

Eight parishes were created by the act, covering the then settled areas of the small colony. The area around Savannah was, of course, named Christ Church Parish; the land lying next to Christ Church Parish to the north along the Savannah River "as far as the Beaver Dam" was named St. Matthew's Parish; northward from St. Matthew's along the Savannah to the Augusta District was St. George's Parish; and the Augusta parish area was named St. Paul's. To the west and south, three parallel parishes stretched from the line of the first three down to the Altamaha River: St. Philip's, St. John's, and St. Andrew's. The eighth parish, St. James's, consisted of Frederica town and district, including St. Simon's Island.

The next important section of this measure "incorporated" the Rev. Mr. Zouberbuhler and future Savannah ministers as rectors of Christ Church Parish, and provided similar legal status for the seven other parish rectors whenever they should be appointed. Zouberbuhler was named "the Rector and Incumbent of the said Church of Christ Church, and he is hereby incorporated and made one Body Politic and Corporate, by the Name of the Rector of Christ Church . . . and shall be and he is hereby enabled to Sue and be sued by such Name, in all Courts within this Province, and shall have the Cure of Souls within the said Parish, and shall be in the Actual Possession of the said Church, with its Cemetery and Appurtenances, and shall hold and enjoy the same to him and his Successors, together with the Glebe Land, already granted to him . . ."

The Parish of St. Paul in Augusta was specifically provided for as in the manner of Christ Church above, except that no minister was named. For the remaining parishes, the statute included enabling legislation for churches to be built and ministers appointed for each. Churchwardens and vestrymen were to be elected in each parish on every Easter Monday by "the Inhabitants of the said several Parishes respectively, being Free Holders within the same, or Householders, and of Ability to contribute to the Public Taxes and Charges thereof. . . ." It will be noted that nothing was said about these voters being Anglican communicants. ". . . Not less than five, nor more than Ten . . . sober and discreet Persons," were to be elected vestrymen in each parish, and, at the same election, two other "discreet" free-holders would be chosen as Churchwardens.

Vestrymen and wardens were authorized to tax their parishes to the amount of thirty pounds where churches existed and ten where there were no churches, for these expenses: church repairs, "providing Bread and Wine for the Holy Eucharist, the payment of Salaries of the Clerk and Sexton, and the making provision for impotent Poor Persons." It was clearly stipulated that each rector was to be a member of his parish vestry. Further, church wardens were told to provide a parish Registry Book in which, upon notice by the "Masters or Heads of the Several families," would be recorded births, christenings, marriages, and deaths.

A final provision in the law clearly stipulated the roles which clergymen were to occupy in the new order: "no Rector or Minister, is or shall hereby be invested with any Power or Authority to exercise any Ecclesiastical law or Jurisdiction whatsoever." Apparently the Royal Legislature was seeking to establish vehicles for local governmental operations; certainly in the implementation of this system the principal colonial power remained that of the Governor and Council in Savannah.

In 1765, the territories of Georgia having been extended down the coast from the Altamaha to the St. Mary's, the Royal Legislature created four new parishes, stretching roughly parallel to the river lines. These were St. David's, St. Patrick's, St. Thomas', and St. Mary's. Thus twelve parishes existed by 1765, and they remained the local administrative units until the American Revolution.

But Georgia was still basically a frontier province. Only at Savannah was there a semblance of urbanization. Up the Savannah River to Augusta lay the only other organized church, St. Paul's; and here the congregation was having its difficulties. When Jonathan Copp accepted a call to South Carolina in 1756 he left St. Paul's without a rector. This condition lasted for five years.

In November, 1762, the Reverend William Duncanson appeared in Augusta and applied for the rectorship. Feeling that they had obtained "a valuable man and a good Minister," the vestry accepted Duncanson. But it took no more than six weeks to show that he was far from being "valuable" or "good." Duncanson proved that the rumors which had led the vestry of Christ Church to refuse him many years earlier were well founded. He was anything but reverent in his conduct, displaying profanity, intemperance, and a violence of manner and temper. In 1762 he was relieved of his appointment and again Augusta was without a rector.

At length the Society for the Propagation of the Gospel sent the Reverend Samuel Frink. When he arrived in 1764, however, he found that a clergyman named William Teale had been serving the parish for a few months on a trial basis. So now, after being without any minister for some time, Augusta found itself with two! However, Teale had made himself somewhat unpopular by attempting to undermine Frink's interests before he could arrive from England. Despite the fact that the vestry of St. Paul's released him, Teale remained in town for some time, trying unsuccessfully to depose Frink by stirring up opinion against him. With some justification, Samuel Frink was disturbed by conditions in his parish when he arrived. Not only did he have the Teale situation to deal with, but the general religious situation in Augusta depressed him. He noted that "the lower sort of people in Augusta have but little religion, and public worship is kept up principally by a few gentlemen and their families."

When Bartholomew Zouberbuhler died in 1766, Frink was named as his successor at Christ Church in Savannah. Thus Frink seems to have earned an excellent reputation as a minister in Augusta and had improved the religious situation there somewhat. When he resigned in 1767 to go to Savannah, he reported that about one-third of the population seemed to be religiously inclined—which, if not an extremely hopeful prospect, still constituted some improvement on the situation at the time of his arrival.

Frink was succeeded at St. Paul's by another devoted clergyman, one who has been termed "the most distinguished of the Georgia

Missionaries [of the colonial period]." He was the Reverend Edward Ellington. He too found the religious situation critical in the Augusta area. On the 30th of June, 1768, he described the conditions of St. Paul's and his efforts to bring Christian enlightenment to the area:

Round about my dwelling there is a famine—not a famine of bread nor a thirst for water, but of hearing the word of the Lord; for I may, with the Father of the Faithful, lift up my eyes and look from the place where I am northward and southward, eastward and westward, and there is not one place of worship of any denomination within a hundred miles either way. Therefore, as God has enabled me, I have endeavored in some way to remedy this inconvenience. I have been thrice at St. George's Parish, in this province. I generally set out of a Monday, travel between twenty or thirty miles that day, perform Divine Service on Tuesday, Wednesday, and Thursday at three different places about ten miles wide of one another, and return home on Friday.

Despite Augusta's plight, Ellington accepted an appointment in 1770 as President of the Bethesda Orphanage in Savannah.

During the era from 1745 to 1766 Christ Church Parish at Frederica was served by Bartholomew Zouberbuhler, who seems to have expended the same energies when visiting that parish as he demonstrated in his regular duties in Savannah. After 1766 the church work at Frederica dwindled steadily. Records do not indicate whether a vicar was assigned to that community; the next known Anglican minister there was a Reverend Dr. Best, assigned to Frederica about 1800. Yet it seems difficult to believe that Anglican activity disappeared entirely in this parish. In the first place, the garrison of troops was not removed until 1767, and some sort of chaplain must have been available for the soldiers. Also, Christ Church of Savannah was not too far away; it seems reasonably certain that at least occasional visits must have been made to St. Simon's by the Savannah ministers.

Meanwhile steps had been taken to create two new churches in Georgia. The first of these was Sunbury, in St. John's Parish. Here the principal impetus came from John Alexander, a Dissenting Minister. Becoming interested in the possibilities of the establishment of an Anglican church there, and being himself interested in that faith, Alexander went to England in 1765 and sought Holy Orders at the hands of the Bishop of London. After Ordination, he was named Anglican Missionary to Sunbury where he had high hopes of carrying out his objective. When he returned to Sunbury in August, 1766, however, he found that sickness had caused much emigration. Then, very shortly, more of the population departed, this time to take up residence in East Florida. Only a handful of Anglicans remained, considerably outnumbered by other religious groups. Apparently Alexander's good resolves left him in the face of these misfortunes, for after a few months he was reproved for poor conduct by the Society for the Propagation of the Gospel. About 1770 he abruptly left Sunbury for South Carolina, leaving St. John's Parish without a rector. In 1771 a minister named Timothy Lowton visited Sunbury on his way to East Florida. He liked Sunbury, and apparently this was reciprocated, for the vestry of St. John's asked him to stay and become their rector. He was described as "a gentleman well calculated for that meridian, sober and sedate, yet with a facetious and winning deportment, a man of candour and a good preacher." Obviously influenced by such characteristics, Governor James Wright appointed him minister to both St. John's and St. Philip's Parishes.

The second activity leading to the establishment of a new church was in St. George's Parish, where both Mr. Frink and Mr. Ellington had labored from their headquarters at St. Paul's. The parish was organized shortly after Mr. Frink preached there in 1767; but it was rather weak, and it needed a resident priest. In anticipation of obtaining a minister, the parishioners made plans to build a small church and a vicarage, and applied to the Society in England for aid in paying a vicar. They had someone in mind, an Alexander Findlay, who had been in Georgia for three years and who desired Holy Orders. Governor James Wright wrote to the Bishop of London on July 2, 1770, praising Findlay: "In justice to him I Cannot Avoid declaring that he has Acted as a Schoolmaster in this Town for about 2 years & 3 Months last past, during Which time I believe he has done great Justice to the youth that have been Under his care, And has always behaved in a very Worthy Proper Manner. . . ." The Bishop of London ordained Findlay, who returned to Georgia and began work at St. George's in May, 1771. But he was dissatisfied with conditions there, and soon accepted a call to South Carolina. Findlay's uncle, the Reverend Alexander Keith, of St. Stephen's Parish, South Carolina, wrote to the Bishop of London on May 31, 1771: "Mr. Findlay arrived safe in Georgia this Spring, & his parsonage house not being erected, nor his Church finished, he came to this Province, & will no doubt be chosen to succeed me as Rector of this Parish, being on the point of leaving . . . and going to a healthier Climate. . . ."

For two years, St. George's was without a minister. Then, in December, 1773, the Reverend John Holmes arrived, but found a disturbing lack of interest—as he described it, "Not above sixty have yet attended Divine Service at any one time." Soon he too left, to go into retirement. During the Revolutionary era, St. George's did not have another minister until 1780 when the Reverend James Brown became rector. But he soon went to Savannah for temporary work, and from there became a chaplain in the British army.

Meanwhile, in the colony's pioneer parish of Christ Church, Bartholomew Zouberbuhler was nearing the end of a long service. In the last year of his life, 1766, the Colonial Assembly appropriated three hundred pounds for improvements to the church building, including repairs and enlargements. The first church organ in Georgia was presented to Christ Church by Col. Barnard of Augusta. There had been some talk of building a new church, but the projected cost of three thousand pounds seemed far beyond what could be raised.

Bartholomew Zouberbuhler died in 1766. He left an interesting will, one which reflects his strong interest in missionary work among Negro slaves. 1237 acres of land, forty-three Negro slaves, and all of the income from his estate were left to a group of trustees to be used in employing a qualified person to teach Anglican Christianity to Negroes. The teacher was to live on the estate, and "there do Teach and instruct the negroes thereon and thereunto belonging and cause them to Attend and join in Morning and Evening devotions and all other Christian duties and divine Services. . . ." Children born to his slaves were to be baptized and "taught to read and be instructed in the Saving truths of the Gospel. . . ." Should any of the Negro males show an interest in converting other slaves, the trustees were empowered, if convinced of the sincerity of such would-be teachers, to manumit and employ them for that purpose. If the income from his estate were sufficient, Zouberbuhler desired that "the said Trustees do bestow a Competent recompence on a second Catechist or School-master at Savannah who shall be obliged to teach and instruct all other Negroes or so many as the said Trustees . . . shall direct. . . ."

These trustees, Francis Harris, James Read, John Smyth, Joseph Clay, and N. W. Jones, hired Cornelius Winter as the catechist and teacher for Zouberbuhler's slaves. After about a year, feeling that they had "full proof of his Abilitys and Fidelity in duly discharging his Duty," they recommended him to the Bishop of London for Holy Orders, "by which, he will be enabled fully to comply with the Intention of the Testators Will." They also asked the Rev. Mr. Frink, Zouberbuhler's successor, to endorse Winter. On December 7, 1770, Frink wrote such an endorsement to the Bishop of London.

Not much is known of Samuel Frink's service as Zouberbuhler's successor. He bitterly opposed George Whitefield, whose last visit to Savannah was in 1770. Indeed, Frink's letters about White-field are vitriolic and vituperative. Frink died on October 4, 1771. His church wardens wrote to the Society in England that he was "much lamented by the inhabitants, which appeared in the countenances of great numbers of people who attended his funeral, which was so great that the Church was not sufficient to contain them."

Frink's successor at Christ Church was the Rev. Timothy Lowton, who had been pastor at St. John's, Sunbury. In Savannah his period of service was from December, 1771, to 1774, when he was succeeded by the Rev. Haddon Smith.

George Whitefield died in 1773. The most memorable of his activities in Georgia was probably the Bethesda Orphanage. His will placed the orphanage and its management into the hands of the Countess of Huntington and James Habersham; the latter was then President of the Royal Council in Georgia. Although the Countess handed the reins of actual management over to Habersham, she proposed an interesting plan to add to Bethesda's function that of a missionary college, "to furnish Missionaries to carry the Gospel not only into the Provinces, but also into the back settlements and among the heathen tribes." She found success in promoting this idea in England; and in Savannah Habersham was able to put the plan into effect for a time. Ellington had moved to South Carolina by this time, and the new President of Bethesda, the Reverend William Piercy, named seven young men as the first of the missionary students, who were "solemnly set apart for their Mission."

General reaction in Savannah to this program was favorable; and in November, 1772, seven mission students began the new phase of Bethesda's work. But disaster struck this promising activity barely six months later. On May 30, 1773, during a severe storm, lightning hit the central building at Bethesda and it burned to the ground. Partially salvaged were the two wings, which had been recently added. But the financial loss was considerable, and, more important to the future of Bethesda, the morale of its directors was lowered. Disheartened, the Countess of Huntington took less interest in the school. In the meantime, Bethesda passed into the hands of the new state government. In December, 1791, thirteen trustees were named to govern the affairs of the orphanage-school, under the leadership of George Houston.

When the Reverend Mr. Ellington left Augusta to become President of Bethesda, he was succeeded at St. Paul's by the Reverend James Seymour. In 1771, Seymour had gone to England for ordination. He returned as a priest in 1772, assigned to Augusta. He remained there almost throughout the Revolution. When the patriots captured this frontier post in 1780, Seymour fled to Savannah, where he found it necessary to support his family by teaching school.

By the 1770's, the Anglican Church in Georgia had grown to respectable proportions. Undoubtedly much of the credit for this progress belongs to Bartholomew Zouberbuhler. His hard work and deep sincerity stabilized Christ Church in Savannah, which in turn brought similar influences to the other Anglican churches in the colony. But ahead lay difficult times.

CHAPTER
✤ · III · ✤

THE AMERICAN CHURCH BECOMES
INDEPENDENT

WITH THE approach of the American Revolution the Anglican Church was in a precarious situation. Long associated with the English government, it became one of the symbols of the enemy to patriots. Most Anglican ministers resisted the revolutionaries stoutly, preferring to suffer denunciation as "Tories" or "Loyalists" and sometimes physical and often economic torments. Typical of this pattern are the experiences of the Rev. Haddon Smith of Savannah's Christ Church.

Governor James Wright officially installed Mr. Smith as rector of Christ Church in 1774. At this particular time, agitation was underway which eventually produced a revolutionary movement in the American colonies, and echoes of this emotion were heard and felt in the small Georgia colony. Articles and letters appeared in the *Georgia Gazette* supporting opposition to the crown, or arguing an intellectual position against England. Ardently loyal, Haddon Smith could not stand by idly in this crisis. Using the *nom-de-plume* of "Mercurius," Smith sent several articles to the *Georgia Gazette* which were published in 1774 and 1775. On July 10, 1775, after armed resistance to English authority had occurred in the North, Smith preached a strong loyalist sermon which aroused much opposition and anti-Anglican prejudice among the patriots. Governor Wright had ordered a day in July to be a day of "fasting, humiliation, and prayer, for a speedy and happy reconciliation between Great Britain and her colonies"; and it was this occasion which Smith was honoring. However, the Provincial Congress proclaimed July 20 as a day of fasting and humiliation in the name of the revolutionary movement. Smith recorded that on July 17 "one Stephen Biddulph came . . . and delivered . . . a written Paper from some Persons assembled in this Town under the name of a Provincial Congress." The paper was a notice of a resolution passed unanimously by the Congress asking Smith "to preach a Sermon on Thursday next suitable to the present unhappy differences subsisting between Great Britain and the Colonies." The note further explained that the Continental Congress had requested that all the colonies have such a religious observance to further the revolutionary cause.

Smith's reply was firm:

> In answer to your request beg leave to remind you that his Excellency the Governor has appointed Wednesday next for a Day of fasting, humiliation, and prayer to Almighty God on account of the unhappy differences at present subsisting between these Colonies and the Parent State, when I purpose to discharge the duties of my Profession in obedience to that Authority. Nothing hurts me more than being under the disagreeable Necessity of refusing any Thing that is politely requested of me; but, as a Clergyman of the Church of England, I think myself bound in Conscience not to do any Thing of a public Nature without the express Authority of my lawful Superior. I sincerely and ardently wish a reconciliation between us & our Parent-State, and shall sincerely & heartily pray for it; but must beg that you will excuse one in not complying with your request upon the present occasion.

The Provincial Congress was insistent. On the same day, Biddulph returned with another message. This one asserted that since Smith lived in one of the colonies associated in the Continental Congress, it was proper that he accede to their request and observe the fasting day which was specified. They concluded with this thinly veiled threat: "We therefore must inform you that we think it neither will be decent or safe for you to stand in opposition to the People of this Country and the united Voice of America." Disregarding the threat, Smith replied, "I am sorry that the Reasons I gave you in Answer to your first Message seem not to be approved of. I think them decent & proper, and chuse to abide by them, as they are my real sentiments."

Such forthright expression and subsequent demonstration of his "real sentiments" cost Smith his cure. He did not conduct a special fasting and prayer service for the patriots. Therefore, on the morning of July 22, he was visited by a committee from the Provincial Congress. He came down to the front door of the rectory and there saw "Peter Tarling of St. John's Parish, Jonathan Cochran of St. Andrew's Parish Planters; Edward Telfair of Savannah, Merchant; George Walton of Savannah Esqr., and Oliver Bowen of Savannah Merchant & some others." Smith reported that Tarling held up a document and read from it as follows: "Sir. From your late Conduct in Disobeying the Orders of the Congress, you are deemed an Enemy to America; and by order of the Committee we are to inform you, that you are to be suffered no longer to officiate in this Town." Smith then stated that the group turned and left without giving him an opportunity to "reply or ask for the Paper. Since which this Deponent hath not thought himself safe in doing his duty as Rector."

On the following day (July 23), the Sexton of Smith's church, John Neidlinger, was ordered by Biddulph to report to the home of a patriot where he was told by the Committee "that he should not ring the Bell of the Church without their Orders, or abide by the Consequences." Further, Neidlinger stated that when he was about to report this to Smith, the committee informed him that he was "not to deliver the Key of the Church door without their orders to any Person whatever, and they would support him." Because of these events, Neidlinger "was afraid to ring the Church Bell." Later the committee sent a carpenter named Philip Allman into the Church to fasten the back door, to which Smith had a key. After this Neidlinger locked up the front door and took the key home and did not send it to Smith. When the rector went to the church that day, he found himself locked out.

Within twenty-four hours, Haddon Smith, the "Enemy to America," as the committee had termed him and the *Georgia Gazette* had echoed, was threatened with bodily harm. During a mob action in Savannah on the 24th of July, a sailor named John Hopkins was picked up by a crowd, tarred and feathered, and then carried around in a cart. According to his description of this experience, he overheard some of them say, "if they could lay hold of the Parson they would put him along side of this Deponent in the Cart." They told Hopkins that "Mr. Smith should be next; and they intended to continue on until they had tarred and feathered all the Tories."

Evicted from the parsonage, Smith hastened to flee Savannah so as to avoid the mob. He took his family to Tybee Island; and after a week, managed to catch a ship bound for Liverpool. In this atmosphere, Smith was fortunate to escape physical injury. Yet he had suffered. He and his family had lost most of their personal belongings and had felt personal humiliation. The coursing events had uprooted them from their home in Savannah and had sent them to begin a new life far away with few resources save Smith's training and abilities.

The experiences of Haddon Smith in Savannah in 1775 well illustrate the plight of the Anglican Church in America during the Revolution. Most clergymen were denounced, reviled, and exiled, some suffering physical harm in the process. Left without ministers, most congregations themselves conducted services depending on the tenor of the patriot opinion.

In Savannah Christ Church for a time, save for its physical appearance, lost its Anglican character. Governor James Wright reported to the Royal Council on August 15, 1775, that "a Layman has been appointed to preach in Christ-Church, by the Committee of Christ Church Parish, of which I apprehend some of the Members, are Persons professing the Jewish Religion and others, Members of the meeting of the Independents of Savannah."

Shortly after, James Wright was removed from the office of Royal Governor by the patriots and sent back to England. Christ Church was closed. It did not again have Anglican services until the British recaptured Savannah in 1779. Wright was then reestablished as Royal Governor; and on December 4, the Reverend Edward Jenkins was installed as rector of Christ Church. Jenkins conducted services, with the occasional assistance of the Reverend James Brown and Smith's curate, the Reverend John

Stewart, until July, 1782. During this month the British were again driven out of Savannah, and Christ Church again was closed by patriot action.

During the agitated and often disheartening times between the beginning of the Revolution and the adoption of the United States Constitution in 1789, the Anglican Church came to the end of its particular and somewhat peculiar existence in the thirteen colonies. Yet Anglicanism, as such, did not die—despite the considerable challenges which it faced. In the same year in which the new government was organized under the American Constitution, the Protestant Episcopal Church of the United States of America was organized. Thus its spirit and basic doctrines survived revolution and political crisis; and Anglicanism, shorn of its political associations, became firmly rooted. Anglicanism now flourishes as the Protestant Episcopal Church in the United States of America. (Once every ten years, on the invitation of the Archbishop of Canterbury, the Bishops of the Episcopal Church meet in the Lambeth Conference with the Bishops of the Church of England and the Bishops of the several other national churches which constitute the Anglican Communion. At this Lambeth Conference common principles and opportunities of the Anglican Communion are discussed.)

The Declaration of Independence severed the Anglican Church from its normal governmental process. It was true that during the colonial period there had never been an American Bishop. The Anglican Church had been under the supervision of the Bishop of London; and many affairs had been directed by the Society for the Propagation of the Gospel in Foreign Parts. Yet despite this rather tenuous governmental system, the Church did exist in America; and a regular source for new ministers was available. When the Revolution brought an end to this arrangement, Anglicans in America faced a harsh crisis. The Society rather justifiably withdrew its support, and most of the clergy returned to England. Those who remained were either patriot or loyalist. The latter closed the doors of their churches rather than conduct services which omitted prayers for the English monarch; while the patriot clergy, while omitting these prayers and making other adjustments necessitated by the times, faced many local difficulties because of the old associations which their Church had with the English crown.

The individual parishes, too, faced difficulties. Their members were divided by differing beliefs. Some remained strongly aristocratic and "high church." Some favored tolerance as opposed to rebellion, while others were fervently patriotic. Naturally these ideas colored their views on the American Revolution and political developments. Usually the patriot crowd could engender much public antagonism against their more conservative fellow parishioners; and such developments heightened the crisis of Anglicans.

By 1780 the Church of England in America was gravely weakened. Local factionalism, dwindling clergy, the continuing success of the Revolution, the loss of a source of new ordinations— all were phases of the problem. Church government tended to become parochial, and most parishes were unable to cope with the situation. Many of the patriot members left, preferring no church or new faiths to "an enemy church." As the patriot cause improved, a number of Loyalist members left as well, leaving, in most parishes, mere handfuls of parishioners.

The State of Georgia adopted a new constitution on February 5, 1777. One of its provisions did away with the parish system of local government. The counties of Wilkes, Richmond, Burke, Effingham, Chatham, Liberty, Glynn, and Camden replaced the previous eight parishes. This action further hurt the Church of England in Georgia; for while the church of each parish had never become fully "Established" in the normal sense of that term, yet there had been obvious benefits to the Church's operation.

One logical answer to some of the trouble besetting Anglicans involved renaming their Church and creating an American organization. The first movement to bring it into being in America came in Maryland. This development was largely the work of Dr. William Smith, a minister who moved to Maryland in 1779. He brought together leading Anglican clergy and laity of that state in a convention in 1780, which adopted the name of "Protestant Episcopal Church." This was apparently the first use of this term for the Anglican faith in America. But more positive action was delayed until the Revolution was concluded.

In 1783 Maryland called another convention, this time sustaining greater success. The Protestant Episcopal Church of Maryland did several important things, including the appointment of six men to serve as readers until a regular method of ordaining clergymen could be obtained. They even attempted to make Dr. William Smith a Bishop by sending him to Europe for that purpose. However, too much overseas opposition was encountered, and he was never consecrated.

Meanwhile in other parts of the United States attempts were being made to establish a general American organization of the new church. Despite the objection that none but a Bishop could govern a group of Episcopal churches, a general feeling grew that the most logical step would be to set up a pattern of organization similar to the new American government under the Articles of Confederation. Each parish would send representatives to a General Assembly of the church. Arguments for, and a description of, this plan were published by the Reverend William White of Philadelphia in a pamphlet which was widely circulated and discussed among American Episcopalians.

White's proposal for a federal organization gained momentum in the 1780's, especially among the Middle Atlantic States. In the South there had been a greater tradition of "high church" tendencies, or the churches themselves were too weak to take positive steps in this direction. The New England churches largely supported the proposal most often associated with the Reverend Samuel Seabury of Connecticut. The "ecclesiastical plan," as his system was termed, urged that Bishops were necessary to control churches, to preside over conventions of churches, and so that native American clergymen could be consecrated in America. Seabury spent several years in England seeking consecration as a Bishop; eventually he had to obtain his Episcopal orders in 1784 from Scottish Bishops who apparently were quite willing to thwart the objections of the English prelates.

The result of William White's labors for a federal organization was a meeting in New York on October 6 and 7, 1784. Present were clergy and laity from Massachusetts, Rhode Island, Connecticut, New York, New Jersey, Pennsylvania, Maryland, Delaware, and Virginia. This group resolved to draw up a general constitution for the united Episcopal churches in America, and agreed to meet again the following year. The next meeting occurred on September 27, 1785, attended by Maryland, Pennsylvania, New York, New Jersey, Virginia, and South Carolina. The New England delegations were absent "because of their loyalty to Bishop Seabury." Georgia and North Carolina were still too feeble to organize their state groups, and sent no delegates to either of these conventions.

Despite the lack of a Bishop to preside over their discussions, the Convention proceeded to the work of organizing a national church. The problems were serious, and threatened to disrupt the entire movement. The most basic issue was that of whether they could proceed without a Bishop or whether they should call in Bishop Seabury and establish a system under a strong episcopate. The convention decided to petition the English church for the consecration of three American Bishops and at the same time to repudiate Bishop Seabury's consecration. Some members of the convention withdrew when this was adopted. Other dissension arose over the question of the proposed American Prayer Book, which contained serious liturgical changes.

Meanwhile the English Bishops responded favorably to the request for consecration of the American Bishops, but stated that they must be satisfied with the liturgy adopted in America. This presented fresh difficulties, for the English churchmen soon found that the proposed Prayer Book was not to their liking. Hoping, however, that the consecrations might occur anyhow, the American convention nominated three clergymen to be elevated to the Episcopate: Samuel Provoost of New York, William White of Pennsylvania, and David Griffith of Virginia. Provoost and White left for England late in 1786; but Griffith could not get away for three years, and he died in 1789 without having been to England.

The two who went to England were consecrated in 1788. However, three Bishops were necessary in order to consecrate an American Bishop in America. Consequently the two conflicting groups in the American church sought to find unity so that Bishops White and Provoost could work harmoniously with Bishop Seabury. Also, die-hards in both camps tried to establish their own separate organizations, while sensible leaders looked for any means to avoid schism. Thus, until 1789, the Episcopal church in America continued in a spirit of conflict and confusion.

In 1789 the new Constitution of the United States of America was ratified and a new government established. Interestingly enough, it was also in 1789 that the Episcopal Church found its union in a new ecclesiastical organization which has lasted equally long. Nearly all the states sent delegates to a general convention in Philadelphia which met from July 28 to August 8 and again from September 30 to October 16. Georgia still was not able to furnish a delegation. The principal obstacle to union was removed when the convention agreed to accept Bishop Samuel Seabury. Further, a constitution was drawn up which would permit Connecticut to have a state convention without lay delegates according to their preference. This constitution and the canons represented compromise views all along the line. The official date of the union was October 2, 1789, from which time dates "The Protestant Episcopal Church of the United States of America."

A new Prayer Book and an approved liturgy were also adopted by this important convention. Essentially there were no serious changes in theology or worship. Nonetheless, the English Prayer Book of 1662 was rewritten. The first point of alteration pertained to, as is pointed out in the Preface to the Episcopal Prayer Book now in use, "these alterations in the Liturgy which became necessary in the prayers of our Civil Rulers, in consequence of the Revolution." The "principal care" of the Prayer Book writers was to make these prayers conform "to what ought to be the proper end of all such prayers, namely that 'Rulers may have grace, wisdom, and understanding to execute justice and to maintain truth'; and that the people 'may lead quiet and peaceable lives, in all godliness and honesty'." Then the convention utilized the "happy occasion which was offered to them (uninfluenced and unrestrained by any worldly authority whatsoever) to take a further review of the Public Service, and to establish such other alterations and amendments therein as might be deemed expedient."

The "alterations and amendments" which they "deemed expedient" included these: obsolete expressions were modernized; lesser Saints' Days were omitted from the church calendar; the Athanasian Creed was omitted altogether; new prayers were introduced for various occasions; and various other changes were made. Probably the most important alteration, however, came with reference to the Eucharist. Going beyond the English worship service as adopted in 1662, the American convention of 1789 utilized a central Consecration prayer which was very similar to that appearing in the first Prayer Book of 1549. This earlier version was in the Scottish Prayer Books, and its appearance in the American liturgy was undoubtedly the result of Bishop Seabury's influence. A major modern chronicler of Episcopal worship and doctrinal developments, Powell Dawley, characterizes the adoption of the 1549 type of Consecration prayer in these words: "The change greatly enhanced the beauty and enriched the meaning of the liturgy, bringing into the American Communion Service not only the western Latin tradition through the 1549 Prayer Book, but also such elements of Eastern Orthodox liturgies as had been incorporated into the Scottish revision."

Not all of the American church's problems were ended by the Convention of 1789. But the threatened schism seemed ended, and other developments of the next five years extended the harmonious spirit which the union engendered. Connecticut Episcopalians, during the period 1790 to 1794, gradually changed their church government to the more democratic type in which laity could sit, discuss, and vote. Finally, for the first time, America acquired in 1792 a native American Bishop consecrated by American Bishops. He was the Reverend Thomas J. Claggett of Maryland, who was consecrated by Bishops Seabury, White, Provoost, and Madison (the latter had succeeded Griffith as Virginia's nomination to the Episcopate, and was consecrated in England.)

In the meantime, what of the church in Georgia during this period? Following the final expulsion of the British from Savannah in 1782, only spasmodic services were held at Christ

Church for the next four years. There was no resident rector; some services were conducted by visiting missionaries. In 1786, Christ Church again had a rector, the Rev. Mr. Nixon. Two years later he was succeeded by the Rev. Benjamin Lindsay, during whose term Christ Church was officially chartered by the State of Georgia, December 23, 1789. According to the Official History of Christ Church Parish, this was the first such charter granted by the State of Georgia.

In 1792 the Rev. Edward Ellington became the Rector of Christ Church. Already well known in Savannah for his work as President of Bethesda Orphanage, Ellington soon became well respected and loved in his new assignment. He served only a few years, however, before his death.

Thus by the 1790's the Anglican Church in Georgia had survived, if but feebly. As the English Church found a new name, new organization, and new Bishops for a United States Church during the troublesome years after the Revolution, Georgia was too weak to participate. But when the Georgia Church found itself again after the turn of the century, and parish life could be resumed, efforts could begin toward establishing relationships with the American Church.

PART TWO

· ✿ ·

The Episcopal Church In Georgia
From Revolution To Division

CHAPTER
✿ · IV · ✿

THE YOUTH OF A NEW CHURCH
1790-1840

IN 1790 THERE was but one active Episcopal Church in Georgia. This was Georgia's pioneer parish, Christ Church of Savannah. During the troubled years of rebellion and new-found loyalties which characterized the Revolutionary period, other Episcopal churches became dormant.

In the meantime the Episcopal churches of the United States had by 1789 consummated a national Convention of the Episcopal Church. The first Georgia connection with this body came when Georgia's only active church took steps to utilize the new American Prayer Book, although with some reservations. The Vestry of Christ Church voted on December 23, 1793, as follows: "Resolved That the Book of Common Prayer of the Protestant Episcopal Church of the United States of America, ratified by the said Church and made of force on the 1st of October 1790, be adopted for the present church, subject to such alterations as shall hereafter be agreed on by the minister of Christ Church and the Vestry thereof."

Until Georgia could establish a Diocese of its own, it was in a very weak condition, and expansion would be difficult. Diocesan supervision of the area came largely from the neighboring Bishop of South Carolina. After the Diocese of Georgia was organized in 1823, the South Carolina Bishop presided at Georgia Conventions until a Georgia Bishop was chosen. In 1826 Bishop Nathaniel Bowen of South Carolina reviewed this supervision as he addressed the Georgia Convention of that year:

Having had his attention invited to the condition of Congregations of our Communion in this State [Georgia], Bishop [Robert] Smith, of South Carolina, as early as 1798—and from that time forward, until his death in 1802—by correspondence, sought to cherish and preserve them in soundness and stability. . . . From 1802, until 1812, the Episcopal office was vacant in South Carolina; and it was not until 1815, that any acts, proper to that office, were performed [by South Carolina] in behalf of your Congregations. In the Spring of that year, the late Bishop [Theodore] Dehon visited Savannah, consecrated the Church there, then recently rebuilt . . . and administered confirmation, about fifty persons having, on that occasion, been presented to him as subjects of the rite.

Actual union with the Protestant Episcopal Church of the United States of America did not occur until 1823, when the first Diocese of Georgia was established. This pioneer Diocese consisted of three parishes: Christ Church, Savannah; Christ Church, St. Simon's Island; and St. Paul's Church, Augusta. An examination of the development of these churches during the generation after the Revolutionary War is necessary here in order to appreciate properly the nature of the Church's growth in Georgia.

That the Episcopal thread in Georgia continued in existence during the meager years before 1820 is due primarily to the interest and efforts of a few faithful churchmen in scattered parts of the state. The prejudice against Anglicans did not die out when the Revolution ended. Churches had difficulty securing legal status from the state government; and problems of recognition among townspeople also existed.

Although the Savannah church building—so long delayed in construction—burned to the ground in 1796, the congregation continued to hold services elsewhere until a new edifice could be constructed. At first rentals and then sales of glebe lands belonging to Christ Church helped raise money for the new church building. For example, in January, 1802, notice was given to the public of such a sale of land at the price of $6,025. Although disheartened by a hurricane which in 1804 flattened the incomplete new building, the parishioners of Savannah, under the leadership of their rector, a Rev. Dr. Best, began again the following year to achieve a church structure. On May 23, 1808, they received assistance from the Georgia General Assembly, which passed legislation allowing Christ Church to conduct a lottery to obtain construction funds, although the law-makers stipulated that not more than ten thousand dollars could be raised in this manner. In addition, an act was passed which enabled the vestry and wardens to offer certain lands held in trust by the church at public sale. Gratified at the latter opportunity, the church leaders did not hold a lottery. Instead, they sold the land as authorized and obtained five thousand dollars which was applied toward the church structure. In 1814 the building was completed, a white-pillared, red-brick church with belfried steeple. The rebuilt Christ Church was dedicated in 1815 by Bishop Theodore Dehon of South Carolina.

The Rev. Dr. Best served Savannah's Christ Church from about the turn of the century until he resigned in 1807. There was no rector for the next four years, during a period of financial difficulties at Christ Church. The Rev. Dr. Theodore B. Bartow became minister in 1811. During his term, 1811 to 1814, the new church building was completed. When Bishop Dehon consecrated this structure, the Reverend Walter Cranston was rector, and he remained so until 1822.

Physical deterioration of the chapel of Christ Church at St. Simon's Island and a gradual departure of the principal parishioners during the Revolutionary era brought a temporary end to its status as an independent parish. It became a mission church, operated out of Christ Church in Savannah. Early in the nineteenth century a group of wealthy indigo planters who had lately come to the island decided the parish should be re-established. An early account states that during this period services at Frederica were held by Savannah's Dr. Best "in an unoccupied tabby building . . . fitted up for the purpose, and a goodly number were always present." The necessary legal status of the reborn church was assured when, in December, 1808, the Georgia General Assembly passed a law incorporating the parish. At this time it contained three town lots and a hundred acres of garden land. This latter territory was leased by the planters, whose rent money was accumulated to help pay for a new church building. Under the leadership of their rector, the Reverend Edmund Mathews, the new Christ Church of St. Simon's Island was finished in 1820 and formally dedicated that same year.

In the meantime, the Episcopalians of Augusta, although lacking a church building of their own at the beginning of the nineteenth century, were not without vigor and spirit. Their doctrinal belief was a holdover from the English institutions which the patriots had fought to overthrow; and considerable prejudice against these institutions lingered after the war. Indeed, in 1781 the church building of St. Paul's had been confiscated, along with the grounds and cemetery. From 1786 until 1818 St. Paul's Parish was forced to utilize an inter-denominational wooden building made available to the Episcopalians for worship but not ownership. For five years (1804-1809) even this building was taken from them and rented to Presbyterians. There had also been occasions in the late eighteenth century when the old St. Paul's church building was used for public services in connection with the state government—for Augusta was then capital of the state.

The devotion of a few Episcopalians nourished the church during these troublesome years. St. Paul's historian William K. Miller sympathetically describes the situation:

> Divine services at St. Paul's were continued by a *faithful few,* and they were so few that they practically took care of each other. Their faith and combined effort kept the Church alive, while time—the great arbitrator—rightfully adjudged their claim against the State. As time rolled on the feeling against the Episcopal Church, as a relic of the English Crown, began to subside. The 'faithful few' had, in the meantime—from 1781 to 1816—grown into a large[?] society. They had no Rector, but their continuous efforts for good resulted in their acquiring a considerable influence in the community—so much so that the public authorities thought such should be recognized."

In the year 1816 the parish was given corporate status by the Georgia General Assembly and two years later a new church building was begun. When completed, St. Paul's Church in Augusta was a handsome structure, ninety-four by sixty-four feet in dimensions, and costing thirty thousand dollars. Of Grecian Doric design, the church, boasting 124 ground floor pews and

CHRIST CHURCH, Frederica (St. Simon's Island)
Organized 1736

CHRIST CHURCH, Savannah
Organized 1733 (oldest Episcopal Church in the Diocese of Georgia)
Church built 1840

CHURCH
OF
THE ATONEMENT
Augusta
Organized 1850
Church built 1850

ST. PAUL'
Augusta
Organize
Present C
built 191

ST. ATHANASIUS'
Brunswick
Organized 1855
Present Church
built 1898

CHURCH OF THE GOOD SHEPHERD, Augusta
Organized 1869 • Present Church built 1897

TWO OF THE
NEW CHURCHES
in the
DIOCESE OF GEORGIA

ALL SAINTS', Savannah Beach
Church built 1959

ST. GEORGE'S, Savannah
Organized 1959 ● Church built 1960

fourteen in the gallery, was proudly characterized by a parishioner: "in point of chasteness, simplicity, and beauty [it is] scarcely exceeded by any church in our country." In 1821 South Carolina's Bishop Bowen consecrated the new St. Paul's. When the Reverend Hugh Smith became Rector of St. Paul's in 1818, the little parish numbered but four communicants (hardly a "large society"). By 1826 this number had grown to seventy, with many baptized children besides.

Until Georgia could have a Diocese of its own, it could not participate actively in the American Church. In 1811, for example, the Reverend John V. Bartow, rector of Christ Church, Savannah, turned up in New Haven at the General Convention of the United States Church. He showed a certificate entitling him to attend the Convention as a representative of the "Episcopal Church in the city of Savannah, State of Georgia." This brought some discussion, and the Convention finally resolved that "the Protestant Episcopal Church in the State of Georgia, not being organized, and not having, in Convention, acceded to the constitution of the Protestant Episcopal Church in the United States of America, the Reverend Mr. Bartow cannot be admitted a member of this House, but he [shall] be allowed the privilege of an honorary seat."

By the early 1820's, Georgia's three Episcopal churches were gaining strength. They each had rectors: Abiel Carter at Christ Church, Savannah; Edmund Mathews at Christ Church, St. Simon's Island; and Hugh Smith at St. Paul's, Augusta. Under the leadership of these clergymen and interested laymen, the three parishes made a highly significant move in 1823. Without the services of a directly superior Bishop since the Revolution, the Georgia churches now took steps to create their own Diocese and achieve union with the national Church. In February Carter, Mathews, and Smith assembled with lay delegates for this purpose. From Savannah came Dr. J. B. Read and Peter Guerrard; John Course, Edward F. Campbell, and Dr. Thomas I. Wray represented St. Paul's; no laymen from St. Simon's Island were present. This group of eight Episcopalians constituted the first Diocesan Convention in Georgia.

The most important order of business was the drafting of a

constitution for the new Diocese of Georgia. The clergymen and three of the laymen comprised the committee which drew up the document. This constitution, so important in the history of Georgia Episcopalianism, provided:

The several congregations of the Protestant Episcopal Church in this State, now represented in this Convention, shall be considered one Church or Diocess [sic] . . . with a view to union with the Protestant Episcopal Church in the United States of America. A standing committee shall be chosen at each annual meeting of the convention, to consist of three clerical and three lay members, of the time and place of whose meetings, due notice shall be given . . . at least four weeks before the time of such meetings. At a meeting thus notified, any four members (provided one be a clergyman) shall form a quorum. . . .
The *general* powers and duties of the committee shall be such as are designated by the general constitution of the Church.

The committee's draft of a constitution was accepted by the Convention, and thereby became the fundamental law of the Diocese. The next order of business was the consideration of necessary canon laws which would effectuate the new constitution. Four canons were adopted. The first provided for the establishment of new churches in the Diocese:

1. Whenever any number of persons in this State shall associate to form an Episcopal Church, and shall elect 2 wardens and any number of vestrymen at discretion; and shall properly signify by their association for this purpose, to the officers of the standing committee, or to the Bishop, if there be one, they shall be recognized as an episcopal congregation duly organized, subject however to the usual disciplines of the Protestant Episcopal Church of this State: and it is hereby recommended to all congregations that may be thus organized to obtain as early as possible, a legislative act of incorporation.

The second canon specified that the Standing Committee's President should be responsible for stipulating the nature of business to be transacted whenever special church conventions were called.

Certain important parish records were the subject of the third canon:

3. It is hereby required that every settled minister . . . in this state shall keep an accurate register of marriages, baptisms, and funerals he

has solemnized, during the last year—and that he shall render to the convention at each annual meeting, a written account of the same.

Finally, the Convention's fourth canon directed that each church in Georgia should contribute "the sum of fifteen dollars annually, for defraying the incidental expenses of the convention."

Anxious to affiliate with the national Episcopal organization, the Diocese of Georgia in the 1823 Convention agreed that the Constitution of the Protestant Episcopal Church of the United States of America was acceptable to the new Georgia Church, and they chose a delegate to attend the next General Convention of the American Church to announce the activity in Georgia. Another step taken was the drafting of a general letter to "all the scattered members" of the Episcopal Church in Georgia. The initial paragraph of this document interestingly summarizes the threshold upon which the little Georgia Diocese found itself:

The present, brethren, is an interesting era, in the local history of our venerable Church. It marks the dawn of a brighter day upon her prospects. She now appears as a "city that is at unity in itself." Her spiritual building is now "fitly framed together, that it may grow into a holy temple in the Lord." Duly and harmoniously organized, she is now about to exchange the feebleness of individual, separate action, for the strength of united, concentrated effort. She is about to take a name, and a station, among her sister Churches in our country, and to form a component part of that glorious body, of which Christ Jesus . . . is the glorified head.

The letter continued by asking all Episcopalians in the state to aid the Church's progress. Groups of churchmen should organize in all areas, no matter how small the group. All should join and contribute to the Diocese, the letter concluded.

Although Diocesan status for the Georgia churches was thus assured by these activities in 1823, it was not until 1840 that a local Bishop was secured. During these seventeen years, the Church grew slowly but steadily. Expansion into the interior of Georgia followed the pattern of the state's expansion into Indian lands, obtained by treaty.

Most of south and central Georgia lay in the hands of the Creek Indians. Immigration into the previously ceded areas occurred rather rapidly after the Revolutionary era. By 1800 thirteen new counties had been created in interior Georgia. The state's population rose from 82,548 in 1790 to 162,686 in 1800. Similar growth continued in succeeding years, as this list of the creation of new counties indicates: 1800-1809, fourteen; 1810-1819, nine; 1820-1829, twenty-nine; and 1830-1839, seventeen.

In 1802 the State of Georgia concluded an agreement with the United States government by which, among other terms, the federal authorities promised to remove the Indians from Georgia at the earliest possible time "by peaceable means." From Georgia's standpoint, this removal was all too slow during the years which followed. The lands of the Creek and the Cherokee Indians were desirable territories for expansion, and when she grew impatient for these regions, Georgia took steps on her own. In each case United States agents eventually arranged treaties satisfactory to Georgia, and removal proceeded under federal supervision. The Creeks were removed finally by the Treaty of Indian Springs in 1827 and the Cherokees by the Treaty of New Echota in 1835. Save for scattered individual Indians in the state, Georgia was free of red men by 1840. By then, white settlers had begun to move very swiftly into former Creek and Cherokee lands.

But while the new territories enabled Georgia to extend its limits to the Alabama, Tennessee, and Carolina boundaries, the state's internal expansion was featured by a splattering of settlements. County seats for the new counties which had been formed out of Indian lands were often merely hamlets. Travelers in Georgia reported passing only a few scattered houses while crossing miles of territory.

In general, these pioneer Georgians were non-Episcopalians. Baptists, Presbyterians, Methodists, and some Quakers predominated, especially in the backwoods and farming communities. Early expansion of the Episcopal Church from the three parishes of Savannah, St. Simon's, and Augusta occurred in the more populous communities which were well behind the lines of the frontier.

The first of these new Episcopal churches in Georgia was established in Macon. This came about as a result of an exploratory and investigative tour in 1825 by the Reverend Lot Jones, a representative of the Protestant Episcopal Society for the General Advancement of Christianity in the State of Georgia. One of the places which he thought a likely spot for a new Episcopal church was Macon. The settlement on this site was long known as a trading post on the Ocmulgee River, and when its surrounding territory was freed of Indians the community grew rapidly. Bibb County was founded by the Georgia General Assembly in 1822; at the same time, the county seat was surveyed and laid out by state commissioners. Because so many settlers were from North Carolina, the town was named for Nathaniel Macon of that state.

Macon grew as its citizens capitalized on the growing value of the cotton crop. Macon's warehouses bulged with this product, for the city's strategic location on the river (and later the railroads) brought both produce and money into the city's commerce. At the time when the Reverend Lot Jones visited Macon (in 1825), the town was barely three years old, and he found it ripe for Episcopal evangelization.

Macon was without churches at this time. Jones met with important citizens and with them established the first new Protestant Episcopal Church in the state since the Revolutionary period. C. B. Strong and Dr. Ambrose Baber were elected Wardens of Christ Church, Macon. The Vestrymen included a future governor of Georgia, Brigadier General Charles J. McDonald, and other prominent Maconites. The initial enthusiasm for membership in this new church dwindled somewhat when the legislature incorporated churches of other denominations in Macon. However, in 1826 the Diocesan records show that Christ Church had nine communicants and fifty pupils in Sunday School. The Rev. Mr. Jones reported in that year that he had baptized one child and performed one marriage. An encouraging report on Macon had been given late the previous year. The editor of the *Savannah Georgian* visited the town in December, 1825, and wrote: "I was delighted with the place and its growing prosperity. Last March two years ago, it was a wilderness. It has now thirty-two stores; has cotton stored from sixteen counties, and perhaps nothing characterizes its refinement more conclusively than the fact that it maintains an Episcopal minister."

Despite this promising beginning, however, Lot Jones departed from Macon the next year. This surprising event was brought on by a development which, while heartening for some denominations, brought discouragement to the Macon Episcopalians. A wave of revivalism sponsored by the evangelistic churches resulted in a widespread increase in the membership of these churches, including some who withdrew from Christ Church. This church's membership, although promising for the future, was so small in 1827 that these withdrawals left it with but a handful of Episcopalians. Mr. Jones seemed to be unable to cope with the new situation, for he left Macon by the end of the year.

For the next few years the laymen of Macon's Christ Church strove valiantly to keep the little congregation together, to organize and hold services, and to find a minister. The Diocesan records for 1830 indicate that the parish, urgently seeking a rector, announced that Macon was "a town of 3,500 in a healthy, hilly country with a northern climate." One of the difficulties faced by the Macon parishioners was the lack of a church building. During their early years most services were held in a bank's basement or in the Bibb County Courthouse. Some reorganization of the little parish occurred in 1831 when new church officers were elected. With this new set of leaders, the church made determined efforts both to secure a minister and to build a church. For both purposes it was decided to secure money through sale of the lot which had originally been granted to them by the General Assembly of Georgia. This transaction realized the sum of $2,400, which, together with money already on hand, boosted their treasury to $3,000.

But Macon's church was still without a clergyman. The tenth Annual Convention of the Diocese met with the Maconites in May, 1832. The Parish Report made by Christ Church's Wardens and Vestry stated that "their diligent endeavours to procure the services of a resident minister, have thus far been unsuccessful." If this situation continued, they reported, church membership would fall off even more than it had already. They asked that ministers and missionaries be informed about Macon, because "as this portion of the State is not often visited by ministers of our Church from abroad, they are probably ignorant of the field for usefulness which is here presented."

In the year 1833 a rector arrived for the Macon parish. He was the Reverend Seneca Bragg, a native of New York, who was to serve Christ Church nearly fourteen years. He and his new congregation worked to attain a church building of their own. A lot on Walnut Street had been purchased for $700, and subscriptions and donations were being collected for the building. Contributions came in from all parts of Georgia and from the Diocese of South Carolina as well. On Sexagesima Sunday (February 3), 1834, public services in the new church were held for the first time. The official history of the parish describes the church as follows: "It was built in the form of a Roman Cross and was surmounted by a dome. There was a gallery at the end opposite the chancel and the Church contained sittings, in all, for between three hundred and four hundred people. The pews were all rented from the day that they were offered for that purpose, with the exception of four pews which, by resolution of the Vestry, dated December 5, 1833, were set aside for strangers."

In 1838, with the church's debt completely paid, the new structure was consecrated. On March 25 the Right Reverend Jackson Kemper, Missionary Bishop of Missouri and Indiana, performed the dedicatory service. Macon's Episcopalians then totalled forty-two, with a Sunday School enrollment of thirty students. An event of great importance to Episcopal Church history in Georgia occurred during Bishop Kemper's visit: he conducted the first Confirmation services ever held in Middle Georgia. On this significant occasion, the Bishop brought twenty new communicants into the congregation of Christ Church, Macon. Although this new church's growth in the next few decades would, in accordance with the frontier development, be slow, it would be steady.

In its struggle for financial security, Christ Church in Macon had appealed to a recently organized Georgia Episcopal missionary organization. This was the Protestant Episcopal Society for the General Advancement of Christianity in the State of Georgia. Founded in 1823 at the first Diocesan Convention, the Society's stated purpose was to extend "the ordinances of the Church, to its destitute members in the different parts of the state." Later, the experience of the Macon parish led the Diocese to amend the Society's objects to include "assistance of such Churches as may be unable, without aid, to support the ministry." At the same time, it was voted to step up missionary activity in other regions of Georgia. For this effort, the following amounts were pledged: Christ Church, Savannah, five hundred dollars; St. Paul's, Augusta, three hundred dollars; Christ Church, St. Simon's Island, one hundred dollars; and, as indication of its progress, Christ Church, Macon, one hundred dollars. Finally, this Convention passed a resolution that more ministers should be secured by the Standing Committee and placed within the Diocese at needful places.

The next new church in the Diocese of Georgia was Trinity Parish in the new frontier town of Columbus. Although it may seem a "minor" circumstance to some (Columbus's historian Nancy Telfair states that "minor happenings" of the year 1834 "included the first cargo of ice, the establishment of the Episcopal Church, and the first bank failure."), this was a major step for Georgia's expanding Episcopal Diocese. Right behind the removing Creek Indians came Georgia's land surveyors in 1826, who laid out the future town of Columbus on the Chattahoochee River near the Coweta Falls. Here in Georgia's western frontier outpost the new town by 1828 was a trading center which boasted more than a thousand inhabitants; and a continued steady growth brought into the community a number of Episcopalians anxious to begin their own church. Dr. E. L. de Graffenreid, one of the founders of Columbus and a city health officer, was one of these interested churchmen. On August 17, 1834, he held a meeting at his home in which plans for the new church were formulated. Macon's rector, the Reverend Seneca Bragg, conducted the first Episcopal service for the Columbus public. This meeting, on September 6 of the same year, was held at the Presbyterian church.

From these beginnings grew Trinity Church in Columbus. In 1835 the parish was formally presented to and accepted by the Diocese at its thirteenth Annual Convention. Trinity received a missionary priest the next year in the person of the Reverend William D. Cairns from North Carolina. Meanwhile the congregation had been active in securing loans for, and constructing, an Episcopal church. On June 3, 1838, Cairns read the first service in the new edifice; and later that year the church was consecrated by Bishop Jackson Kemper. The Columbus parishioners had built well and they could be justly proud of the result. "It was a beautifully appointed church of forty-six pews with carpets, hangings, marble baptismal font, a pair of elegant stoves, hanging lamps and a three thousand dollar organ of fourteen stops." Rental at public auction brought a revenue from the pews of $3,369 for 1838.

The next few years brought extreme financial difficulty for the new Columbus parish. In the very years of its church building and consecration the country underwent a major depression (the Panic of 1837) which was devastating to the cotton farmers and land speculators in and near Columbus. In 1839 the church's income was almost depleted, and in October of that year a suit was brought against Trinity Church for failure to meet a payment on the building loan. Income from pew rentals fell to less than a thousand dollars in 1839 and again in 1840; and vestry records show that a special committee was organized to stave off the legal action which the suit of 1839 had initiated.

The establishment of new churches in Macon and Columbus was not the only missionary activity going on in the Georgia Diocese in these times. The Protestant Episcopal Society for the General Advancement of Christianity in the State of Georgia, the Domestic Committee of Missions of the General Church, and the missionary interests of the Standing Committee of the Diocese of Georgia were all active in spreading the Episcopal Church into the frontiers of Georgia. Usually these groups worked independently of each other—yet there was a spirit of cooperation manifested by the results of all the endeavors.

An example of this activity occurred in 1836 when the Domestic Committee sent the Reverend John J. Hunt as a missionary to Clarke County. In the previous year Mr. Hunt had been brought to Georgia through the missionary activity of the Standing Committee and stationed in Savannah where he served as Sunday School superintendent. In his new assignment, Hunt settled in Athens, and shortly thereafter reported: "Though our scattered band is small, and few (in this part of Georgia) united

with our peculiar worship . . . yet I have found more Episcopalians than I had expected."

Further expansion of the Episcopal Church into north and
west Georgia, now possible with the expected removal of the
Cherokee Indians in 1838-39, was under consideration by the
various missionary groups. The Rev. Edward Neufville of Christ
Church, Savannah, who was at that time Chairman of the Standing Committee of the Diocese, was able to render a first-hand
report of conditions and opportunities in this undeveloped area.
He toured the region for seven months, "traveling chiefly in
the upper part of the State, and officiating occasionally, as opportunity offered, for the scattered members of our communion
and others who were destitute of regular ministration." He noted
that "Clarkesville and Milledgeville present a field for Missionary labour."

A problem of peculiar consideration was that of evangelization.
Personal and emotional appeals such as characterized missionary
efforts of other denominations were apparently repugnant to
Episcopal missionaries. This point of view was rather strongly
expressed by the rector of St. Paul's in Augusta. The Reverend
Hugh Smith observed, "The disgusting and degrading acts of
studied proselytism are foreign to our institutions, and to our
social spirit. We do not propose to open an asylum, for our own
spiritual outcasts, and for *others* who have no spiritual home."

With the feeling that too much scattered missionary effort was
underway, the Diocese moved in 1838 to consolidate activities.
All Episcopal missionary work of various societies and groups
operating in Georgia would come under the direct supervision
of the Diocesan Convention. At the meeting in 1838 a new
canon was adopted which established a central Missionary Committee as one of the regular Diocesan committees.

While Athens was still in the missionary stage, a movement
was launched to establish a church at Clarkesville in Habersham
County, in the region which Dr. Neufville had suggested as a
promising mission field. At the seventeenth Convention of the
Diocese in 1839, held at St. Paul's in Augusta, a lay delegation
from Habersham consisting of George R. Jessup and Richard
Habersham, Jr., reported on the progress of their infant parish.

A missionary named E. B. Kellogg from New York arrived in Clarkesville on October 28, 1838. Using the local Methodist Church for his meetings, Kellogg began to build a parish around the three Episcopal families in Clarkesville. In the summer of 1839 "large congregations" attended the services, which were being held twice-monthly still in the Methodist building. A year-round Sunday School with forty-two pupils was being conducted in the local schoolhouse. According to the report, this was the only Sunday School in Clarkesville. Meanwhile the local vestry-men of the new Grace Church had obtained for five hundred dollars a building site, and through contributions and pledges, $715 from St. Paul's in Augusta and Christ Church in Savannah, to be used by Mr. Kellogg in his parish work.

While helping to build the Grace Church Parish at Clarkes-ville, Mr. Kellogg was also laying the foundations for another Grace Church. This was at Gainesville, whose Episcopalians shared missionary attention from Kellogg with a mission at Nacoochee.

In 1839 Georgia's Episcopal leaders received word that the Diocese of Florida desired to join with Georgia and Alabama in the creation of a union so that they could procure a Bishop. At the Georgia Diocesan Convention of that year, the matter was discussed favorably in committee. However, a careful study of the situation in Georgia led the Convention to the conviction that they could obtain their own Bishop. In all likelihood, the Florida suggestion pushed the Georgia Diocese into a quicker determination to secure an Episcopate.

A positive program of church growth in Georgia was difficult to achieve without a Bishop; and Georgia's Diocese was still lack-ing in this leadership. The three parishes which survived the Revolution had created the Diocese in 1823 and in seventeen years had brought three other organized churches into their number: Christ Church, Macon; Trinity Church, Columbus; and Grace Church, Clarkesville. In addition, several missions showed promise. The naming and consecration of a Bishop of the Diocese of Georgia would be the most dramatic development in the ante-bellum years and would presage a new era in the history of the Episcopal Church in Georgia.

CHAPTER

✤ · V · ✤

GEORGIA'S FIRST BISHOP AND HIS DIOCESE

THE EIGHTEENTH Annual Convention of the Diocese of Georgia met in Clarkesville in 1840. Here, on the ground of Georgia's newest Episcopal Church, the delegates unanimously elected an outstanding clergyman to the newest office in the Diocese, that of Bishop of Georgia. He was the Reverend Stephen Elliott, Jr., of South Carolina.

Although comparatively young, and with limited experience as a priest, Stephen Elliott possessed a wide background of interests and training which would be of considerable advantage in his important new assignment in a Diocese so largely a frontier one. He was born August 31, 1806, the son of Stephen and Esther Habersham Elliott of Beaufort, South Carolina. His mother was formerly of Savannah. Reared in his native state, young Elliott graduated in 1825 with third honor from South Carolina College in Columbia. He had been tutored for first year college work in Charleston and had attended Harvard University his sophomore year. Proceeding into his then preferred profession, Elliott read law in the office of a prominent South Carolina lawyer, James L. Pettigru. In 1827 he was admitted to the bar in Charleston and later practiced in Beaufort. But apparently the ministry held a strong attraction for him, because in 1833 the Episcopal Church admitted him as a candidate for orders. Two years later Bishop Nathaniel Bowen ordained the young aspirant to the Diaconate, and Elliott reported to the Parish of Wilton, South Carolina, for duty. Hardly had he begun work here, however, when he was called to his alma mater, South Carolina College. He became the College Chaplain and Professor of Sacred Literature and Evidences of Christianity. In 1836 at Columbia, he was ordained to the priesthood.

It seems especially interesting to note that when Stephen Elliott came to Georgia to accept the call to become Bishop, he received this bid in Clarkesville, seat of the county bearing the same name as that of his mother's family. More appropriate, however, was that the budding young Diocese should receive a young and vigorous leader at a time when strong leadership was needed. The six churches (at Savannah, Augusta, St. Simon's, Macon, Columbus, and Clarkesville) were, except for Christ Church, Savannah, not strong. Indeed, it was Savannah's pledge of four hundred dollars for the ministry at Clarkesville which made that church possible and gave Georgia the six churches necessary to elect a Bishop.

The resolution to elect a Bishop came from the Rev. William D. Cairns of Columbus: "Whereas, in the good providence of God, the Church in this Diocese is now entitled to proceed in the election of a Bishop, and whereas, there is good reason to believe, that by the liberality of our congregations generally, the requisite provision will be made for his support—it is therefore,

"Unanimously Resolved, that we gratefully acknowledge the mercy of God in this event, so propitious to the best interests of the Church; and with the Divine blessing, will proceed at this Convention of the Diocese to the election of a Bishop to preside over us. . . ."

Elliott was unanimously nominated by the clergy and unanimously elected by the entire Convention. In solemn ceremony at Christ Church, Savannah, Stephen Elliott was consecrated Bishop on February 28, 1841, by Bishops William Meade of Virginia, Levi S. Ives of North Carolina, and Christopher E. Gadsden of South Carolina.

Bishop Elliott's salary was a matter of concern to the Episcopalians of Georgia and especially to those of Savannah. Christ Church there pledged an extra thousand dollars a year for this purpose, to be added to the sixteen hundred already pledged by the Diocese (largely by Savannah, Augusta, St. Simon's Island, and Macon). Trying to get the salary level higher, the men of

Savannah in 1841 formed a new church, the Parish of St. John's, whose rector was to be Bishop Elliott. With seven churches supporting the Episcopate, one of which was his own, the new Bishop seemed certain of receiving about three thousand dollars annually.

Bishop Elliott found his Diocese in a state of weakness which might have discouraged a lesser man. Christ Church in Savannah was considered financially sound and was competently led by the Rev. Edward Neufville, who had succeeded Abiel Carter in 1827. St. Paul's in Augusta seemed promising; but the others needed immediate attention or the work of the church in those communities might dwindle away. The vestrymen in Columbus were still greatly disturbed about the suit in civil court over the church's debt; Macon reported small offerings owing to "pecuniary embarrassments of this section of the country"; and Grace Church in Clarkesville had been unable to complete a church building and the people were still using the Methodist Church in evenings and the local academy in the morning services.

Yet the difficulties of the older churches and missions did not dim the desires of the Episcopalians of other communities to found their own churches. When Stephen Elliott became Bishop, he found three missions under way. At Springfield, in Effingham County, the Rev. George White of Savannah had established the mission of St. Michael's, whose vestrymen were planning to build a church in the next few months. An Episcopal minister named Ford had six families attending a mission at Lexington; while the Rev. John J. Hunt, discouraged by lack of funds in Athens, found some support for missionary activity at Oglethorpe.

The new Bishop must have felt especial satisfaction from his first official missionary activity in Georgia. Of course, the establishment of his own parish of St. John's in Savannah marked the first situation in post-Revolutionary Georgia where two parishes existed in a single city. Then, during a visit to St. Simon's Island, conversations with a leading Episcopalian from Darien proved fruitful. Dr. James Troup encouraged Bishop Elliott to found a new church in Darien, St. Peter's (later re-named St. Andrew's). Here an enthusiastic congregation proceeded with plans for a commodious church. The building was completed in 1844, and has been described as follows: "It was a plain wooden building with an attached vestry room, there was also a belfry, which held a bell, then thought as necessary as a pulpit. The church had a large seating capacity, larger than the seating capacity of today, a spacious chancel with mahogany furniture. The interior was well-lighted by large windows and was painted a pearl gray and the outside a lead color. The pews and trimmings were brown. The church was built by subscription, the subscribers furnishing the money for the material and sending their colored servants, carpenters and masons to perform the work." The first minister to St. Andrew's, the Rev. Richard Brown, arrived in 1844.

St. Stephen's in Milledgeville was the next new church. An Episcopal group there suggested the creation of such a church, and the Bishop himself conducted the first several services in the buildings of Methodist and Presbyterian faiths.

In such vigorous fashion did Georgia's first Bishop proceed to enlarge his Diocese. Seventy-six persons were confirmed during his first year. Altogether, his Diocese numbered three hundred and eighty-two communicants with three hundred and sixty-two Sunday School pupils.

But the physical expansion of his Episcopate was not his only concern. Near Macon the Bishop took steps to realize a dream. At Montpelier Springs he established the Episcopal Institute of the Episcopal Church of Georgia. The Bishop's plans were made possible by Col. G. B. Lamar's gift of a large tract of land located about sixteen miles west of Macon. The donation included Montpelier Springs, a noted health resort of the early nineteenth century. Concerning the site, Bishop Elliott wrote that it just suited his purpose, for it was "in a remarkably healthful region, its 800 acres affording grounds for amusement and exercise of the students, free from all intrusion." The Bishop hoped that large cash endowments might be forthcoming from other interested Georgia Episcopalians, so that Montpelier could develop into a great Southern Episcopal educational center. The Bishop himself gave freely of his own money and time to aid the school's early years.

Montpelier began as a girls' school. Although the Bishop tried to initiate a boys' school there as well, this latter movement never got off the ground. The Institute for Boys lasted only from 1842 to 1849. But the female training proceeded briskly, and many Georgia girls from prominent Episcopal families received precollege training there. In 1842, as the school began, Bishop Elliott wrote enthusiastically, "the Girls' school is flourishing beyond all expectations, there being 43 students." During the 1840's and 1850's young ladies at Montpelier Institute were exposed to a variety of curriculum offerings, including Italian, French, Latin, English, painting, botany, philosophy, trigonometry, geometry, algebra, history, chronology, astronomy, theology, Bible, music, and others. Such courses were taken during two yearly sessions, January to May and June to December, with vacations in May and December. Tuition, board, and lodging were $250 per year.

Victoria Hunter [later Clayton] of Alabama was one of the young ladies who attended Montpelier. In a book of memoirs she describes life at the Institute charmingly and interestingly:

In my fifteenth year, . . . my father . . . an Episcopalian, took me to the school of Bishop Stephen Elliott. The Bishop at that time had the supervision of Christ College, a female institute . . . situated at Montpelier, about fourteen miles from Macon. There I remained two years and learned to love God's Holy Church. This love has grown day by day in all these succeeding years. The school generally numbered about one hundred girls from our best families, and they were all devoted to the dear Bishop and lovely Mrs. Elliott.

Many of our teachers were from the North, and were very intellectual and highly cultivated ladies, and I was much attached to several of them. Some of my happiest days were spent here at Montpelier, and memory still retains some lovely pictures of our life in these classic halls. The school was conducted somewhat unlike most boarding schools. It was divided into sections, each section consisting of about twelve girls. One teacher had special charge of a section. She was expected to look after the girls under her care with regard to their welfare in every way. Each teacher had a parlor, called her section room, where all of her girls were obliged to assemble at the ringing of the bell, very soon after the evening meal. Here the girls were required to bring some sewing, fancy work, or plain sewing, as each wished, and, while we were learning the use of the needle, one of the girls would read aloud. In this way the section room became an important feature in the education of the girls. Here we read Milton's *Paradise Lost,* and many other standard works.

Apparently there was deep mutual affection between the Bishop and his students, as this passage from Mrs. Clayton's book indicates:

I shall ever remember the day Bishop Elliott became forty-one years old. We all knew when his birthday was. For several weeks beforehand we were making preparations for the surprise and happiness of this "man of God." When he awoke in the morning, the first thing that greeted him was a pair of chamber slippers with a dainty note of love from the section composed of the smaller girls; then in the sitting-room there awaited him a token of love from each teacher and her girls. When he entered the breakfast room, the table was all wreathed in flowers. The Bishop then made us a little speech, expressing his appreciation, and school duties were suspended for the day. How happy we all were!

Despite these pleasant experiences, however, the endowments which the Bishop had hoped to receive for Montpelier never came, and the Diocese was severely taxed to maintain the school. Finally the Institute was forced to end its role as a church school. Reporting to the Diocesan Convention in 1856, Bishop Elliott remarked: "Possessing no endowment it required an unfailing number of pupils to pay current expenses. Those pupils could not be regularly counted upon, any epidemic that might pervade the country, any idle report, any change of superintendence subjected us to loss of pupils and the hazard of incurring debt for which there was no recourse save the purse of the church. At a meeting of the board of trustees in December [1855] it was unanimously determined to close Montpelier Institute."

Meanwhile, in 1840 Christ Church in Savannah enjoyed the privilege of moving into a new church building. Three years earlier Dr. Neufville and the vestry had decided that since the old building seemed to be unsafe for long continued usage, a new structure should be projected. The former church was torn down, and on February 26, 1838, the corner-stone of a new building was laid by the rector. Compared to the efforts of the preceding century, the construction of this Christ Church building proceeded rather rapidly. After about a year, the parish was able to conduct its Easter services in the new church's basement; and on March 22, 1840, the building was complete. Consecration ceremonies were conducted by North Carolina's Bishop Levi S. Ives, with the assistance of Bishop Philander Chase of Illinois.

Frederica's Christ Church had also been concerned with its church building. By 1840, the structure had deteriorated to the point where it was necessary to repair or rebuild; but enough money for either did not seem to be available. Then one day someone noticed a large swarm of bees buzzing about the little church's steeple. It was found that almost the entire steeple was filled with honey. The honey was turned into money, and enough income was obtained to make the needed repairs on the church. From this incident, there came into being at Christ Church, Frederica, the "Bee-Hive Missionary Society"; and the church itself was thereafter known as the "Bee-Hive Church."

Of course the Diocese was not in idyllic circumstances, despite these developments and the fact that Macon and Columbus were recovering from monetary crises. By the end of 1842 the long-standing mission at Athens still lacked a clergyman and a church building of its own. Grace Church in Clarkesville, without a rector since the departure of Mr. Kellogg, was experiencing difficulty in finishing its church. Also without a church was St. Andrew's in Darien. The sickness of the Rev. Theodore Bartow on St. Simon's Island prevented the holding of services there for a time.

Yet 1842 offered some hopeful signs. St. Michael's in Springfield reported the completion of its chapel. Trinity Church in Columbus, faced with a court order involving some eleven hundred dollars, found unexpected succor when its rector, the Rev. William D. Cairns, paid the amount due out of his own pocket, hoping for reimbursement later as soon as the parish and the Diocese could help him. Although Augusta's new rector, the Rev. Edward E. Ford, complained of the "drainage effect of emigration" on the church's membership rolls, the parish was able to boast of seventy-four members, and two Sunday Schools of fifty white and eighty Negro slave children. The latter Sunday School reflected the Bishop's charge to all parishes to begin religious education for young slaves. The Bishop also had called on Georgia Episcopalians to establish churches for the religious benefit of all their slaves. One such church was already functioning, St. David's in Glynn County.

The year 1844 saw the ordination to the priesthood of one of the most interesting clergymen in Georgia Episcopal history. He was William Bacon Stevens, who had settled in Savannah in 1837 to practice medicine. A man of wide and varied interests, Dr. Stevens helped to found the Georgia Historical Society and shortly thereafter began to write a history of Georgia. He developed a close association with Bishop Elliott, and soon was able to realize an ambition of long standing: the Bishop gave him personal training in preparation for the ministry. He was admitted to the Diaconate in February, 1843. One month later he received an appointment as missionary to Emmanuel Church in Athens, an assignment which he probably welcomed. Bishop Elliott advanced Stevens to the priesthood in the following January.

In Athens, while ministering to the needs of Emmanuel Parish, Stevens became Professor of Oratory and Belles Lettres at the University. Also, he continued with his history of Georgia, the first volume of which finally appeared in 1847. As a minister, Stevens became well-known for his sermons, some of which were published. At the Diocesan Convention in 1844, he was elected Secretary of the Convention. During the next few years he travelled widely in the Atlantic Coastal area, preaching frequently en route. One of these visits was to St. Andrew's Parish in Philadelphia, where he made such an impression that in 1848 he received a call from that Church. On July 30, he gave his farewell sermon at Emmanuel Church and shortly thereafter left for Philadelphia. In 1857 the second and concluding volume of his Georgia history appeared. This work, although taking the colony and state development only to the year 1798, was, in the words of Dr. E. M. Coulter, currently Georgia's leading historian, "a scholarly work, far beyond any other history which had ever appeared in Georgia or in the majority of other states, and has not yet been superseded."

Recognizing the extraordinary clerical ability of Stevens, the Diocese of Pennsylvania elevated him to Bishop in 1865, and he held that office until his death twenty-two years later.

Other changes in the ranks of the Georgia ministry were numerous and are worthy of examination here since they reflect the increasing vigor and complexity of the new Diocese. Additional ordinations were those of Thomas F. Scott, previously a Presbyterian missionary, and John Fielding, who had been a Roman Catholic priest. New assignments included that of Dr.

John A. Vaughn, from the Diocese of New York, to the mission at St. David's; another New Yorker, Rufus M. White, as Deacon of St. Stephen's in Milledgeville; E. P. Brown to Christ Church, St. Simon's Island; A. J. Berger to Grace Church, Clarkesville, from Maryland; and R. T. Brown as rector at St. Andrew's in Darien. A new area in which mission work was begun was Floyd County; Carter Page of Virginia was assigned to this work. In addition, five Georgians were seeking Holy Orders by training in various seminaries.

The growth of the Church in Georgia necessitated a clearer interpretation of the Diocesan Constitution. To this end, the twentieth Convention enacted Canon V as follows:

Section 1. Whenever any number of persons shall associate to form an Episcopal Congregation they shall adopt articles of association for their government, in which they shall accede to the Constitution, Canons, doctrines, discipline and worship of the Protestant Episcopal Church in the United States of America, and the Constitution and Canons of the Diocese of Georgia, they shall assume a suitable name by which their Church or Parish shall be designated, and elect two Wardens and any number of Vestrymen, at discretion, not exceeding eight. A Certified copy of the articles of Association of the proceedings at their adoption, signed by the Wardens, shall then be laid before the Convention, and if approved by that body, delegates from such congregation or Parish may take seats in the Convention and subject to its decisions.

Section 2. Every Parish so organized, shall annually, on Easter Monday, elect the same number of Vestrymen and Wardens. . . .

St. James' Church of Marietta joined the Diocese in 1843. It was organized by a group of railroad men. C. F. M. Garnett, Chief Construction Engineer of the Western and Atlantic, a railroad contractor named Denmead, Assistant Engineer Cooper, and several others, including Col. S. H. Long, brought St. James' into being. Bishop Elliott attended a meeting of these men at Col. Long's home on May 23, 1842, and was so encouraged by the prospects that he volunteered to furnish Diocesan missionary money for the new church to match whatever should be subscribed locally. Within twenty-four hours enough was pledged "to determine the Vestry to proceed forthwith to the erection of a Church."

Until a church building was ready, Bible classes were held on Sunday afternoons at the home of William Root, another leader in the group of Marietta Episcopalians. However, services in their own church building became possible for the parishioners of St. James' in one of the shortest periods in Georgia Episcopal history. On May 28, Col. Long donated the lot; on September 8, the building contract was let; on October 13, the cornerstone was laid. Before the year 1842 was out, the church had been incorporated by the state and the parish officially named St. James' in honor of St. James' Church in Philadelphia, where Root had been a member. On Palm Sunday (April 9), 1843, Bishop Elliott consecrated the church building. A week earlier, the Rev. Thomas F. Scott began his service as the first rector of St. James', Marietta. When the first delegation from this church attended the Diocesan Convention in 1843, they reported a total of eight communicants in the parish.

Four other new churches entered the Diocese of Georgia in 1843: St. Luke's, Montpelier; St. Andrew's, Darien; St. David's, Glynn County; and Emmanuel, Athens. St. Luke's, which had been a mission serving the Episcopal Institute, numbered among its congregation the faculty, students, some neighbors, and several slaves. St. Andrew's and St. David's were two churches whose principal activity was servicing the missionary needs of the many slaves found on nearby plantations. The establishment of Emmanuel Church at the seat of the University of Georgia was the fruition of six years of missionary activity through periods of alternately encouraging and depressing reports from Athens. When the recently ordained William B. Stevens offered his services as rector, and a preliminary congregational meeting at the home of Mrs. R. D. Moore, niece of the Bishop of Virginia, promised success of the parish, Emmanuel Church was born.

Emmanuel was a very small parish in early years, and with the small income from pew-rentals and Communion alms it could hardly support its rector. Therefore Bishop Elliott, although he intended to obtain as much help as possible for Emmanuel through the Diocese, sought an additional means of supplementing Stevens' income by successfully encouraging the University to offer him a professorship. Emmanuel's church building was begun on June 3, 1843, and was completed within the year. Bishop Elliott consecrated the church on November 19, and Emmanuel Parish was off to a good start.

1844 was another good year for the Bishop. Two new churches were firmly established, one of which brought especial satisfaction since it was located in the state capital, Milledgeville. This was the parish of St. Stephen's. The other new church was St. Michael's at Springfield, then a popular summer resort. St. Michael's had been operated as a mission out of Savannah for some time; the Rev. George White, with the help of a lay reader, conducted services there for summertime transients from Savannah.

Several efforts began in 1844 toward new churches which would bear fruit later. One of these mission fields was Albany, where recent immigrations of cotton planters had populated and enriched the region. Two of the planters were Episcopalians (Phineas M. Nightingale and a Mr. Johnson) who organized a small mission activity under the Rev. Jonathan B. T. Smith to serve their slaves. Meanwhile Bishop Elliott, convinced that a white church would prosper at Albany, initiated the parish of St. Paul's there. He was encouraged in this effort by the contribution of $750 collected by Baker County Episcopalians. Dr. Meals, Albany's first mayor, was named to attend the next Diocesan Convention and represent St. Paul's in an official capacity. Unfortunately Dr. Meals could not attend the meeting, and by a curious quirk of fate the church's official organization papers were misplaced. Seven years elapsed before St. Paul's in Albany gained union in the Diocese!

The oldest parish record of St. Paul's in Albany gives, in its first paragraph, this account of the curious circumstances surrounding the church's early failure to join the Diocese:

In the year of our Lord 1844 sometime in the spring the Parish was organized by the election of wardens and vestrymen and would have been admitted into the convention with the Diocese but for the providential prevention of Dr. Meals from attending the convention which that year met in Augusta. By some means the papers were mislaid. The Parish was occupied by the Rev. Mr. Ellis for about one year after which time he left it and the members and friends of the Parish either removing and being discouraged let the Parish die out. And five years after scarcely a vestige of what had been done could be found to tell that a faithful minister had been among the people. As difficult as it is to establish the Church in a floating and scattered population it would seem bad policy to undertake it unless our Church had more ministers.

Bishop Elliott reported to the Diocesan Convention in May, 1844, that on the previous January 1st, he had visited Baker County where the Rev. Jonathan B. T. Smith had just assumed the duties of minister. On the morning of that New Year's Day the Bishop held services on the plantation of J. M. Nightingale; then he drove seventeen miles to Albany for an evening service. One night later, at a gathering of Albany citizens, Bishop Elliott discussed the liturgy and beliefs of the Episcopal Church; the result of the meeting was the organization of St. Paul's of Albany. The men present pledged $750 for a church building, which they promised to have ready for consecration in December.

Another area of new ground cleared for plowing by Bishop Elliott in 1844 was in Cass County. Accompanied by Marietta's energetic rector, the Rev. Thomas F. Scott, the Bishop met with and preached to a group of North Georgia Episcopalians in a Baptist church at Pettis Creek near the Etowah River. Sixty acres of land were bought and plans made for the construction of a church, school, and parsonage before the Bishop continued on his missionary journey into the northern part of the state. (Later the Rev. Frederick Elwell began a thriving school at the parsonage.) Rome was the next stop, where the parish of St. Peter's was begun. The Rev. Carter Page was entrusted with the mission work here, but his departure shortly thereafter, and the infrequency of Mr. Scott's visits, left the little mission on shaky foundations.

The principal developments of 1845 concerned educational activities and efforts to bring further religious instruction to the slaves of Georgia's Episcopalian planters. At Montpelier Institute, reported Bishop Elliott in some discouragement, the boys' school had closed; strong objections had been raised because it was considered to be too close to the girls' school (!). Still desirous of a religious school for boys, the Bishop looked hopefully at Mr. Elwell's school in Cass County. Meanwhile another girls' school had been founded by St. James' in Marietta. The

Kennesaw Female Seminary, supported strongly by the vestry and other Mariettans, obtained $550 by subscriptions for the school itself, as well as $250 for a rectory and an additional $146 to meet church expenses. Mr. Scott was well pleased with this school's prospects, and reported that based on his observations in Cobb, Cass, and Floyd Counties, the future of the Episcopal church in North Georgia seemed bright indeed.

The religious instruction of Negro slaves was a continuing interest of the Bishop's. The year 1845 showed some of the fruits of this effort in two areas of the state. In Glynn County the work carried on by St. David's Church was being done by the Rev. Theodore Bartow. Mr. Bartow, a Navy chaplain on leave, reported much progress in the services and instruction given to the slaves in that county. The Rev. Edward Brown was directing the same sort of work at St. Simon's Island. A decrease in the number of slaves in Darien, caused by a declining agriculture, slowed down the Negro instructional program of St. Andrew's Parish.

Continued spread of churches, the migration of some Episco-palians within Georgia, and the emergence of two important parishes from financial indebtedness were the principal highlights of the year 1846. A new mission church, St. Mary's, was opened in Camden County with the Rev. Joseph A. Shanklin as missionary. Another new mission gave further indication of the willing response to the Bishop's call to instruct slaves. When William C. Williams, a protege of Bishop Elliott's, was ordained, he began working with slaves on the north side of Great Ogeechee River. Meanwhile, progress in the Negro work in Baker County was so favorable that when the Bishop visited there he was able to confirm sixty-five of the slaves.

While it was pleasing to Episcopalians to see the opening of new missions and new churches in Georgia, it must have irritated them somewhat to realize that some of these resulted from the migrations of Episcopal parishioners *within* the state, thus weakening older churches. In the 1840's and 1850's Georgia experienced a considerable reshuffling of its population. The removal of the Cherokees in 1838-39 rid the state of its last major Indian group and opened up vast new extents of territory for white settlement. Of course, a number of Georgians had pushed

ST. JAMES', Marietta
Organized 1842
Church built 1843
Parish House built 1956

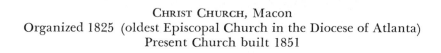

CHRIST CHURCH, Macon
Organized 1825 (oldest Episcopal Church in the Diocese of Atlanta)
Present Church built 1851

GRACE CHURCH, Clarkesville
Organized 1838
Church built 1842

TRINITY CHURCH, Columbus
Organized 1834 • Present Church built 1890
Parish House built 1925

SOME OF
THE OLD CHURCHES
in the
DIOCESE OF ATLANTA

St. Stephen's, Milledgeville
Organized 1841
Church built 1843

Emmanuel Church, Athens
Organized 1843 • Built 1899

CHURCH
OF THE
REDEEMER
Greensboro
Organized 1863
Church built 1868

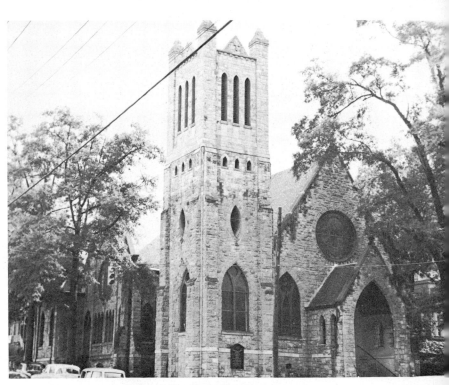

ST. PETER'S, Rome
Organized 1844 • Church Built 1900

St. Philip's Church—First Church on Hunter Street
Built 1847

THE
CATHEDRAL
of
ST. PHILIP

THE
CATHEDRAL
of
ST. PHILIP

FIRST PRO-CATHEDRAL ON PEACHTREE STREET
BUILT 1933

into the Cherokee lands as far back as 1832, when a gigantic distribution of the land took place in a land lottery. But it was not until the main body of the Cherokees was formally removed that the migration into northwest Georgia could proceed with vigor. When it was proposed to lay a railway from the little hamlet of Marthasville, later Atlanta, through North Georgia to Chattanooga, a large-scale expansion of the population into this area was assured. Even St. Paul's in Augusta, once considered a frontier parish itself, felt the vacuum of emigrating Episcopalians who left the more established areas of the state for the newer lands in the north and west.

The parish of St. James' Church in Marietta had enjoyed much of its early growth when the vanguard of the railroad construction used the city as a base. As the iron rails and wooden ties pushed further north, some of the Episcopal congregation moved on to set up new headquarters further up the tracks; and the little parish faced some staggering difficulties in trying to maintain its existence. But by 1846 the vestry proudly reported that the church was prospering and its church building was owned with clear title, along with the school, parsonage, and twenty acres of glebe land. Likewise formerly troubled by finances, Trinity in Columbus reported in 1846 that it had triumphed over its financial difficulties and its congregation now numbered one hundred and twenty-five church members.

By the time of the annual meeting of the following year, Bishop Elliott reported that the Georgia Diocese was widely dispersed. Young churches like St. Stephen's in Milledgeville, and Emmanuel in Athens were struggling, largely successfully, to keep going, while two new churches had been added to a Diocese whose members were scattered from Savannah to Rome and from St. Simon's Island to Clarkesville. The mission operations in Cass County had successfully produced the new Church of the Ascension; while mission developments at Georgia's newest booming railroad center, Atlanta, produced yet another new church, St. Philip's.

The history of St. Philip's dates back to May of 1846 when a meeting was held at the Richard Peters house in Atlanta. Present were railway men including the Chief Engineer of the Western Railroad, C. F. M. Garnett of Virginia, who had also been instrumental in the founding of St. James' at Marietta. His colleagues at this meeting were J. E. Thompson, the Georgia Railroad's chief engineer (and later Pennsylvania Railroad president); Samuel G. Jones, railroad surveyor; and William Stockton of New Jersey. From this meeting came the organization of St. Philip's Parish, which was formally established a year later, May 2, 1847. At this time the vestry elected Richard Peters, Samuel G. Jones, and Guy L. Warren, as the parochial delegates to the next Diocesan Convention. In the following year St. Philip's was consecrated. Bishop Elliott was impressed with the humble appearance of the "28 feet by 42 feet frame building." He urged other new churches to build cheaply so that more money could go into needed mission and religious work. Better churches could be constructed later when funds were available for such purposes, he noted.

Two new churches entered the Diocese in 1848. One of these, Zion, in Talbotton, received considerable help from the Episcopalians of Savannah, who showed their continued interest in church mission work by donating eighteen hundred dollars to the Rev. Richard Johnson for the building of this new mission. The Church of the Messiah at St. Mary's was the other fresh mission.

Emigration continued to trouble the well-established churches, especially Christ Church at St. Simon's. Also, the outlook for educational activity seemed clouded in view of the lack of support being given the Montpelier project by Georgia Episcopalians. The parish there, St. Luke's, still did not have a chapel; and the Bishop's plea for sufficient contributions to make it possible did not seem to meet with favorable response. But if the Bishop were concerned over the Montpelier situation, he could look with pride at the educational work which had been initiated in Savannah by St. John's Church. Its rector, the Rev. Rufus M. White, reported that he had established a school and asylum for orphans, with the assistance of the women of his parish.

As the Episcopal Church of Georgia moved into mid-century, it enjoyed a feeling of solid progress under its first Bishop. Stephen Elliott's achievements in ten years of service to his Diocese were impressive.

CHAPTER
❧ · VI · ❧

THE GEORGIA CHURCH IN THE 1850's

THE YEAR 1850 marked the tenth anniversary of the Episcopate of Bishop Stephen Elliott. By the end of that year his flock numbered twenty-one churches and 870 communicants. Leading in membership and in support of the Bishop's entire program of church activity and expansion was Christ Church, Savannah, with 160 members. Second was St. Paul's, Augusta, with 136. St. John's, Savannah, had 109, while close behind was Trinity Church, Columbus, with 105. The other 377 members were divided through the state as follows: Christ Church, Macon, 80; St. James', Marietta, 48; Emmanuel Church, Athens, 31; St. Andrew's, Darien, 26; Church of the Messiah, St. Mary's, 25; Christ Church, St. Simon's, 23; St. Peter's, Rome, 22; Church of the Atonement, Augusta, 18; Ogeechee Mission, 17; Grace Church, Clarkesville, 12; St. Stephen's, Milledgeville, 11; St. David's, Glynn County, 10; Church of the Advent, Madison, St. Philip's, Atlanta, and Zion Church, Talbotton, 8 each; Church of the Ascension, Cass County, 7; and St. Paul's, Albany, 6.

The newer of these churches were the Church of the Advent, in Madison, and the Church of the Atonement, in Augusta. The new church at Madison, like those of Marietta and Atlanta, was founded through the work of railroad men. Despite the transient nature of these communicants, the church got off to a good start with a large group attending the meetings at the local town hall, where the Rev. B. Elliott Habersham held services.

A step toward democratization of the Episcopal Church in Georgia occurred in Augusta in 1850 when the Church of the

Atonement was founded. In an age when pews were customarily rented to church families—certainly a deterrent to visitors and poor alike—the new Augusta church featured free pews. A fund established by Mr. and Mrs. Hallowell Gardiner and Miss Mary G. Jones made this possible. The church was to be located in "the upper part of the city" (northwest Augusta) to serve the families in a new manufacturing area. The petition by the Gardiners and Miss Jones for the establishment of the new church was approved by the vestry of St. Paul's on May 1, 1850, and the cornerstone of the Church of the Atonement was laid by Bishop Elliott on May 27. A year later, April 21, 1851, the church was organized as a parish, and on January 29, 1852, the completed church building was consecrated. While the practice of renting pews guaranteed some income to Episcopal Churches, it must have hurt them in the eyes of Georgians during an age of new and greater American democracy.

It is axiomatic that clergymen, like other men, will come and go, some by transfers and some by death. Yet when a particular Episcopal minister died on January 1, 1851, he was mourned by Episcopalians all over Georgia. He was the Rev. Edward Neufville, for twenty-three years the rector of Christ Church, Savannah. Despite nomination of his own name for the post, he had sparked the movements which led to the naming of Stephen Elliott as Bishop of the Diocese; and as President of the Standing Committee and the Missionary Committee his voice had been an influential one in Diocesan affairs. Bishop Elliott remarked of Dr. Neufville: "His labors and his cares had brought the diocese to a condition which called for a bishop of its own, and he might well have claimed the post as his by right of creation. But this was not our brother." Neufville was succeeded at Christ Church by the Rev. Abram Beach Carter of New York, son of Neufville's predecessor, the Rev. Abiel Carter. In the same year, 1851, the Diocese also lost the services of another veteran, the Rev. William Cairns of Trinity Church, Columbus.

Other new priests in the Diocese by 1851 were Joseph A. Shanklin at Christ Church, Macon; James D. Gibson at the newly consecrated church of St. Peter's, Rome; and James H. George in Baker County.

1850 and 1851 were years of building and rebuilding of church structures in the Diocese. Also, new parishes and missions were created. All of these reflected the prosperity of the times and the continued Episcopal growth. Macon was growing so fast that a new church on the edge of the town was being contemplated, and Christ Church itself was considering the possibilities of a new building to meet the demands; St. John's, in Savannah, was likewise considering a proposed new building; new missions in Griffin, LaGrange, and Albany were under discussion by Bishop Elliott; the success of the Ogeechee Mission in serving large groups of slaves on six plantations led to the establishment of a new slave mission on the Savannah River.

In the year 1851 St. Paul's in Albany was finally admitted to the Georgia Diocese, thus completing a new-church movement which had come to naught seven years earlier. Again on New Year's Day steps were taken to organize St. Paul's. In this case it was done by the Rev. James H. George. The little congregation which gathered together invited Bishop Elliott to preach on Easter Day of 1851. The next day the Bishop proceeded to re-organize St. Paul's formally. P. M. Nightingale was chosen Senior Warden and Y. G. Rust Junior Warden; other vestrymen were C. J. Harris, R. R. Hines, Garrett Andrews, W. W. Cheever, John Brooks, and W. S. Lawton.

Perhaps it would not be amiss to observe Mr. George's operations during his first year at Albany and Baker County, as indicative of the experiences of a new church in South Georgia of the 1850's. Mr. George reported on arrival in the county that churchmen were "hungering and thirsting" for Episcopal services. His weekly schedule during 1851 was an active one. "1st Sunday, at Nightingale's plantation, where a house had been provided for services. 2nd. Sunday, at the plantation of Major Nelson, Major Fishburn, Mr. Hill; 3rd Sunday in Albany; 4th Sunday, the house of Mr. A. Colquitt. And every Friday night he conducted services in Albany."

During Bishop Elliott's tour of the county in January of 1851, he had baptized and confirmed a number of Negro slaves on the various plantations. Mr. George continued to work with slaves; this is reflected in the statistics of his county membership by the end of 1851. Sixty-eight of eighty-eight communicants were Negro. The Albany Episcopalians were busy with church building plans, and several plantations were preparing houses for use in church worship. Altogether, reported Mr. George to the Diocesan Convention in 1851, "I know of no wider sphere of ministerial labor than that which presents itself in this section of the state." Albany's church was completed and consecrated on May 16, 1855.

The new structure for Christ Church, Macon, was consecrated by Bishop Elliott on May 2, 1852. It was a Gothic building of 4,438 square feet in floor space, topped by a pinnacled tower of one hundred feet in height. Much of the old brick from the former building went into the new church; and an affectionate spirit was expressed by the Macon Episcopalians who laid some of these brick themselves.

By the 1850's Bishop Stephen Elliott had built an enviable reputation. He was deeply respected and loved by Georgia Episcopalians, and under his leadership the Church grew proportionately. Georgia's Bishop had powers of persuasive eloquence which put him in demand as a speaker and orator on both religious and public issues. He was a versatile man of many interests, not the least of which was horticulture. Convinced that Georgia should expand its outlook on agriculture, floriculture, pomology, gardening, and architecture, Elliott gave speeches on these subjects and practiced his own ideas at Montpelier.

An important characteristic of the high purpose of Georgia Episcopalians in the mid-nineteenth century was reflected in the humanitarian and missionary work to which many of the state's churches dedicated themselves. In the field of humane endeavor there were special missions for the poor, for the afflicted, and for Negro slaves. In addition to the orphans' school and asylum conducted by St. John's Church, Savannah, another for both widows and orphans was begun in Augusta in 1852 by St. Paul's. Here, as in Savannah, most of the initial costs were met by the parish women's organization through special money-raising projects. Meanwhile Savannah was the scene of another phase of the Diocese's humanitarian work. In 1852 a mission was opened in the state's pioneer Episcopal city to serve unfortunates of all denominations—poor, physically afflicted, and others in need. The Rev. Thompson L. Smith was assigned to serve this mission whose pews were free to all. Also, a free school was begun by the ladies of Trinity Church in Columbus, utilizing a brick building which cost one thousand dollars.

The activity of bringing Christianity to Negro slaves had long been a special interest of Bishop Elliott's, and the mid-century accomplishment in this field proved no exception to previous progress. The Great Ogeechee Mission, under the Rev. W. C. Williams, numbered 250 pupils in its mission school, while the travelling ministry of Mr. Williams served more than a thousand slaves in surrounding territory. A chapel for the Ogeechee Mission, St. James', was consecrated by Bishop Elliott on February 10, 1856; and he had the pleasure of confirming a total of 148 Negro slaves, including numerous young people who had received training in the mission schools. This brought the total membership of the Ogeechee operation to 298 communicants.

The mission on the Savannah River was equally active, serving as many slaves as Ogeechee, on seven plantations on both sides of the river. Missionary S. W. Kennerly reported that the slaves seemed interested in the church service and that full cooperation was being received from their masters. Meanwhile the various churches in the plantation areas carried on with the program of serving nearby slaves. When on May 16, 1855, Bishop Elliott consecrated St. Paul's in Albany, he noted that three-fourths of its seventy-five communicants were Negroes. Two weeks later St. Andrew's in Darien was consecrated. There the Bishop found that of ninety-one communicants, fifty-four were bondsmen.

The Rev. Joseph A. Shanklin, who had succeeded Seneca Bragg of Macon in 1846, reported to the Diocese in 1853 that his parish was experiencing some interest in the Church by Negroes. "The Rector reports with gratitude and pleasure the addition of four colored communicants to his flock. The attendance of this class upon our service has been increasing, and it is hoped that a work has been commenced among them which will go on until numbers are brought within the fold of a Church so admirably adapted to their wants."

The Georgia Diocese obtained a Chapel for Negroes in Savannah in 1856 when the parishes of Christ Church and St. John's established St. Stephen's. Served by the Rev. S. W. Kennerly who also was in charge of the Savannah River Mission for Negroes, St. Stephen's boasted forty-five members and over a hundred pupils in the Sunday School.

Something of Bishop Elliott's approach to his cherished program—that of bringing Negro slaves into the orbit of the Church—is revealed in a part of his message to the Convention of 1852. Discussing the confirmation of some Negro slaves at Major Fishburn's plantation near Albany, the Bishop remarked:

This confirmation . . . terminated one of the most interesting series of services in which I have ever been engaged. It was made peculiarly so from the fact that it was a deliberate withdrawal from the miserable system under which they had been living, and a voluntary transfer of their religious allegiance to the Church, and this done, not too hastily nor unadvisedly, but after several years of faithful instruction and earnest thinking. It is a very idle superstition to imagine that our services are not suited to this class of people. They seize upon them with avidity so soon as anybody will take the pains to win their confession and confidence and enlighten their ignorance; but it would be worse than useless to waste one's time in dealing with them, except upon the determination of devoting one's self to their instruction.

The manner in which many Southern women of the Episcopal Church approached the responsibility of bringing religious instruction to their slaves is interestingly detailed by Victoria Hunter Clayton:

As to their religious training, every Sunday morning the mothers brought their little ones up to see me. Then I could satisfy myself as to the care they gave them, whether they had received a bath and suitable clothing for the holy day. Later the larger children presented themselves to be taught the Catechism. I used the little *Calvary Catechism,* prepared by Mrs. D. C. Weston. The adults were permitted to attend the different churches in town as they pleased, but . . . [in the evening] all were compelled to return home to feed and care for the horses, cows, etc. When the evening meal was over my dining room was in readiness for the reception of all the grown [slave] members of the family. They gathered there and took their respective seats. They were taught the Creed of the Holy Apostolic Church, the Lord's Prayer, and the Ten Commandments; that is, all who could be taught, for some of them never could learn to repeat them, but understood the meaning sufficiently to lead a right life. Sometimes I would read a short sermon to them. They sang hymns, and we closed with prayer to our Heavenly Father.

The consecration of new missions and churches continued in the early 1850's. St. Paul's of Augusta, Christ Church of Macon, and Trinity of Columbus were supporting missions in Rome and nearby Cave Spring. The latter effort culminated in the consecration of the Church of the Good Shepherd of Cave Spring on August 12, 1853. St. John's of Savannah held a formal dedication of a new building in the same year, a church which cost them $35,000 to build. When the Rev. Abram B. Carter departed from Christ Church in Savannah in 1852, after serving barely a year, he was succeeded by Georgia's prelate, Bishop Stephen Elliott, who thereby shifted his rectorship from one church to another in the same city. Christ Church remained the Bishop's parish throughout his life (to 1866).

One of the oldest present-day churches in Middle Georgia was consecrated by Bishop Elliott in 1853. In the town of Talbotton a mission effort had been active since 1848, supported in part by Christ Church of Macon. The small group of Episcopalians from Talbotton and nearby communities built a little church whose simple beauty and architectural perfection still attract visitors each year. Zion Church, as it was named, is considered to be a superb example of a small country church done in English Gothic style of the Tudor period. The wooden building was constructed in the first year of the mission with money furnished by a group of South Carolina planters because of their great interest in the missionary activity of a friend, the Rev. Richard Johnson, who initiated the Episcopal work at Zion. Eleven townsmen of Talbotton organized Mr. Johnson's church and helped him construct the beautiful little building. From its consecration in 1853 until today the church has never had a large membership. Yet this Episcopal monument, in a grove of cedar trees in Talbotton, reflects in the dim interiors of its wooden pew-boxes and slave gallery the personification of the mid-century missionary movement.

At the thirty-second and thirty-third conventions (1854, 1855), Bishop Elliott challenged the Episcopalians of his Diocese to think deeply of the serious problems which he saw in mid-century. It seemed to him that the Church was associated too often with persons of wealth, position, and influence—despite, as the records would indicate to anyone interested enough to look, the serious and constant need for money to support new missions and some of the older but thinner congregations. Many Georgians, observed the Bishop, tended to associate the Episcopal Church with those institutions which the patriots of the American Revolution had sought to destroy. Such customs as the renting of pews, a highly formalized service with Prayer Book and robed clergymen, and a seeming distaste for personalized, emotional evangelism, denied to the Church the opportunity to expand more quickly into rural areas or even to attract a larger membership in more settled communities. Bishop Elliott offered no proposals for changing any of these time-honored customs. But he did call upon Episcopal clergy and laymen to think about the situation and to make suggestions as to means by which the Church might be able to broaden its appeal.

Another area of consideration opened by Bishop Elliott concerned Georgia's position as a member of the Protestant Episcopal Church of the United States of America. In his view the state had been virtually ignored by the rest of the Church during the state's infant years after the Revolution until the creation of the Diocese in 1823, and scarcely recognized after that until his election seventeen years later. He deplored this generation of neglect; and he charged the Diocese with the responsibility of accelerating the Church's progress in order that the Episcopal movement in Georgia might meet its responsibilities. Yet the Bishop noted with concern the effects of emigrations on churches like St. James' in Marietta, where early departures left the rector with but one family of members. That the church in Marietta had succeeded despite this crippling early blow was due in great measure to the dedication of the Rev. Thomas F. Scott, its minister. There seems little doubt that other rectors could emulate Mr. Scott's example with pride; for the House of Bishops had already recognized Mr. Scott's accomplishments by appointing him Missionary Bishop to Oregon in 1853.

One of Mr. Scott's cherished projects, the seminary "for the education of ladies," was completely severed from St. James' Parish in 1858. In November of that year the property was sold for $3,500, save for a small plot on which a rectory was to be constructed. Financial crises were too heavy for the parish to continue the school.

New churches in the later 1850's were St. Mark's, Brunswick, which joined the Diocese in 1858; St. John's, Americus; St. George's, Griffin; and St. Paul's Free Chapel, Savannah. This free church had an interesting history. Founded in part on the terms of a legacy of a Mrs. Dorothy Abrahams of Savannah, and the generosity of the parishioners of Christ Church and St. John's, the chapel was built with an accumulated sum of fifteen thousand dollars. For the first time in Savannah, and with very little precedent in the rest of Georgia, an Episcopal church was to be supported by the contributions rather than from the rental of pews.

The history of St. Mark's in Brunswick dates from April of 1858, when a group of local Episcopalians determined to organize a church. They had been meeting together for worship during several years, utilizing such neighboring clergymen as would come to Brunswick for the special services. At the April meeting a delegation was named to attend the May Convention of the Diocese; and during the Convention sessions, St. Mark's of Brunswick was admitted to the Diocese. Serving as Minister-in-Charge of St. Mark's during 1858 was the Rev. E. T. Brown, at that time rector of Christ Church, Frederica.

During this period a mission of some twenty years' history received an unexpected boost. A staunch Churchman, Col. George Harvey Hall, moved into Gainesville from New England. He showed immediate interest in the struggling mission and donated a church building which was completed by 1860. Until then, services were often held in the Hall residence. A year later (1861) Bishop Elliott's Journal records that "the church at Gainesville is thriving, with fourteen members."

In the late 1850's Bishop Elliott, although disappointed at the discontinuation of his beloved Montpelier as a church school, put fresh energies into a new educational project—that of creating an Episcopal college for young men in the South. Bishop Leonidas Polk of Louisiana and other Bishops in the South were also interested in such a college; and when Polk enlisted the support of his warm friend, Elliott, the project was off to a good start. Elliott translated Polk's ideas into powerful sermons which produced sufficient donations so that on October 10, 1860, the corner-stone was laid for the University of the South at Sewanee. Elliott had been instrumental in the selection of this beautiful Tennessee site in the plateau of the Cumberland, and he further aided in the landscaping by submitting proposals for beautification of the campus.

In 1860 Bishop Elliott could look back on twenty years of steady growth in his frontier Bishopric. The original six-member Diocese which had called him in 1840 had grown to twenty-eight members, while the number of communicants in Georgia had increased from three hundred to two thousand.

CHAPTER
⚜ · VII · ⚜

THE GEORGIA CHURCH
IN THE CONFEDERACY

THE CLIMACTIC events of the 1860's represented a real challenge for the Episcopal Church in the South. The relentless toll of war would reach into all churches and resulting adjustments would bring critical problems. Political separations would inevitably involve existing religious affiliations, and new outlooks and approaches would bring new alignments. Georgia's Bishop, having been consecrated in 1841, would enter the war years as one of the three senior Southern Episcopal leaders (the others were Bishops Leonidas Polk of Louisiana and William Meade of Virginia).

Because of its healthy growth in Georgia in the ante-bellum years, the Episcopal Church by 1861 stood in fifth position in membership among other Georgia churches. The Baptists and Methodists had more than all the others put together. In third place were the Presbyterians, while fourth position was occupied by the "Union Churches," or those operated jointly in sparsely populated regions by several denominations. In sixth, seventh, and eighth places were the Christian, Lutheran, and Roman churches.

Following the secession of South Carolina in December, 1860, five other Southern states had seceded by February: Florida, Georgia, Alabama, Mississippi, and Louisiana. During the month of February Texas seceded, and these seven states organized the provisional government of the Confederate States of America; and their representatives began to appeal to the other states of the South to secede and join the new government.

In anticipation of the passage of a secession ordinance in Georgia, Bishop Elliott suggested to his clergy that when secession was announced in the state, they should omit the term "the President of the United States" from the prayers and substitute in its place "thy Servant, the Governor of the State of Georgia."

With a serious crisis concerning their allegiance to the General Convention of the Episcopal Church facing the Southern churches, Bishops Elliott and Polk resolved to call a special meeting of Southern Episcopalians to consider the situation. From a conference held at the newly established Church College at Sewanee in March, the two Bishops issued an important letter summarizing the needs for such a meeting and inviting the other Bishops to assemble:

The rapid march of events and the change which has taken place in our civil relations, seem to us, your brethren in the Church, to require an early consultation among the Dioceses of the Confederate States, for the purpose of considering their relations to the Protestant Episcopal Church of the United States, of which they have so long been the equal and happy members. This necessity does not arise out of any dissension which has occurred within the Church itself, nor out of any dissatisfaction with either the doctrine or discipline of the Church. We rejoice to record the fact, that we are today, as Churchmen, as truly brethren as we have ever been; and that no deed has been done, nor word uttered, which leaves a single wound rankling in our hearts. We are still one in Faith, in purpose and in Hope; but political changes, forced upon us by a stern necessity, have occurred, which have placed our Dioceses in a position requiring consultation as to our future ecclesiastical relations. It is better that these relations should be arranged by the common consent of all the Dioceses within the Confederate States than by the independent action of each Diocese. The one will probably lead to harmonious action, the other might produce inconvenient diversity. We propose to you therefore, dear brethren, that you recommend to your Diocesan Convention, the appointment of three clerical and three lay deputies, who shall be delegates to meet an equal number from each of the Dioceses within the Confederate States, at Montgomery, in the Diocese of Alabama, on the third day of July next, to consult upon such matters as may have arisen out of the changes in our civil affairs.

We have taken it upon ourselves to address you this Circular because we happen to be together, and are the senior Bishops of the Dioceses within the Confederate States.

A "P. S." to the letter explained that the "late date" of July 3 was necessitated by the June meeting of the South Carolina Diocese.

Several points in this interesting circular letter clearly indicate the nature of the ecclesiastical problem. The Bishops stated emphatically that the crisis in relations with the General Convention did not arise out of ecclesiastical dissension or doctrinal differences, but that "political changes" necessitated action. Further, the writers indicated a preference for joint action by southern Dioceses rather than individual states.

The group action which resulted from this letter brought into being the "Protestant Episcopal Church of the Confederate States of America," which would remain in existence until late 1865. Meanwhile, the dioceses in the seceding states examined their positions. Louisiana followed Bishop Polk's rather extreme opinion that "the Church must follow nationality," and decided that since Louisiana was seceded from the United States the Episcopal church in Louisiana had been rendered asunder from the Protestant Episcopal Church of the United States, and was therefore an independent Diocese. Other southern churches generally followed the position of Georgia's Bishop Elliott, who said that the Bishop should go with his jurisdiction; that since secession had occurred the proper procedure was to amend the individual Diocesan constitutions so that the southern churches could preserve their unity and at the same time satisfy jurisdictional necessity. The Georgia Bishop argued:

He is a Bishop of the Protestant Episcopal Church, not because he is a Bishop of the Church Catholic, but because he is the Bishop of Maine, or of New York, or of New Jersey . . . . When the jurisdiction, therefore, of a Bishop declares itself, in the exercise of its rightful sovereignty, to be thenceforth and for ever separated from the other jurisdictions which make up the Protestant Episcopal Church in the United States, it forces him necessarily into a like separation . . . The separation of his jurisdiction severs him at once from the Protestant Episcopal Church in the United States, not simply because the Church must follow the nationality, but because the Church of the United States has trammelled itself with constitutional and canonical provisions, which force the Church and its Bishop into this attitude.

An important part of Bishop Elliott's view was that the seceding states had exercised "rightful sovereignty" in their actions.

The attitude of most Episcopal leaders in Georgia concerning secession was probably similar to that of the Rev. George H. Clark, Rector of St. John's Church in Savannah. In a sermon delivered to his congregation on November 28, 1860, before any secessions had occurred, Clark stated that the possibility of the dissolution of the United States seemed a terrible one indeed, but if no other answer seemed available, then by means of secession "we will sing the requiem of these United States."

The Dioceses of South Carolina, Georgia, Florida, Alabama, Mississippi and Louisiana sent four Bishops, fourteen other clergymen, and eleven laymen to the meeting in Montgomery. No representatives from Texas appeared. Although four other southern states had seceded by the time of the meeting, they had not been among the original invitees, and their Dioceses had not had sufficient time to take the necessary action to attend. Georgia's Bishop Elliott was the senior Bishop present and was elected presiding officer.

A committee was appointed to decide upon the agenda of the conference. Clergymen favoring the immediate adoption of a new constitution to be sent to the Episcopal Dioceses of the seceded states found themselves in a minority; the Bishops and the laymen preferred to hold off permanent action until a General Convention could be held in the following summer. A compromise proposal was adopted: the Montgomery group would prepare a draft of a constitution and appropriate canons, which would be presented to another meeting to be held in Columbia, South Carolina, three months later (October 16, 1861). For the present, it was agreed that measures should be taken to secure a continuing missionary effort, both domestic and foreign. To that end, two South Carolinians were appointed treasurers to receive donations from southern Dioceses for missionary expenditures.

Finally, the Episcopalians in Montgomery adopted this important resolution:

"*Resolved,* That the secession of the States of Virginia, North Carolina, South Carolina, Georgia, Florida, Alabama, Mississippi, Texas, Arkansas and Tennessee from the United States, and the formation by them of a new government, called the Confederate States of America, renders it necessary and expedient that the Dioceses within those States should form among themselves an independent organization." As the Convention ended, Presiding Bishop Elliott remarked, "We have done, brethren of the Convention, enough at this meeting, and yet not too much."

Meanwhile, within Georgia itself, Bishop Elliott was actively supporting the Confederate cause. In sermons which were published and widely circulated, the Bishop urged not merely sympathy for the Confederate position, but active participation and support. On June 9, 1861, speaking to the Pulaski Guards in Savannah, he concluded with these remarks: "And now, Soldiers, I send you forth with the Church's benediction . . . Your cause is just . . . . Who can doubt the issue if you will but keep the Lord on your side?" Again, a week later, he stated publicly that the Confederacy was engaged in "one of the grandest struggles which ever nerved the hearts . . . of a heroic race." In August, the Bishop urged that all of the Georgia clergy utilize a suggested program which he mailed out calling for a reorganization of the Georgia Church, and he further hoped that they would all cooperate with defense preparations in case of possible invasion. These were his words:

Each Parish to organize under its Rector, and some gentleman who will act as treasurer and secretary . . . . The purpose . . . shall be to prepare . . . clothing . . . medicines and nourishment . . . and . . . hospital attention when sick and wounded, if the troops [are] from Georgia.

Each Rector to exhort every person in his Parish to do what he can towards this prospective fund by contributions in . . . clothing, in blankets, provisions, medicines, money. . . .

Each Parish to report monthly to the Bishop . . . the condition of the Parish, the articles and funds collected, distributed, and on hand. . . .

During these months of 1861 the war was far away from Georgia. Bull Run had come and gone, the South had enjoyed a glorious victory, and the long privations and suffering that lay ahead for Georgians and other southern families were yet undreamed of. Like other institutions, Georgia's churches would experience the terrible effects of war gradually. Meanwhile, enthusiasm for the southern cause ran high generally throughout the Confederacy, and the attitude of Episcopal clergy and laity proved no exception.

On October 16, 1861, the Confederate Episcopal Church resumed its efforts to organize. At a five-day conclave in Columbia, South Carolina, delegates continued the adjourned Montgomery meeting. Leonidas Polk of Louisiana was the only Bishop absent; otherwise, all eleven southern states which by this time were engaged in a war against the United States were represented. Bishop Meade of Virginia, who had seniority, presided over the meetings. The first order of important business pertained to the constitution which the committee from the Montgomery meeting offered for approval. Essentially, the new document was but an adaptation of the one by which these Churchmen were formerly governed. One specific point of departure was the adoption of provisions which crystallized a trend that many had wanted added to the previous constitution. This concerned the use of "Provinces" in cases where more than one Diocese existed within the bounds of a state. The provincial system appeared to be a logical development to systematize the growth of the church. The delegates wrangled somewhat on this point; but finally settled on the state provincial plan, if the several Dioceses which might exist within a state desired so to unite.

One of the discussions which occurred at this meeting reflects the attitude toward the former association with the Protestant Episcopal Church of the United States of America. A motion was made and seconded that the term "Protestant Episcopal" be dropped (along with "United States of America") in favor of "Reformed Catholic." Of the three Bishops supporting this idea, Bishop Atkinson expressed an interesting view: he averred that "Protestant" suggested a "spirit," while "Reformed" indicated a "fact." However, the motion did not carry.

Another change considered was a suggestion that some term other than "Convention" be used to designate the annual Diocesan meetings and the triennial national assemblies of the church. The new constitution which this group adopted contained references to these meetings as "Councils," with the additional title of "General Council" for the national body. At the next meeting of the Georgia Diocese, the term "Council" was used, and this continued until the meeting of 1866.

The Constitution of the Protestant Episcopal Church of the Confederate States of America, as adopted by the Columbia Convention, was sent to the various southern states for ratification. Georgia adopted the document within the year, as did Virginia, North Carolina, South Carolina, Alabama, Mississippi, and Texas. Arkansas approved it in November, 1862, and Florida in December, 1863. The fortunes of war prevented Tennessee and Louisiana from holding Diocesan Councils until the end of hostilities, so that these two states were never formally joined with the Confederate Church.

The Right Reverend William Meade, Bishop of Virginia, died on March 14, 1862. At his death the mantle of leadership and seniority fell upon Georgia's distinguished Bishop, Stephen Elliott. (The other possibility, Bishop Leonidas Polk, was on active duty as a Confederate General.) Six months later, Bishop Elliott issued a "Declaration and Summons" to the southern Dioceses, quoting in full the proposed constitution and announcing its ratification by seven Dioceses. The "Summons" portion of his bulletin called upon the Confederate Dioceses to send Bishops, clergy, and laity to a General Council of the Confederate Church, to meet in November, 1862, in Augusta, Georgia, with St. Paul's as the host parish.

The General Council of 1862, which met in Augusta under the presidency of the Bishop of Georgia, was the only such Council in the short history of the Confederacy. Its first and most pressing order of business was the preparation and adoption of canons, those necessary by-laws which would make its Constitution a practicable and working document. Here again the Confederate Episcopalians produced church regulations which differed only in details, not in principle, from the canons of the Church of the United States. One previous canon was completely omitted: "Of the Use of the Book of Common Prayer." Presumably, those Dioceses which should adopt the Constitution of the Confederate Church would use the Prayer Book automatically.

The General Council in Augusta also sought to continue the

same interest in missions which southern churches had always shown. Resolutions were adopted which indicated an interest in "Missionary labor coextensive with the limits of fallen humanity"; and in providing "for the spiritual wants of that class of our brethren, who in the providence of God have been committed to our sympathy and care in the national institution of slavery." But despite the desires to participate in foreign missionary activity, reports were already arriving as to the effect of the Federal blockade upon the Confederacy. A committee of three Bishops was named to the responsibility of "prosecuting of Foreign Missions so far as it may be able," but if the program was hindered by the war, donations for mission purposes "shall be securely invested." As for the Negro missions, it was deemed "next to her own expansion, the Church's greatest work in these Confederate States. The religious instruction of the negroes has been thrust upon us in such a wonderful manner, that we must be blind not to perceive that not only our spiritual but our national life is wrapped up in their welfare. With them we stand or fall, and God will not permit us to be separated in interest or in fortune."

Certain changes in the Prayer Book were necessitated by politics and by the action of the General Council. A committee was directed to make two substitutions throughout: "Confederate" for "United" and "Council" for "Convention." The committee was to consider other possible changes, but to make none which would involve a change in the "Doctrine or Discipline of this Church." Not only was the committee to prepare a Prayer Book for regular use, but one was desired for the Confederate armed forces as well.

The need for a Prayer Book, or at least a manual of prayers and services, for Episcopalians in the Confederate forces was serious. Before the General Council in Augusta resolved that one should be prepared, Bishop Elliott had already taken steps to make a Prayer Book available. Early in 1862 he made arrangements with an Atlanta printer to produce five thousand copies of a collection of prayers and services which the Bishop called the "Mission Service." He told a friend that this work "contains much more . . . than is contained in the N. York publication and . . . will contain all that will be needed in Camps, Navies, Hospitals, besides being a substitute for the Book of Common Prayer until we can see our way clear to the publication of a perfect edition." But the Bishop was somewhat less than pleased when he saw the result. Quickly he wrote the printer that the pamphlet was not produced according to specifications. He complained that the "commonest newspaper trash" was used for the paper stock. The item which aroused the greatest ire in Georgia's prelate was an announcement which appeared on the cover. Elliott told the printer not to distribute any further copies which bore "the advertisements of a firm," and to substitute plain paper for future covers. This Prayer Book for military use included Morning Prayer, Evening Prayer, the Litany, the Ante-Communion, a few hymns and Psalms, several selections of "Prayers and Thanksgivings," the "Office for the Burial of the Dead," and "Prayers to be used at Sea."

One decision of the General Council of 1862 was that a "Pastoral Letter" should be composed and dispatched to all Episcopal churches in the Confederacy. The Bishops of Georgia, Virginia, and North Carolina were named a committee to prepare the letter. This document, which apparently was written by Georgia's Bishop, contains a classic expression of the crisis faced by Episcopalians during the difficult times of the early 1860's. Calling attention to the urgency of their problems, the letter in a rather long sentence sought to justify the Church's position:

Forced by the providence of God to separate ourselves from the Protestant Episcopal Church in the United States, a Church with whose doctrines, discipline, and worship we are in entire harmony, and with whose action, up to the time of that separation, we were abundantly satisfied, at a moment when civil strife had dipped its foot in blood, and civil war was desolating our homes and firesides, we required a double measure of grace to preserve the accustomed moderation of the Church in the arrangement of our organic law, in the adjustment of our code of canons, but above all in the preservation, without change, of those rich treasures of doctrine and worship, which have come to us enshrined in our Book of Common Prayer.

In rich and glowing tones, the letter summarized the work of the General Council, explaining the various constitutional, canonical, and Prayer Book changes. If anyone were to find defects

in the Prayer Book, the letter urged that "their removal had better be the gradual work of experience than the hasty action of a
body convened almost upon the outskirts of a camp . . . ." Then,
moving into the considerations of "the points to which our efforts
as a Christian Church, should be specifically directed," the Pastoral Letter recommended several aims and objectives. Concerning relationships with churches out of the Confederacy, the letter
directed that "Our first duty is to send forth from this Council our
greetings of love to the Churches of God all the world over . . . .
Whatever may be their aspect towards us politically, we cannot
forget that they rejoice with us in . . . the one God and Father
of all . . . . Any note of man's bitterness, except against sin, would
be a sound of discord . . . ." But, the letter continued, none should
forget "that special love is due by us toward those of our own
household. To us have been committed the treasures of the
Church, and those of our own kindred and lineage. . . who are
now united with us in a sacred conflict for the dearest rights of
man, ask us for the bread of life. They pray us for . . . the Gospel
of the grace of God . . . . Their petition is that we will . . . give
them the means of Grace . . . . They pray us not to let them perish
in the wilderness; not to permit them to be cut off from the
sweet communion of the Church . . . ."

Domestic missionary effort was also needed, Bishop Elliott
wrote. "Unless we take care that the Gospel is sent to these isolated children of the Church, who will heed their cry?" Then, in
conclusion, the Bishop asked "May God's gracious Providence
guide you in safety to your homes, and preserve them from the
desolations of war." The "isolated children of the Church" to
whom the Bishop referred included not only the regular mission
opportunities of the Episcopal Church in those places of Georgia
without parishes. There were also crises among churches whose
rectors had gone into chaplain's gray or where vacancies could
not be filled. For these unattended churches and also for the
continuance of missionary work, Bishop Elliott appointed the
Rev. Mr. Pinkerton of Darien as General Missionary for the Diocese. One of the vacant churches was St. Stephen's of Milledgeville, and this parish was used by Pinkerton as his resident station
for a time during the early years of the war. Other temporary

rectors followed at Milledgeville throughout the war and reconstruction period (the first to remain as long as ten years was the Rev. J. M. Stoney, 1873-1884).

One new church during Georgia's Confederate era was St. Luke's in Atlanta. In 1863 the Confederacy sent a Tennessee chaplain and physician, Dr. Charles Todd Quintard, to Atlanta to serve southern soldiers and civilian transients there. Chaplain Quintard soon became the center of a devoted congregation, many of whom were former parishioners from Tennessee; and from this nucleus St. Luke's was launched. Services at first were conducted in a Methodist Church on Garnett and Pryor Streets while a church was being built. On April 22, 1864, Quintard held the first services in the new building, located on Walton Street (present site of the Grant Building). Four months later, during the Siege of Atlanta, an artillery shell brought sudden cessation of the very promising St. Luke's Mission. When the dust had settled, the church building was found to be completely destroyed. Not until 1870 would another St. Luke's in Atlanta again emerge in organized church work.

Another church destroyed by military action during this war was St. Andrew's at Darien. Much damage was suffered by shelling, and when Federal troops entered the town the church building was burned to the ground. (It is an interesting sidelight that five years after the war the rector, Rev. Robert Clute, and a layman published in the New York *Times* an account of this burning, attributing the blame to a Colonel Robert Shaw. Relatives of Col. Shaw not only denied the charge publicly—offering the name of another officer instead—but sent St. Andrew's the sum of $1,000 for rebuilding.)

Late in 1863 Bishop Elliott visited LaGrange to celebrate Communion for a new mission in that city. On the following Easter Sunday (March 27, 1864) the congregation organized officially as St. Mark's and was admitted into the Diocese in May. Services were held variously in Baptist, Methodist, and Presbyterian Churches. The first rector was the Rev. Charles W. Thomas.

In most Confederate states, church societies and special groups made religious materials available to soldiers. All of the major religious denominations in Georgia cooperated in the organization of a Soldiers Tract Association, to provide short sermons, inspirational readings, and prayers for the military. In January, 1863, Bishop Elliott announced that "The British and Foreign Bible Society . . . has . . . generously placed a large amount of Bibles at the disposal of parties in the Conf. States, who are taking means to have them introduced thro' the blockade."

Another manner in which some Episcopal clergymen served the armed forces was by going into service as chaplains. Eight Georgia priests are known to have been on regular duty as chaplains, while a number of others served sporadically. Six of the Georgia clergymen-in-uniform were Richard Johnson, with the First S. C. Cavalry; Samuel J. Pinkerton, with the Atlanta Hospital; and George Easter, William T. Helms, Telfair Hodgson, and J. M. Meredith. Clergymen as such were exempt from Confederate conscription, although many saw service during the war.

The role of the chaplain was a trying one, indeed, especially in the dying days of the Confederacy. An Episcopal clergyman from Mississippi, serving on the staff of the Confederate General Hardee, wrote from Atlanta an interesting description of some of his difficultes. He was the Rev. John W. Beckwith, later to become the second Bishop of the Diocese of Georgia. In a letter to his wife dated June 26, 1864, Chaplain Beckwith stated:

> I have asked Hardee for a candid opinion as to the ability of a Missionary to do work in the Army while this Campaign is going on, and he tells me it is simply impossible . . . . He says that if the men were brought together for service it wd. at once attract the attention of the enemy who wd. open fire upon us . . . and cause a useless sacrifice of life. He therefore advises me to confine my operations to the Hospitals, for nothing can be done here outside of his Staff . . . . I had an interesting service this morning: the Gen. and Staff were around me and joined in the services. I did not preach, and the service was short, for fear of interruption, no man being able to tell what a half hour may bring forth.

Chaplain Charles T. Quintard had considerable success on a high level. In 1864, during the Atlanta Campaign, on Quintard's urging four Confederate generals were baptized and confirmed by Bishop Elliott. These leaders were Joseph E. Johnston, Braxton Bragg, John B. Hood, and William J. Hardee.

Although of a different nature, problems besetting the civilian clergy were no less difficult. Not only concerned with the troubles of his parish at Christ Church and the other established churches of the Diocese, Bishop Elliott continued with the missionary program for which he had been noted in pre-war Georgia. But throughout the war period only two new churches were admitted to the Diocese, raising the number to twenty-seven. One of these new churches was St. George's at Griffin, organized as a parish by Bishop Elliott in 1859. Its mission status dated back to 1848. During the war, St. George's development was slow. The Rev. J. H. George reported in 1861 that there but three communicants, Mrs. John McIntosh Kell, Mrs. C. W. Thomas, and Mr. Andley Maxwell. By 1864 the parish was reorganized, and with a sufficiently large membership was admitted to the Diocese.

Church finances presented a serious challenge. In an 1863 letter, Bishop Elliott summarized some of these difficulties: "My own salary and travelling expenses have been fixed heretofore by the Domestic Committee at $1800. I am content to receive anything the Church may give. I have no other income . . . . I have been obligated, since the war began, to apply to the salaries of the missionaries and of myself, a special fund solicited personally by me and not intended to be thus applied. Of this there remained some $700, which I desire to use for the assistance of feeble Parishioners." Many sources of income were no longer dependable. "The Missionary Committee has not been idle," he wrote during the third year of the war, "but the distances by which we are separated and the slowness of the mails makes communication very tedious and prospects very slow."

Although the war had a generally disruptive effect upon the churches of Georgia, there is at least one occasion in which a military operation stood still during an Episcopal church service. A company of Confederate infantry was marching through Gainesville early in the war at a time when a wedding was about to take place at Grace Church. The commanding officer, Captain Daniel Chandler, received and accepted an invitation for the entire company to attend the nuptials. The soldiers altered their direction of march, stacked arms outside the Chapel, and filed into the building where they stood throughout the service. Upon its conclusion, they filed out of the building, took up arms, and continued their original march.

Georgia churches of all denominations extended themselves to support the war effort, and in this sacrifice Episcopal churches played a full role. A few examples will illustrate this trend. In May, 1862, the vestry of Christ Church, Macon, resolved to donate their church bell to the Confederacy. Informed of this gesture, Captain Richard M. Cuyler responded that until the bell was needed, he would not call for it. However, in October, 1863, the need was felt, and the bell was turned over to him.

Support of the war effort also included loans to the government, usually in the form of investments of church monies in Confederate bonds. On July 7, 1862, the vestry of St. James' Church in Marietta voted to purchase $2,100 worth of the bonds "until further permanent investment should be decided upon." Like Macon's Christ Church, St. James' had also donated its church bell to the Confederate need for iron. Shortly thereafter the town of Marietta placed its own town bell in St. James' tower so that proper warnings could be given in time of crisis.

In June, 1864, Marietta's town bell in St. James' steeple rang vigorously and often—for Sherman's massive hundred thousand were flanking and marching through North Georgia. Episcopalians in Marietta knew especial sadness on June 14 when the body of Lieutenant General Leonidas Polk, Bishop of Louisiana, was brought to their town from the battlefield of nearby Pine Mountain.

Two weeks later, on a Sunday morning, Federal forces entered Marietta hard on the heels of evacuating Confederates. The vestry records of St. James' indicate that six communicants attended morning services, but "the excitement was so great that no service was held in the afternoon." A few days later, Union officers asked the rector, the Rev. Samuel Benedict, if he would "use the prayer for the President of the United States." Both Benedict and his assistant, the Rev. J. J. Hunt, refused and as a consequence the church was ordered closed and the two clergymen placed under technical arrest. At one time during August, Benedict and Hunt were confined in a room of the Marietta Hotel for twelve days. On September 1, Mr. Benedict moved his family to the North "under orders of banishment."

An oft-told end-of-the-war tradition in Trinity Church of Columbus is that communicants were at the altar praying for victory on Sunday morning, April 16, 1865, when word came that Union cavalry forces were entering the city. At once the male members of the congregation left the church and went directly into unsuccessful battle against the invaders.

Thus the Episcopal Church in Georgia, like other churches in the South, donated its treasure, goods, and men to the Confederate cause. But still another type of support was given. A student of religion in the Confederacy, Dr. W. E. Wight, asserts that the various southern churches exerted one of the strongest of all influences attempting to sustain the cause of the South among its people. Religion merged with nationalism provided the firmest possible basis for the maintenance of morale and enthusiasm. In this activity the Episcopal Church of Georgia cooperated thoroughly.

CHAPTER
✤ · VIII · ✤

THE POST-WAR YEARS
(1866-1890)

DESPITE all the progress which the Church would make in the first full year after the War Between the States, it was a very sad year for Georgia Episcopalians. On December 21, 1866, Bishop Stephen Elliott died in Savannah. The Church thus lost the single leader so largely responsible for the Diocesan success and progress since 1840.

A few months earlier, Bishop Elliott had, as usual, presided at the annual Council of the Diocese, held in Savannah with his own original Georgia parish, St. John's, as host. Since this would prove to be Bishop Elliott's last Council, and because, both in its actions and in the significance of the Bishop's message, it was a critical time, it seems appropriate to devote especial attention to this particular convention.

To the Council of the Diocese the Bishop reviewed the events of the nine months which had elapsed since the last meeting, August 10-13, 1865, in Athens. Bishop Elliott reminded the delegates that in Athens the question of the direction of the Georgia Church's allegiance had been left in the hands of the Bishop, "to be determined according to his judgment and sense of the fitness and propriety of things." The Bishop's "judgment and sense of the fitness" of what should be done led him to a considerable correspondence and exchange of letters with both northern and southern Church leaders. He did not attend the meeting of the General Convention of the Protestant Episcopal Church of the United States of America, which met in Philadelphia in October,

1865, believing that it would be better "not to embarrass its utterances or its action" by being present. Rather, he intended to wait and see what the General Convention's attitude might be toward a reconciliation and a reunion with the dioceses of the southern states. Proudly, Bishop Elliott reported to his Georgia brethren that "instead of anathemas, there were warm greetings of renewed friendship and tears of reconciled love—instead of excommunications, there was hearty welcome and assurances of rejoicing hearts over the healing of the wounds which had been produced by political strife." After all, the Bishop reasoned, the action which had separated the southern Dioceses from the mother Church had not been taken for the "formation of a new church, . . . (God forbid,) but merely an organization for legislative purposes."

Now that the Church in the North had removed all possible hindrances to reunion, the Bishop next met with the General Council of the Confederate States of America, which very soon resolved "that it was entirely consistent with the good faith which any Diocese owed to the Bishops and Dioceses with which she had been in union since 1862, for her to decide for herself whether she shall any longer continue in union with this Council." All the other southern Dioceses had already removed themselves from the Confederate group (or were in the process of doing so), had made the necessary revisions in constitution and canons, and were preparing for the next annual meeting of the Church in the North. The Bishop concluded this portion of his address by remarking that all that remained was for Georgia to take similar steps so as to be rejoined to the national group.

The "similar steps" suggested by Bishop Elliott were taken at the Savannah meeting. A special Committee on Constitution and Canons was set up which reported, on the following day, the necessary revisions which would make the Diocesan constitution and canons acceptable to the General Convention. These revisions were promptly adopted.

Both the Bishop's address and committee reports registered justifiable concern over the status of the Church in Georgia at the end of the war. Complete statistical data seemed impossible to obtain. As a committee phrased it, "Some Parishes are not reported at all; some returns cover a period of twelve months; some of nine. Few Parishes have been regularly worked during the past twelve months of anxiety and disturbance, of political and social change." Fourteen reports were made; and the Convention learned of a total of 244 baptisms, 189 confirmations, 1,998 present communicants, and $7,055.13 in contributions.

Twenty-two parishes were considered the contributing members of the Diocese. Assessments levied against these churches for the Bishop's salary indicate their relative status as to wealth and membership potential for the coming ecclesiastical year, which would be the first real post-war year. Assessed amounts were: Christ Church, Savannah, $1,000; St. Paul's, Augusta, 550; Christ Church, Macon, 400; St. John's Savannah, 400; Trinity Church, Columbus, 250; Emmanuel Church, Athens, 125; Church of the Atonement, Augusta, 100; St. Philip's, Atlanta, 100; St. James', Marietta, 50; St. Paul's, Albany, 50; St. Stephen's, Milledgeville, 50; St. Peter's, Rome, 25; St. Mark's, Brunswick, 25; Christ Church, St. Simon's, 10; St. Andrew's, Darien, 10; St. David's, Glynn, 10; St. George's, Griffin, 10; St. Mark's, LaGrange, 10; Grace Church, Clarkesville, 10; Advent Church, Madison, 10; Church of the Redeemer, Greensboro, 10; and Zion Church, Talbotton, 5.

In the course of his general remarks, Bishop Elliott referred to the dire needs of certain churches which had experienced physical damage from the effects of war. St. James', of Marietta, for example, "suffered very much during the war," and the building was "in sad condition." Columbus had been captured on Easter Day, 1865, and the parishioners of Trinity Church had "suffered very heavily in person and in property." To add to this they lost their rector shortly after. Since his death their general depression had been aggravated by having no services at all, the Bishop noted. St. Philip's in Atlanta had been "horribly desecrated" during the war, and on January 14, 1866, Bishop Elliott performed a special service for that parish. Taken from the Irish Prayer Book obtained by the Bishop from a Pennsylvania minister, the service was an "office for expiation and illustration of a church desecrated or prophaned."

Another church in pathetic condition at the end of the war was St. Andrew's, Darien. Bishop Elliott appointed the Rev. J.

Knowles as Missionary to Darien. On Knowles' arrival, he "found the town in ruins, and the beautiful Episcopal Church edifice in ashes." Most of the communicants, along with most of the town, had gone to a nearby community ("The Ridge") to live, where Knowles held services in the Methodist Church. There "the congregations have been unusually large and serious," he reported, "and we have gathered up communicants, and organized a Sabbath School and Bible Class."

Stephen Elliott's last episcopal message to his Diocese contained an interesting summary of some of the critical problems facing Georgia parishioners in 1866, and is suggestive of the character of this great Church statesman. Near the conclusion of his remarks the Bishop discussed "the transition state in which all opinion seems to be at this moment in the Diocese." He commented on the agitation which the war had produced, with its concomitant readjustments of society, and realization that the systems in which men had believed and rested their beliefs had proved "unsound and unsatisfactory." In this crisis, he believed, lay "the Church's time for action." It was an age of challenge which the Church should capitalize upon "boldly and fearlessly," in guiding the reorientation of men's spirits and minds.

But Bishop Elliott went beyond these philosophical and psychological considerations. He took up the situation brought on by the emancipation of the slaves. Reminding Georgia Episcopalians of the almost constant effort which had been underway long before the war to give Christian instruction to Negro slaves, the Bishop now observed that the freeing of the Negroes had brought "no new obligations" to the Georgia Diocese. Instead, it had "freed her from a fearful responsibility." He listed the sacrifices which had been made to have slaves instructed in Christian education. "No people," he said, "have ever labored more faithfully, more devotedly, with more self-denial, than have Southern Christians to do their best for the slaves committed to their trust . . . Almost every Minister for a half century past has devoted some of his time to these poorer members of his flock, and very many more would have kneeled at our altars, had they not preferred a more exciting worship and a more enthusiastic exhibition of their feelings than we allowed . . . . If a slave did not receive religious instruction it was because he did not care about it, or because he was in some remote position, where the whites were as badly off as himself."

As far as the continued religious education of the freedmen was concerned, the Bishop argued that the Georgia Church should continue to do this work without seeking outside assistance. The former slaves had attended Sunday Schools in the past—they could still continue to do so. If they wished to organize an Episcopal Church for themselves, they would be given every assistance—in Georgia by Georgians, not through help invoked from the outside. "None understand the colored race as well as we do—none care for it as much as we do—none have its confidance as fully as we have," he noted. The Bishop went on to remark that in his heart he was glad that slavery had been abolished, but he thought that it was "the greatest calamity which could have befallen" the Negroes. He stated that he foresaw physical disease and social evils which would cripple them as an independent people.

Elsewhere in his message he commented upon affairs at St. Stephen's Church in Savannah, which was a colored church. On his last visit there he confirmed eight new members; and he commented very favorably upon the work being done at St. Stephen's by James Porter, "a very intelligent and well educated colored man, to whom I have given permission to read, without having actually licensed him in that capacity." He noted that the church had its own wardens and vestry and was capably "managing its temporal affairs" in the absence of the Rev. Mr. Staley who had resigned owing to ill health. Seemingly the war had not affected St. Stephen's, which in his opinion, "could only receive mischief by any intermeddling with . . . . It is quiet, orderly, subordinate to Episcopal authority, and ready to be guided by those whom it has always recognized as its best and truest friends."

On Christmas Day, 1866, Bishop Elliott was buried in Savannah. Apparently he had been in bad health for some months, but whenever queried about it, he usually answered, "It is only weariness." During a meeting with friends in Macon before departing for Savannah just prior to his death, the Bishop was asked in casual conversation what his opinion was in reference to sudden death. He answered, "I consider it the highest mark of favor from God to a Christian, for he is instantly translated into the presence of his Saviour, and the glories of Paradise, without any suffering." And sudden death it was which overtook Stephen Elliott that same day. For hardly had he been reunited with his family when he fell to the floor; and when he was examined, it was found that he had died.

During the burial of Stephen Elliott, the colored vestry of St. Stephen's Church demonstrated "touching and beautiful evidence of love and reverence they bore him." They asked for and received permission to serve as pallbearers. An observer, Thomas A. Hanckel, commented on the incident: "Considering the peculiar and momentous issues of the time, we think it was the grandest and most instructive spectacle, amidst all the solemn, mournful and agitating ceremonies of the day, on which the city of Savannah was hushed to listen to the footfalls of those who thus bore their Bishop to the tomb."

With the death of Bishop Elliott, the rectorship of Christ Church fell upon the shoulders of his long-time assistant, the Rev. Charles H. Coley. Mr. Coley served the parish until 1868, and was succeeded by the Rev. John M. Mitchell, D.D.

In the year 1867 three new churches petitioned for membership in the Diocese. These were the Church of the Ascension, Sparta; St. Mark's Church, Dalton; and St. Stephen's Church, Savannah. The Negro Lay Reader at St. Stephen's, James Porter, was given permission to apply for ordination to the Diaconate. Porter reported to the Diocese that his church membership numbered 87, with 40 enrolled in Sunday School. During the year three adults and eight infants had been baptized; and nineteen communicants added by confirmation. He stated that his routine was to read services "twice every Sabbath, and on other days specially set apart." Although it originally had petitioned the Diocese for membership while the Convention of 1867 was in session, St. Stephen's "asked leave to withdraw its application for admission into union with the Convention." The request was granted.

In May, 1866, the Rev. B. E. Habersham had been sent by Bishop Elliott to begin missionary operations at Sparta. He found there eight communicants; adding to this his own family, several others who moved into the community, and four who were confirmed by the Bishop, his total membership by the following May was sixteen. Habersham preached regularly two Sundays in the month at Sparta, "giving a third Sunday to Col. Johnson's flourishing and interesting school, three miles off, and to occasional services at the Factory and elsewhere." By the end of his year in this area, Habersham had accepted an appointment out of Georgia, and the work at Sparta would have to be continued by someone else.

In Dalton the Missionary-in-Charge was the Rev. John J. Hunt, a man with a long record of missionary activity in the state, commencing with Athens in the 1830's. St. Mark's Mission was begun in 1866 when the newly arrived Col. Ben E. Green stimulated a group of communicants from Dalton, Tunnel Hill, and Ringgold to meet together. Colonel and Mrs. Green gave a lot upon which the first St. Mark's Church in Dalton was built in 1871. Bishop Beckwith held the first services there and commented that "the congregation in Dalton, after many trials, are in possession of a handsome Gothic church with seating capacity of 300."

The applications of Sparta and Dalton were accepted by the Convention of 1867 at its meeting in Macon during the month of May. Initially this Convention conducted several memorial exercises for its departed Bishop Elliott. The Standing Committee of the Diocese reported that it had held an emergency meeting on December 26, 1866, and after expressions of sorrow and appreciation concerning the late Bishop, they had agreed to ask the Rt. Rev. R. H. Wilmer, Bishop of Alabama, "to visit and perform Episcopal offices in this Diocese until the meeting of its next Annual Convention." Bishop Wilmer accepted, and during the Macon Convention he reported on his five months' activity in Georgia. He visited seven churches, ordained one Deacon, Thomas Coke Stanley (formerly a Methodist minister), and confirmed 138 persons. Concluding his report, Bishop Wilmer prayed for divine guidance for the Convention in the "selection of a Bishop who shall emulate the spirit and deeds of your late Bishop, and lead you onward in the good work so auspiciously begun."

The selection of such a Bishop was a prime objective at the forty-fifth Annual Convention. On Saturday, May 11, 1867, two nominations were placed on the floor: the Rev. John W. Beckwith, rector of Trinity Church, New Orleans; and the Rt. Rev. Thomas F. Scott, Missionary Bishop of Oregon and formerly pioneer rector of St. James', Marietta. Beckwith was elected by more than two-to-one, and by motion from the floor he was declared the "unanimous choice" of the Convention.

One other notable feature of the Convention of 1867 was the encouraging prospect apparent from the combined reports of Bishops Elliott and Wilmer, and given by the Standing Committee. They showed an interesting contrast with the figures for the previous year:

	1866	*1867*
Baptisms	244	474
Confirmations	189	314
Communicants	1,998	2,141
Contributions	$7,055.13	$21,199.96

It was reported that three parishes had been reorganized. These were St. Andrew's, Darien; St. Mark's, Brunswick; and St. Luke's, Montpelier, where Elliott had laid the cornerstone for a new church building shortly before he died. The Committee noted that "other points of Missionary labor are still open . . . ." Some of these were Americus, of which Bishop Elliott had reported, "one small congregation keeps well together, and increases, even without the presence of a Missionary"; Flat Shoals, "where, under the care of a Lay Reader, recently ordained Deacon, Rev. Thomas C. Stanley, a congregation is gathered, a large class await confirmation, and a church edifice is ready for our occupancy and possession"; Covington, "where seven persons have been confirmed and nine communicants reside, and a beautiful lot for a church edifice has been donated"; and Thomasville, Bainbridge, Cuthbert, and Hawkinsville.

With considerable regret, the Committee reported the abandonment of one of the oldest missions which served Negroes in the state: the Great Ogeechee Mission. The move, considered "perhaps unavoidable," ceased (at least for the time being) Episcopal operations for "the Church's children on the banks of the Ogeechee."

One of the transitions through which the Georgia Diocese was passing in this era was that of changing the pattern of collections in the church from "Communion Alms" to that of weekly offerings. Of the twenty-four churches in the Diocese in 1867, thirteen gave specific reports of Communion collections. Several others noted the change to weekly alms, while the remainder failed to indicate the source of contributions.

On April 2, 1868, in St. John's Church, Savannah, John Watrous Beckwith was formally consecrated Bishop of the Diocese of Georgia.

Beckwith was born in Raleigh, North Carolina, in 1831. He was graduated from Trinity College, Hartford, in 1852; and two years later, in 1854, he was ordained to the Diaconate. Before the war, he served in North Carolina and Maryland. He was commissioned a Chaplain in the Confederacy and served for a time on General Hardee's staff. After the war, he ministered briefly in two congregations (Demopolis, Alabama, and Deer Creek, Mississippi) before accepting the call to Trinity Church in New Orleans late in 1865. The invitation to serve as Bishop of Georgia was based, at least in part, on the reputation of his "brilliant and marvelous work" at Trinity in New Orleans, which, "in three short years, built up a disheartened, disorganized and poor little parish into one of the foremost in the whole Church . . . ."

Participating in Beckwith's Consecration were Bishops J. P. B. Wilmer of Louisiana, R. H. Wilmer of Alabama, W. M. Greene of Mississippi, Thomas Atkinson of North Carolina, and John G. Young of Florida. Bishop Greene presided. The ceremony was conducted as follows: "The Bishop elect having made the required PROMISE OF CONFORMITY, the *Litany* was sung by the Right Rev. the Bishop of Florida, John Green Young. After the *Examination* was concluded, *Veni Creator Spiritus* was sung, the Bishop of Florida leading. The Presiding Bishop then said the words of *Consecration,* the other Bishops uniting in the *Imposition of Hands.*"

Episcopalians in Georgia soon became very fond of their new Diocesan. One enthusiastic writer characterized him as follows: "Well did the new Bishop do his work. His wonderful voice, bringing out the full meaning of the services, at once arrested the attention of his hearers . . . . His oratory in the pulpit attracted large congregations wherever he went, and the course of his episcopal visitations was like a royal progress."

Bishop Beckwith presided over his first Diocesan Convention during May of 1868, a month after his consecration, with Christ Church of Savannah as host to the 47th annual meeting. The new parishes of St. John's, Bainbridge, and Mediator, Washington, were recognized and received into the Diocese. In his report the Rev. C. A. Grant, rector at Bainbridge, announced that his little church numbered ten communicants and sixteen Sunday School scholars. During his five months there, he stated, he had rounded up another group for confirmation; and he seemed confident that there would be a "decided augmentation" in his membership, which though small then, was "composed of first rate material." The missionary vicar of the Church of the Mediator, Washington, was the Rev. J. Knowles. He reported that "a respectable congregation," including eleven communicants, was active in the Wilkes County church. At present, he announced, "we worship in the Masonic Hall."

One report is particularly indicative of the complex problems facing the Georgia church in the late 1860's. This was a statement of varied activities by the Rev. E. P. Brown:

During the past year I remained at my home in Glynn County, waiting and hoping for the return of my parishioners, who were scattered by the war. But few returned, and those so reduced, nothing could be done in restoring the services of the Church. In the meantime, having received the appointment, I acted as Missionary of the Domestic Board for the negroes upon St. Simon's Island and the plantations bordering the Altamaha, officiating, also, a part of the time, in the Church of St. Mark's, Brunswick, and during the months of September, October, and a part of November, in St. John's, Savannah. In January, having no appointment, I accepted the position of Superintendent of the Union Society for Orphans, at Bethesda, at which point I am still residing, in the meantime performing any service in Savannah, desired . . . Baptisms—Infants, white, 3.

Bishop John W. Beckwith served the Diocese of Georgia for twenty-two and a half years. These were painful years of reconstruction for the Church as well as for the South. Yet it was an era of encouraging growth, as a comparison of the years 1868 and

1890 will show. When Beckwith became Bishop, there were thirty-one churches in his Diocese. At his death, there were fifty-three churches and chapels, and five missions.

During the Bishop's first two years in Georgia, in addition to several very promising missions, two new churches were admitted to the Diocese. These were: Church of the Good Shepherd, Summerville, in 1869; and St. Paul's, Macon, in 1870. Bishop Beckwith laid the cornerstone of the Summerville Church on May 6, 1869. St. Paul's of Macon reported to the Diocesan Convention in 1870 a church membership of eighty-four, seventy-five of whom came from the older church in Macon. The Rev. Henry K. Rees, formerly rector of Christ Church in Macon, moved across town with some of his parishioners and became the minister of the new St. Paul's. In his first annual report, Rees noted three important objectives of St. Paul's: "First, the weekly Eucharist, as the highest act of worship. Second, the weekly Offertory, as an act of worship, and as the means of supporting the Ministry. Third, an open church and free seats for the use of all worshippers." Lacking a regular church building, St. Paul's was using a "rough car shed," which he felt was, by the earnest efforts of his congregation, being transformed "into an orderly church." The church also boasted a Parish School of seventy-five scholars, which was "to a great extent self-supporting," and a permanent teacher who was aided by several volunteer workers.

One church which suffered particularly from the effects of Reconstruction was Grace Mission in Gainesville. Disgusted with the military occupation which accompanied Radical Reconstruction, Grace Church's most important local supporter, Col. George H. Hall, in 1870 disposed of his house and lands, sold the Chapel to the Presbyterian Church, and moved to Brazil. It would be nearly five years before the mission would recover from this blow.

A parish with difficulties of another kind was Emmanuel in Athens. When their long-time rector, Dr. Matthew Henderson, died in 1872, eight years would elapse before a successor would be chosen who remained with the parish longer than two years. Altogether, until the Rev. Jonathan C. Davis of Eufaula, Alabama, accepted a call to Emmanuel in 1881, four priests served short

terms as rector, and during a two-year period services were conducted by lay-readers. Perhaps the chief difficulty lay in parochial
finances, as is evidenced by a decision of the vestry in 1873 to substitute weekly pledges for pew rentals. Thirty-one members of the
church pledged amounts ranging from 25 cents to $2.80 per week,
from which the total to be expected weekly was $28.32. In addi-
tion the Bishop had offered $300 annually from Diocesan mission
funds. These expectations allowed the vestry to promise a weekly
salary for the rector of approximately $30.00, and the Rev. Alex-
ander I. Drysdale accepted. But the pledges for 1874 offered a
total of only $19.60 a week, and when the salary was reduced to
$20.00, Drysdale resigned.

A church which literally "went to town" during the 1870's was
Ascension in Bartow County. Under the leadership of the Rev.
S. J. Pinkerton, with local funds and with contributions from
"parties in Macon, Augusta, Savannah and New York," the Ascension Mission moved into Cartersville from the creek-side location
it had occupied since 1845.

Not long after Beckwith became Bishop, an unexpected benefaction occurred for his Diocese. A close personal friend in New
York, William H. Appleton of the publishing firm D. Appleton
& Company, offered to build a church in Georgia as an evidence
of his affection for the new Bishop. Beckwith suggested instead a
home for orphan girls, children of deceased Confederate soldiers.
Appleton was greatly pleased by the suggestion, and gave the
Bishop warm encouragement. Thereupon Beckwith "begged the
money and bought the land," and Appleton donated $12,500 for
the building and $10,000 towards an endowment.

The Bishop decided that the Appleton Home should be under
the care of a body of Deaconesses. Consequently in 1870 he secured a competent superintendent, Mrs. Margaret Jennings of
New Orleans. Shortly thereafter the Order of St. Katherine was
established at the home. In the words of the Bishop, "this name
was chosen to commemorate the . . . sainted daughter of Mr.
Appleton, who . . . [during a brief life] had devoted herself to
works of charity, especially among children." In its early years
Diocesan support for this venture was slow in developing, and

nearly all of the success of the home in this period was due to Appleton's generosity and Sister Margaret's wholehearted activity.

In 1873 Bishop Beckwith accepted the rectorship of Christ Church Parish in Savannah, as had Bishop Elliott before him. By this time, however, the responsibilities of the Episcopate were so heavy that within a very short time Bishop Beckwith realized that he could not do justice to both parish and Diocese. Accordingly in 1874 the parish accepted the Bishop's resignation of the Christ Church cure, and chose the Rev. George D. E. Mortimer as his successor.

As the Reconstruction Era drew to a close in Georgia and the state began to enter upon a new period of development, the Episcopal Church experienced a similar transition. Under the leadership of Bishop Beckwith, the Diocese saw the admission of five new churches during the next ten years, and there was more than a corresponding increase in mission activities. This increase in new churches is reflected in the list below, based upon the Diocesan Reports during the period 1871-1880:

> 1871 St. Stephen's, Atlanta (changed to St. Luke's, 1872)
> 1873 St. Mary's, Athens; St. Matthew's, Savannah; St. Luke's, Hawkinsville.
> 1874 St. Stephen's, Savannah.

The newest church in Atlanta, St. Stephen's, was begun in 1870 on a basis of hope and expectation for Church growth in the capital city. At the Diocesan Convention of that year, Bishop Beckwith commented on Atlanta's need for a second Episcopal Church: "The rapid growth of this city renders one Parish and one Rector, however zealous, entirely inadequate to the demands made upon the church. It will not be long, I trust, before a new Parish will be organized and in full operation." The organization of St. Stephen's was completed in July, 1870, and concurrently, the Rev. Joseph H. Cross was named as its first rector. Within a year, Mr. Cross was succeeded by the Rev. George Macauley. On May 12, 1871, St. Stephen's was admitted to the Diocese as a parish, although it numbered but five communicants. In the following twelve months, during which the official name of the

THE RT. REV. JOHN WATROUS BECKWITH, D. D.
1868-1890

THE RT. REV. FREDERICK FOCKE REESE, D. D.
1908-1936

THE RT. REV. MIDDLETON STUART BARNWELL, D. D.
1936-1954

THE RT. REV. ALBERT RHETT STUART, D. D.
1954-

parish was changed from St. Stephen's to St. Luke's, the number of communicants rose to forty; and by 1880 there were more than a hundred.

While the five new churches did not strengthen the Diocese as much as Bishop Beckwith had hoped at the beginning of the decade, several administrative changes occurred which did have a strengthening effect. The most important of these reflects a realization that the Diocese was too big for one man to handle without help. At the Diocesan Convention of 1870 a new canon was adopted and slightly amended the next year which established a convocational system within each of four missionary districts. This improvement in the Diocesan organization was designed to relieve the Bishop of some of the responsibility for stimulating, establishing, and maintaining new missions. These regulations asserted the Bishop's control over all mission operations in the Diocese, including the appointment of the missionaries: "He shall divide the Diocese into any number of Missionary Districts not less than four; and shall appoint the Presiding Officers thereof, who shall be styled Deans. The Clergy shall, as far as is consistent with their parochial duties, perform Missionary work within their respective districts, under the direction of the Bishop. They shall also meet in Convocation at such times and places as may be appointed by the Bishop or by the Dean, or by vote of the Convocation, with the Bishop's approval. Any Parish or Missionary Station, within any Convocational District, may send one lay deputy to each meeting of the Convocation . . . ."

The Standing Committee of the Diocese reported very favorably concerning the new system at the 1871 Convention. "It has answered," they stated, "the purpose of a systematic exploration well begun. To the many places where the Church is needed, called on and not yet met, it has opened up the field . . . ." The following were named to head the several missionary districts: the Rev. Messrs. John M. Mitchell, Savannah Convocation; William H. Clark, Augusta Convocation; Henry K. Rees, Macon Convocation; and William C. Williams, Rome Convocation.

In his first report to the Diocese in 1871, Dean Mitchell reported that the parishes in his area had held three convocations, and that the unanimous agreement was that a travelling missionary be named to work the various mission prospects in the area. $1000 had been pledged, and partially raised, to help support this minister. He quoted the following resolution by the Savannah Convocation: "That the Bishop be requested to appoint a general missionary for the Savannah Convocation as soon as he can find an energetic and devoted clergyman to accept the appointment."

Other phases of his report indicate the general interest in Episcopal mission work prevalent in his district. The Ogeechee Mission, originally founded as one of Bishop Elliott's first missions for Negro slaves, had raised $118 for their work, with an additional $100 pledged. Another hundred dollars had been pledged at Valdosta, and Episcopalians there had secured a lot and were at work on the church-building program. The mission at Satilla already had six hundred dollars on hand for church erection, and promised that they would "give liberally toward the support of the missionary." Another pledge for one hundred dollars came from the Isle of Hope, while the St. Mary's Mission offered nearly fifty dollars. At all of these mission points, the report continued, "there have been already, since the creation of this Convocation, ten adults and fifty-two children baptized, and thirty-eight persons confirmed." Further, the Savannah Convocation seemed to have profited from the existence of such an organization which threw them into an extra spirit of cooperation; while the Convocation itself had also sought "to stimulate church feeling and to strengthen the hands of the rectors in the parishes." Altogether, concluded Dean Mitchell, "the experiment has proved eminently successful."

From the Augusta Convocation came a similar report by Dean Clark. Five meetings were held and substantial benefits for mission work in that area seemed to be assured from the new system. Dean Rees reported from the Macon District that three meetings were held, one of which, at Hawkinsville, "excited the deepest interest," and Rees felt that the mission work there was the most promising in his district. Thirteen communicants in Hawkinsville were actively working toward the acquisition of a church lot. Rees observed that if the clergy and congregations of the Macon District *"were only interested* in this work, much more could have been done elsewhere." This interest might result, he added, if the next Diocesan Convention would conduct one entire discussion session on the convocation system of missionary operations.

The final convocational report at the forty-ninth Convention came from William C. Williams of Rome. Showing as much enthusiasm as Dean Mitchell, Dean Williams discussed four meetings of his clergy, all of whom seemed to be "entering heartily into the spirit of the Canon." They had agreed "to devote not less than four Sundays in the year to such destitute points" as might be designated by the Bishop or the Dean.

Subsequent annual reports from the several Deans indicate that the new plan was effective in encouraging and maintaining mission churches, but that the regular assigned clergy found it difficult to attend convocational meetings more often than once yearly. Financing the missionary effort was another problem, since it was readily apparent in all the convocations that the parish clergy were far too busy with parochial duties to give effective missionary service on a regular basis. The Diocese would have to continue its assistance through assignment of a mission minister-in-charge and by financial support.

During the first ten years of the operation of this system, certain revisions were made from time to time to effectuate its success. By 1880 the Diocese had established a Board of Missions in which was vested the entire responsibility for missionary operations of the Diocese. This group consisted of the Bishop, the four Deans, and four laymen, one from each convocation. The Board met regularly during annual conventions, at which time apportionment of monies was arranged, to be distributed "between the feeble Parishes and Mission Stations." Convocations themselves were reorganized somewhat. In addition to "all the Clergy canonically resident within its limits," the membership of each included each parish's lay delegates to the Diocesan Convention as of the time of the Convocational meeting. These meetings were to occur not less than semi-annually, at which time every clergyman in the district was to attend and render a report of missionary operations within his cure. In a move to bring greater financial support for these missionary activities within the state, four regular offerings for Diocesan missions were taken through the year.

The status of the Episcopal Church in Georgia in 1880 is reflected in the Fifty-Eighth Annual Report of the Diocese. Eleven missions were listed, with locations and number of communicants as follows: Barnesville, 10; Cedartown, 7; Fort Valley, 16; Gainesville, 8; Church of the Redeemer Mission, Isle of Hope, 22; St. Paul's Mission, Newnan, 15; St. Mark's Mission on the Ogeechee River, 136; Satilla River, 13; St. Augustine's Mission, Savannah, 55; St. Matthew's Mission, Savannah, 74; and West Point, 22. Thus 378 Episcopalians were being served at these scattered mission outposts of the Diocese.

Thirty-six regular parishes were listed in this report, with a combined active communicant total of 4,055. The overall number of individual church members in the Diocese was 10,155; and 386 teachers were bringing religious instruction to 2,792 Sunday School pupils. The largest of these churches in terms of membership and communicants was St. Philip's of Atlanta, with 2,100 and 564 respectively. Next in size were Christ Church, Savannah (1,200 and 475); St. John's, Savannah (1,017 and 452); Christ Church, Macon (900 and 334); St. Paul's, Augusta (650 and 360); and Trinity Church, Columbus (550 and 252).

In addition to Bishop Beckwith, twenty-nine clergymen were on regular assigned duty in the Diocese in 1880, serving as rectors, assistant ministers, or as missionaries. Two men were listed as Candidates for Holy Orders, and six as Postulants. Some of these clergymen were dividing their time among several parishes and/or missions. The Rev. Edward Denniston, for example, was rector of Zion Church at Talbotton; he also served the missions at Fort Valley, Newnan, and West Point. The Rev. Henry K. Rees was rector of the Church of the Good Shepherd in Cave Spring and the Church of the Ascension in Cartersville; he was also assigned as missionary to the Cedartown Mission.

Mr. Rees reported that the Church of the Good Shepherd in Cave Spring was undergoing extremely difficult circumstances. His summary of conditions there reflects one of the ever-present dangers of over-zealous missionary work: if new missions are thrust out too rapidly or parishes established in missions without sufficient foundation, they become liabilities to themselves and to the work of the Church in general. The Georgia Church had

seen some of this danger realized in the past; and Rees commented on it rather bitterly in 1880:

The condition in which I found the Parish illustrated fully the
inexpediency of organizing Mission Stations into Parishes. Its Church
members were in no condition to call or sustain a Rector, after
twenty-seven years of Parish organization. Its Vestry could not be
gathered as a body, and had held no election for years; the Church
building itself in a state of shameful neglect; its floors and sills rotted;
its windows broken; stove wood and rubbish piled up in the chancel;
and on the outside, the chancel end buried two feet under the wash-
ings and debris of the mountain. By the exertion of the women of
the Church it had recently been shingled, or the building would
soon have been unusable.

Yet despite the pessimism which this report suggests, Rees lec-
tured to his small congregation (49 members, 41 communicants)
and seemed to see a ray of hope for the tiny parish: "My first
sermon forced me to say hard things and to call earnestly for help
to rescue the house of God from this disgraceful condition, and
the work of renovation has begun . . . . A reorganization of the
parish [was] made, and we now trust a new life and interest
will be attained." If the Bishop could come to Cave Spring in
the summer, he noted, "a class awaits confirmation."

Mr. Rees' effort to sustain and improve the struggling parish at
Cave Spring is illustrative of Episcopal Church activities in small
communities in Georgia during the years when the South itself
was struggling to rebuild. Larger churches were, of course, not
entirely free from problems peculiar to the era. Trinity Church
in Columbus, for example, which was sixth largest in the Diocese,
reported in 1881 that "our expenses exceed our income. We still
owe a debt of about $600." In the same year the Rev. George
Macauley, rector of St. Mark's Church, Dalton, thought his church
in "a very healthy and hopeful condition." A total membership
of sixty persons had given $444.50 during the past year. Mr. Ma-
cauley was also conducting missions at Calhoun and Canton. Four
communicants in Calhoun formed the basis of that work; Canton,
although with but three members, seemed to Macauley to be "a
very important point for the Church to occupy. Quite a number
of families from more southern localities pass their Summers here,
and the greater number of them are Church people." Further,

he observed, there were "a number of very intelligent families" in Canton who wanted to see a permanent Episcopal Church there. In summary, he stated that the sum of $500 would firmly establish churches in each of his missions, Calhoun and Canton.

Urban areas of the Diocese continued to find local fields for expansion. In the West End region of the Atlanta metropolitan area, a mission was launched in 1882 which soon became one of the staunchest churches in the Diocese. This was the Church of the Incarnation. In 1895 a site for a church building was donated by Mrs. Mary J. Van Dyke, and the new structure was ready for its first service by April 30th of the following year. When Incarnation moved into this building, it began use of a Church which would extend for sixty years, thus marking it today (1957) as the oldest Episcopal Church structure in continuous use in Atlanta.

In John Watrous Beckwith the Diocese of Georgia was finding a leader cut from (and wearing) the same cloth as Stephen Elliott. Despite the fact that the Diocese could be considered as having already been well-founded by the preceding prelate, Bishop Beckwith faced a challenge in 1867 which would seem to need a Bishop Elliott all over again. That the new Bishop met this challenge with enthusiasm, common sense, and Christian missionary zeal is attested by the steady growth of his Diocese, the administrative improvements which his wisdom recommended and urgent circumstances demanded, and the seemingly universal love and admiration for him which became a cementing factor during the critical post-war years in Georgia. It should also be observed that Beckwith enjoyed a longevity as Bishop which compares with Elliott's; for when an able leader can serve a long time through difficult periods, success seems far more promising.

In his last few annual reports to the Diocese, Bishop Elliott often had included nearly day-by-day accounts of personal activities for part of the year. When Bishop Beckwith began making yearly reports, he adopted this practice and expanded it so that his messages to the conventions included a near-daily diary of the Bishop's work; the remainder of his report concerned his spiritual message and suggestions to the Diocese. These day-by-day accounts have been included in the published reports every year since then, and have become a canonical requirement. They constitute a decided improvement in the Bishop's message, for not only is it easier for his audience to hear and profit from his specific recommendations both spiritual and practical, but every parishioner who can examine the published Journals of the Annual Conventions can read of these daily activities and appreciate the magnitude and importance of a Bishop's function.

For the purpose of gaining a better appreciation of Bishop Beckwith's daily routine, and something of the nature of his contributions to the cause of the Episcopal Church in Georgia, his annual report for the year 1886 87 has been chosen since it marks the end of two decades of his work. On May 11 of 1887 the sixty-fifth Annual Diocesan Convention met at St. Peter's Church in Rome. For the period June 11, 1886 to May 10, 1887, there are seventy-eight entries for specific activities during the reporting year. The Bishop visited a total of forty-three churches and missions. He held forty morning services at St. Luke's (Atlanta), St. Mark's (Dalton), Calvary Church (Mt. Airy), Toccoa Mission (meeting in the Methodist Church), Grace Church (Clarkesville), St. Luke's (Hawkinsville), Calvary (Americus), St. Stephen's (Milledgeville), Zion (Talbotton), St. Andrew's (Darien), St. Mark's (Brunswick), Christ Church (Frederica), St. Simon's Mills Colored Mission, St. Thomas' (Thomasville), St. Paul's (Albany), Church of the Advent (Madison), Gainesville Mission, Trinity (Columbus), St. George's (Griffin), Church of the Mediator (Washington), Emmanuel (Athens), St. Mary's (Athens), St. Philip's (Atlanta), St. John's (Savannah), Ogeechee River Colored Mission, Church of the Atonement (Augusta), Grovetown Mission (meeting in Methodist Church), Good Shepherd (Augusta), St. James' (Marietta), St. Paul's (Macon), and St. Barnabas' Mission (Macon).

During this round of the Diocese Bishop Beckwith also read Evening Prayer fifteen times altogether in these churches: Chapel of the Mission of the Redeemer (Atlanta), St. Philip's (Atlanta), St. Luke's (Atlanta), St. Luke's (Hawkinsville), Sparta Mission (meeting in Presbyterian Church), St. Andrew's (Darien), St. Athanasius' Mission (Brunswick), Satilla River Mission, Church of the Redeemer (Greensboro), St. Augustine's (colored) Chapel (Savannah), St. Paul's (Augusta), and, on the eve of the Diocesan

Convention, St. Peter's (Rome). During his summer and Christmas vacations he preached three times in Clifton Springs, New York; and conducted one service each in Newport, Rhode Island, and Thompson, Connecticut.

In five services, the Bishop baptized six infants. 386 persons were confirmed in thirty-seven services, one of which was conducted in private. He performed six marriage ceremonies. One of the three funerals at which he officiated was that of the poet, Paul Hamilton Hayne, in Augusta. One candidate for Holy Orders was admitted to the ministry.

In addition to his regular Diocesan travels and the vacations mentioned above, the Bishop attended the General Convention of the American Church in Chicago, the commencement exercises at the University of Georgia, and the annual meeting of the Trustees of the University of the South in Sewanee. He gave canonical consent to the election and/or consecration of three American Bishops during the year. "Letters Dimissory" were issued to two clergymen transferring out of the Georgia Diocese; and eight such letters were received for ministers who came into the Diocese.

There seems to be no record of the number of individual conferences held during the year, or specifically of the heavy load of routine office work for which a Bishop is responsible. Certainly this seems to be a busy program of activities for Bishop Beckwith who, at the age of 56, was then in the twentieth year of his episcopate.

John Watrous Beckwith served the Diocese of Georgia for two and one-half more years before death removed him from his field of service. In the Diocesan year 1887-1888 he toured abroad for five months. During this period, in accordance with the canon law of the Diocese, the Standing Committee of the Diocese was authorized by him "to act as the Ecclesiastical authority thereof." According to his annual report of 1888, the Bishop visited in Europe and the Middle East. He preached in Anglican churches in England, France, Italy, Palestine, and Egypt; and on two occasions while in the Holy Land, the Bishop wrote that "I held service in my tent." On Easter Day, April 1, 1888, he "administered the Holy Communion at sea, on board the German steamer 'Ems'."

During Bishop Beckwith's absence the Rt. Rev. E. G. Weed, on Beckwith's invitation, administered to the episcopal needs of the Diocese. Other Bishops also visited the state while Beckwith was away; but he was depending on Bishop Weed for "so much of his time and labor as he could spare from his own work." At the sixty-sixth Convention Bishop Beckwith expressed his gratitude for Bishop Weed's contributions to the several missions in the Diocese. But he had a complaint to register: "I am somewhat disposed to complain that my Rt. Rev. Brother only visited one of the larger Parishes of the Diocese . . . . My indebtedness to him would have been greatly increased had he not deprived the [other] great congregations of the large Parishes of the desired pleasure and profit of hearing him preach . . . . We would lovingly ask that in future when he favors us with his presence he will do the greatest good by ministering, at least to some extent, to the greatest number." However, it should be observed that in addition to ministering to his own Diocese of Florida during these five months, Bishop Weed conducted sixteen confirmation services in Georgia in which he admitted sixty-eight persons to Holy Communion. Further, he consecrated the missions of All Saints' in Sylvania and Christ Church in Valdosta.

A rather remarkable Episcopalian died in Griffin in the year 1890. He was the Rev. Charles M. Thomas. Before becoming an Episcopal clergyman he had been a Methodist minister and a naval chaplain. At the time that Bishop Beckwith assumed episcopal duties Mr. Thomas was rector of St. Philip's in Atlanta. When his health failed, Thomas retired to a plantation near Griffin. But he was not content to remain idle there. Finding that poor health would not permit him to obtain another church, this clergyman then undertook the study of medicine and received the M. D. degree, "hoping thus to increase his usefulness among the poor destitute."

Another death in 1890 marked the end of a long period of unselfish and devoted service. Sister Margaret (Mrs. Margaret Jennings), Superintendent of the Appleton Church Home, died at the age of sixty-nine while in her twentieth year of active duty there.

Bishop Beckwith made his final annual report to the Diocese at the sixty-eighth Convention, held in Milledgeville in May of 1890. His itemized account of activities showed that he was as vigorous as ever during what would prove to be the last year of his episcopate. His recommendations and message to the Convention reflect both the status of the Georgia church in 1890 and the Bishop's love for his Church.

The Bishop's message also shows a feeling of pride in and hope for his Diocese. He told the delegates, "I have not for years looked forward to the future with as much hope as now . . . . All over the Diocese, among clergy and laity, there seems to be an increase in aggressive work on churchly lines." One phase of the "aggressive work on churchly lines" to which he had reference was a new procedure for missionary work in the state which had been adopted the previous year. The position of Diocesan Missionary had been created and an outstanding Georgia clergyman with a long and successful record of mission activity, the Rev. H. K. Rees, was named to the post on June 6, 1889. (It is of interest that several unsuccessful attempts were made to change the name of this official to "Arch-deacon"; Rees referred to himself as the "Diocesan Evangelist.")

Rees' initial report, given at the sixty-eighth Convention in 1890, reflects the spirit with which he approached his task. He had proceeded "to organize Missionary Societies in each Parish and Mission Station. This required a visit to each Parish, occupying a Sunday and three or four days to each place." Working with local rectors, he appointed in each parish a vice-president, secretary, and treasurer, and "a corps of collectors, who were to visit the entire Parish each month, giving every Church member the opportunity to make a monthly offering." These local missionary societies were to meet once each month, discuss their situation and monthly collections, and plan for further improvements. Mr. Rees seems to have had some difficulty with certain churches who preferred "the old plan of assessments upon Vestries," who apparently did not want to adopt his new system; these parishes, he reported, "have not increased their contributions to the Diocesan

Mission treasury one dollar." On the other hand, those who had proceeded to follow his plan were experiencing "a deep interest" in missionary activities. The report of the Treasurer for Diocesan Missions showed nearly twenty-five per cent increase over the previous year's collections: in 1889, $3,407.13; in 1890, $4,235.88. This improvement seems to justify Mr. Rees' claims. Specifically, the financial report showed that sixteen parishes increased their missionary contributions over the previous year, although mission assessments for all parishes were the same both years. Three churches contributed the same amount in 1889 and 1890, while only four gave less. Three parishes made no contributions for missionary work during either year.

At this time the Diocese was supporting ten missionaries in addition to the Diocesan Missionary: the Rev. Messrs. Edward Denniston, T. G. Pond, A. Barnwell, W. W. Kimball, W. M. Walton, A. Forbes, W. R. McConnell, John Gass, M. T. Turner, and A. Prentiss. Rees reported that he "had not visited the Mission Stations under the care of resident Missionaries, because, . . . my relations to the men in charge are too indefinite. I have, as time would allow, gone to vacant Missions." He then proceeded to elaborate on his work with the "vacant Missions." During Holy Week, for example, he was at Blackshear and Waycross, where he held "continuous services." Dalton, Cartersville, and Calhoun were united into a combined mission which had jointly raised $900 for a minister's services. With $600 additional promised from the Diocesan Missionary Board, Rees felt that the three-station mission would be able to secure an able vicar. During the year his attention was directed to "the forsaken and dilapidated Chapel by the wayside at Kingston." He "at once visited the place and appointed a service." Later he made four trips to Kingston, and reported that "the few church people have become inspirited and gone nobly to work; and, with the assistance of their friends, the Chapel has been thoroughly repaired and painted, a handsome altar and lectern placed in the chancel, and the Mission thoroughly organized."

One of the missionaries under Rees' general supervision was the Rev. T. G. Pond, whose activities were spread among Gainesville, Clarkesville, Tallulah, and Mt. Airy. Grace Church at

Clarkesville was his only organized parish. At each of the other three points, Pond reported, "services are held one Sunday in each month. Congregations at each fluctuate." Somewhat pessimistically, he added:

People outside do not seem to desire to learn our forms of service. Although books paged alike are in their reach, and the Missionary has tried the plan of giving out the numbers of the pages as the services progress, they but little and feebly follow with us. And, to say truth, perhaps we ought not to wonder at it, for many of our ministers have with regret, sometimes with discomfort, found out that Protestant Episcopal congregations even, slowly and with apparently much reluctance, use the improvements and changes in our services adopted by the conservative wisdom, and then commanded by the authority of the General Convention.

Bishop Beckwith's annual report to the sixty-eighth Convention in 1890, his last to a Diocesan meeting, expressed his hope that the new missionary scheme, having been tried out for a year, would prove to be the answer to the missionary needs of the Diocese. Further, he saw room for encouragement: "I have not for years looked forward to the future with as much hope as now . . . . All over the Diocese . . . there seems to be an increase in aggressive work on churchly lines . . . ." This optimistic outlook was a fitting ending for the Bishop's last Diocesan Convention. For more than twenty-two years he had been largely instrumental in the church's continual growth during the harsh years of reconstruction and readjustment; as the land in which he lived entered into the era of the New South, so did his Church enter upon a more promising era of development—as he expressed it —"in aggressive work on churchly lines."

Bishop Beckwith became ill late in 1890. On November 13, the Standing Committee of the Diocese met and urged the Bishop to call upon a neighboring Bishop to meet some of the episcopal demands of the Diocese. However, from his sickbed the Bishop told the Committee that they were fully authorized to act in his behalf in governing and administering to the Diocese. Less than two weeks later (November 23, 1890), Bishop John Watrous Beckwith died.

CHAPTER

❦ · IX · ❦

THE GREAT DIVIDE: FROM ONE DIOCESE TO TWO (1890-1907)

FOR THE second time in its history, the Diocese of Georgia had to face the somewhat chaotic conditions caused by the death of its Bishop. As before, and in line with Bishop Beckwith's expressed desire, the Standing Committee stepped into the breach and administered the Diocese. The principal problem was that of filling the vacancy in the Episcopate. After discussing the matter, the Committee resolved to defer the selection of a new Bishop until the next regular Diocesan Convention in 1891.

In the meantime, several nearby bishops made themselves available for duty in Georgia. Bishop Edwin G. Weed of Florida spent ten days in Georgia during the latter part of January during which he traveled from Satilla Mission to St. Peter's in Rome. He preached thirteen times, confirmed 108 persons (including four in private services), made ten addresses, conducted one Communion service, held one funeral, and "set apart a Deaconess." The Assistant Bishop of Alabama also helped. Bishop H. M. Jackson reported that on May 15 he confirmed six at St. James', Marietta, and thirteen others on the same day at St. Philip's, Atlanta.

In the Spring Bishop Weed made several additional visits to Georgia. On April 19 he had a busy day in the several parishes and missions in Savannah. From his first service at 7:30 a.m. through the last at 8:00 p.m. he confirmed seventy-five persons in four Confirmation services; he preached four times and gave addresses to four classes, as well as conducting a service at St. Stephen's. On the following day he confirmed forty-four, preached, and gave an address at Christ Church, in Savannah. Again on May 10, he had a very active Sunday in Georgia. In Brunswick he confirmed twenty-five persons in four services; he ordained J. J. Perry to the Priesthood; and he preached at St. Athanasius', St. Jude's and St. Mark's. In reporting to the Diocese concerning the last-named visits to Georgia, Bishop Weed apologized for asking thirty-seven dollars expense money "for so little work." He averred, however, that he had to travel long distances without having railroad passes "or the entertainment which a Bishop of the Diocese would have . . . . I hope by this time next week you will be in a fair way to be relieved of foreign Bishops . . . ."

Another "foreign Bishop" utilized by the Diocese of Georgia during this period was the Rt. Rev. Hugh Miller Thompson, Bishop of Mississippi. On Sunday, May 10, he conducted three services in Augusta and confirmed a total of twenty-four persons.

When the Diocesan Convention assembled in Savannah in May, 1891, one of the most important items of business concerned nominations for and election of a new Bishop. Three clergymen were nominated: the Rev. Thomas F. Gailor, Vice-Chancellor of the University of the South at Sewanee; the Rev. Chauncey C. Williams, rector of St. Paul's Church, Augusta; and the Rt. Rev. Alexander C. Garrett, Missionary Bishop of Northern Texas. Gailor was elected by majority of both houses of the convention, and the Bishop-Elect was notified by telegraph. On June 4, 1891, Gailor wrote that he could not accept the new position. Although "profoundly moved" by the election, he felt it a "clear and unmistakable" duty to remain as the executive head of Sewanee. "I feel that I have conscientiously done my duty to Georgia and to the whole Church," he concluded, "and I believe in the generosity, the sympathy, the kindness of our people that they will not misunderstand me."

As a consequence of Gailor's decision the Diocese met again in an adjourned session at Macon on July 1st and re-opened the question of the selection of a new Bishop. The names of Bishops Ethelbert Talbot and J. H. D. Wingfield were placed in nomination, the former by the Rev. C. C. Williams who had been runner-up in the previous election. Talbot, Missionary Bishop of

Wyoming and Idaho, was elected, and a telegram promptly dispatched to him. Further, the Rev. F. F. Reese and layman W. K. Miller were named a committee to visit Bishop Talbot.

Once again the Georgia Diocese was destined for disappointment. Reese and Miller met Bishop Talbot on July 24, in Laramie, Wyoming. For three days they talked repeatedly with him, but he was disinclined to state positively that he would accept. Finally the committee agreed that he might take an additional thirty days to make up his mind; also if he accepted, they "would gladly agree to the postponement of his transfer so as to allow him abundant time" to arrange his affairs—the suggested date was January 1, 1892. On September 22, Bishop Talbot informed the Georgia Diocese that he was forced to decline his election on the grounds that he felt "deeply committed to the missionary operations of the Church in this new and growing West."

Upon receipt of Talbot's definite refusal, the Standing Committee issued a call for a Second Adjourned Session of the 69th Annual Convention, to reconvene at Macon on November 11. As this third effort to obtain a Bishop began, it was announced that the clergy in conference desired to present the following slate to the convention: the Rev. Joseph H. Johnson, rector of Christ Church, Detroit, Michigan; and the Rev. Cleland Kinloch Nelson, rector of the Church of the Nativity, South Bethlehem, Pennsylvania. Nelson received majorities in both houses, with scattered votes for Johnson and these Georgia clergymen: the Rev. Messrs. C. C. Williams, W. C. Gray, John Elliott, and J. R. Winchester. Announcement of his election was wired to Nelson; and the convention named W. C. Hunter and Z. D. Harrison to confer personally with Bishop-Elect Nelson.

Thus ended Georgia's effort to secure a successor to Bishop Beckwith. Hunter and Harrison reported that the new electee accepted his appointment; and once again the Georgia Church could resume its normal development under a duly constituted Diocesan.

Cleland Kinloch Nelson was consecrated Bishop of the Diocese of Georgia on February 24, 1892, at St. Luke's in Atlanta. The somewhat poetically inclined Atlanta *Journal* writer who described the ceremonies noticed that the day was perfect, weatherwise: "The mildness of a May morning tempered the February winds into gentle zephyrs. The singing of birds, the beautiful fresh flowers in the hands of the ladies on their way to the cathedral, the bright sunshine and the cloudless sky, combined to make the day a perfect one." Perhaps this writer knew something of the trying circumstances which Georgia Episcopalians had endured in their efforts to bring about the consecration of a new Bishop, and was therefore impressed with the effect of atmospheric serenity on the occasion.

The Bishop-Elect was consecrated in solemn and moving ceremony by these Bishops: Charles T. Quintard of Tennessee, Nelson S. Rulison of Central Pennsylvania, Leighton Coleman of Delaware, Courtlandt Whitehead of Western Pennsylvania, and Theodore B. Lyman of North Carolina. Bishop Rulison preached the Consecration Sermon, and Bishop Quintard conducted the Examination of the Bishop-Elect.

Cleland Kinloch Nelson has been characterized as follows: "A man of imposing stature and physical prowess . . . and every inch a Bishop. With steadiness and insight he gave . . . [the Diocese] true direction . . . . He stood tall among his fellows when looked upon in whatever type of reference."

When Bishop Nelson assumed leadership of his new Diocese, he found it in healthy condition with hopeful opportunity for further expansion. Episcopal churches, chapels, and missions were liberally sprinkled about the state as follows:

1. Organized Parishes

Albany, St. Paul's Church, the Rev. W. E. Eppes, Rector
Americus, Calvary Church (rector unassigned)
Athens, Emmanuel Church, the Rev. J. C. Davis
    "   St. Mary's Church (rector unassigned)
Atlanta, Incarnation (rector not listed)
    "   St. Luke's Cathedral, the Rev. Robert S. Barrett, Dean
    "   St. Philip's Church, the Rev. T. C. Tupper, D. D.
Augusta, St. Paul's Church, the Rev. Chauncey C. Williams, D. D.
    "   Church of the Atonement, the Rev. Charles E. Cabaniss
    "   Church of the Good Shepherd, the Rev. W. M. Walton
Brunswick, St. Mark's Church, the Rev. Henry E. Lucas
Cartersville, Church of the Ascension, the Rev. George E. Benedict
Cave Spring, Church of the Good Shepherd, the Rev. H. K. Rees
Cedartown, St. James' Chuch, the Rev. George E. Benedict
Columbus, Trinity Church, the Rev. William C. Hunter

Dalton, St. Mark's Church, the Rev. James B. Craighill
Darien, St. Andrew's Church, the Rev. Robert M. W. Black
Frederica, Christ Church, the Rev. A. G. P. Dodge, Jr.
Greensboro, Church of the Redeemer (rector unassigned)
Griffin, St. George's Church (rector unassigned)
Hawkinsville, St. Luke's Church, the Rev. F. F. Reese
Macon, Christ Church, the Rev. Frederick F. Reese
"   St. Paul's Church, the Rev. H. Orrin Judd
Marietta, St. James' Church, the Rev. C. T. A. Pise
Milledgeville, St. Stephen's Church (rector unassigned)
Newnan, St. Paul's Church, the Rev. E. Denniston
Rome, St. Peter's Church, the Rev. Charles B. Hudgins
St. Mary's, Church of the Messiah, the Rev. A. G. P. Dodge
Savannah, Christ Church, the Rev. Robb White
"   St. John's Church, the Rev. Charles H. Strong
"   St. Paul's Church (rector unassigned)
"   St. Stephen's Church (colored) (rector unassigned)
Talbotton, Zion Church, the Rev. E. Denniston
Thomasville, St. Thomas' Church, the Rev. C. I. LaRoche

2. Organized Chapels and Missions

Atlanta, Mission of the Good Shepherd, the Rev. R. S. Barrett
"   Mission of the Holy Child, the Rev. T. C. Tupper
Augusta, Christ Chapel (Harrisburg), the Rev. W. M. Walton
"   St. Mary's Chapel (colored), the Rev. C. E. Cabaniss
"   Union Chapel, the Rev. W. M. Walton
Bainbridge, St. John's Chapel, the Rev. W. H. Phillips
Blackshear, All Saints' Mission, the Rev. J. R. Bicknell
Brunswick, St. Jude's Chapel, the Rev. D. W. Winn
"   St. Athanasius' Chapel, the Rev. J. J. P. Perry
Clarkesville, Grace Chapel, the Rev. T. G. Pond
"   Holy Cross Chapel, the Rev. T. G. Pond
Chatham County, St. Mark's Chapel, the Rev. W. R. McConnell
"   St. Bartholomew's Chapel, the Rev. W. R. McConnell
Columbus, St. Mary's Chapel, the Rev. W. C. Hunter
Darien, St. Andrew's Chapel on the Ridge, the Rev. R. M. W. Black
"   St. Cyprian's Chapel (colored), the Rev. F. M. Mann
Decatur, Holy Trinity (rector not listed)
Frederica, St. Perpetua's Chapel, the Rev. A. G. P. Dodge
"   Chapel of the Transfiguration (St. Simon's Beach), the Rev.
            A. G. P. Dodge
"   St. Ignatius' Chapel, St. Simon's Mills (colored), the Rev.
            A. G. P. Dodge
Gainesville, Grace Chapel, the Rev. T. G. Pond
Grovetown, Church of the Heavenly Rest (missionary unlisted)
Kingston, St. Andrew's Chapel, the Rev. J. B. Craighill

Macon, St. Barnabas' Chapel, the Rev. F. F. Reese
"   St. John's Chapel, the Rev. F. F. Reese
"   Mission of the Good Shepherd, the Rev. H. O. Judd
Madison, Church of the Advent (missionary unlisted)
Marietta, St. James' Mission Chapel (colored), the Rev. C. T. A. Pise
"   Union Mission (Marietta Road), the Rev. C. T. A. Pise
Mt. Airy, Calvary Chapel, the Rev. T. G. Pond
Owen's Ferry, Camden County, Church of the Messiah, the Rev D. W.
          Winn
Pooler, St. James' Chapel, the Rev. W. R. McConnell
Satilla Bluff, Camden County, Chapel of the Messiah, the Rev. D. W.
          Winn
Savannah, St. Michael's Chapel, the Rev. D. W. Winn
"   St. Augustine's Chapel (colored), (missionary unlisted)
Sylvania, All Saint's Chapel (missionary unlisted)
Tallapoosa, St. Ignatius' Chapel (missionary unlisted)
Tallulah Falls, St. James' Chapel, the Rev. T. G. Pond
Valdosta, Christ Chapel, the Rev. W. H. Phillips
Washington, Church of the Mediator (missionary unlisted)
Waycross, Grace Chapel, the Rev. J. R. Bicknell

3. Unorganized Missions

Atlanta, The Redeemer
"   St. Paul's
Bailer's Mills
Baysden's Bluff
Bridge Hammock
Calhoun
Convict Camp, near Brunswick
Crispin Island, near Brunswick
Fort Valley
Guyton
Isle of Hope
Jamaica
LaGrange, St. Mark's
"   Factory Hill

Lower Mills, Union Chapel
Pinora
Rockmart
Sand Hills, Camden Co.
Sparta
Spring Bluff
Toccoa, Habersham Co.
Union Point, Ga. R. R.
Waynesboro
Way's House, Camden Co.
West Point

Within fifteen years after Nelson became Bishop, the continued expansion of the Church in Georgia would bring one of the most important developments in its history: the division of the state into two Dioceses. To Bishop Nelson, of course, goes much of the credit for bringing the Church to this prosperous condition. However, no Bishop, even one as indefatiguable as Cleland Kinloch Nelson, could have done it alone. Thousands of loyal laymen and the dedicated missionary work of many clergymen helped to make it possible.

Bishop Nelson sounded the keynote for this expansion when he addressed the seventieth Convention on May 19, 1892, some ten weeks after he had begun his great work. "The proper attitude of the Church in Georgia," he told the Convention, "is best described by the word aggressive as opposed to the idea predominating in older Dioceses of conserving energy already existing. While therefore, the parochial clergy are engaged in strengthening from within, we, the Bishop and missionary clergy, are charged with the responsibility of awaking to life dormant stations and entering immediately upon a lively campaign in quarters where the Church has as yet no foothold."

Specifically, the Bishop named areas which needed "to be attacked (to use the warlike phrase proper to a militant church), and to be strongly manned." These were Cordele, Abbeville, Tifton, Montezuma, Butler, Guyton, Tennile, Sandersville, Rockmart, Jesup, "and a hundred other towns of 600 to 2,500 population." Further, he noted, "one hundred counties in the State are yet unrepresented in our assemblies . . . ."

Urban areas were also targets for the Church's expansion in the 1890's. An example of this interest is found in the missionary work in Decatur, begun originally as an Unorganized Mission by Bishop Beckwith. In 1895 the Holy Trinity Mission was organized by Archdeacon W. M. Walton, and within a year a Chapel had been constructed.

In the Spring of 1893 Bishop Nelson initiated a mission in the Washington Heights region of Atlanta. Numerous communicants in the area responded to the Bishop's interest; and, with the particular help of Mrs. Mary D. de Graffenreid and Mrs. J. D. Battle, the Church of the Holy Comforter was organized and held its first service in a small building on Washington Street, July 21, 1893. During 1896 and 1897 the Rev. Allard Barnwell, Canon of the Cathedral and City Missionary in Atlanta, was Priest-in-Charge of Holy Comforter. The mission suffered a temporary setback in 1898 when they lost both their missionary and the use of the building on Washington Street. Holy Comforter was "held together only through the untiring efforts of the Woman's Guild" until Archdeacon William M. Walton gave it his personal attention. Then in 1902 the Rev. Gilbert A. Ottman was given charge of the mission, and using a chapel on Pulliam and Atlanta Avenues, Holy Comforter resumed its growth. By 1906, communicants numbered 93.

With a practical view to the financial responsibilities which such an expansion would bring, Bishop Nelson asked for, over and above regular annual missionary funds, $2,500 from each convocation, or a total of $10,000. The results over five years time, he argued, "will surprise the most sanguine, and approve our policy to every thinking business man." Business men should be appealed to strongly, he said. "If we want their assistance, we must prove to men of brain and ability that the Lord's business is managed with the same energy, fidelity and enterprise that distinguish advance from retrogression in worldly undertakings."

Bishop Nelson chose Atlanta for his cathedral city, believing that the capital of the Church should be in the capital of the state. Among other justifications for this choice he listed Atlanta's "accessibility, healthfulness, the opportunity of the Church in the formative condition of Atlanta, and the present weakness of the Church in the midst of a population increasing daily." St. Luke's became his Cathedral and the Reverend Robert S. Barnett its Dean. Two years later the Cathedral site was shifted to St. Philip's.

One parish in the Diocese enjoyed a happy benefaction during this era. When Mrs. Eliza Lewis Clinch of Savannah died in 1903, her legacies included $40,000 for St. Paul's Church in that city. Two years later the Vestry took steps to have a new Church built; this structure, located at the corner of 34th and Abercorn streets, was consecrated on the Feast of St. Paul's in 1908. A year earlier the Rev. S. B. McGlohon had accepted a call to St. Paul's. Mr. McGlohon served this parish for twenty-four years.

Another new church building in the Diocese about the same time was St. Andrew's at Fort Valley. Stimulated largely by the initiative of an English cabinet-maker named George H. Harrison, the new mission soon grew large enough to attract Diocesan support. A Gothic style chapel was soon built, with much of the interior construction being done by Mr. Harrison, and consecrated in 1897. The mission was named for St. Andrew's Church in Uxbridge, Middlesex, England, where the Harrisons had been communicants. The first missionary to serve St. Andrew's in Fort Valley was the Rev. Edward Denniston, then living near Phenix City, Alabama. A long-standing inspirational tradition at St. Andrew's about Mr. Denniston is that "having no conveyance he walked from his home to St. Andrew's and back again, serving Zion Church in Talbotton en route." In between these walking visits, Lay Readers Harrison and Charles T. Eberhardt conducted services.

The extent to which the Bishop applied his militant views and the nature of the response by Georgians resulted in substantial expansion of missions. The year-by-year growth from 1893 to 1906 in missions and total Diocesan communicants, despite a decrease in the number of parishes, is indicated by the annual reports:

	Parishes	*Missions—All Types*	*Communicants*
1893	29	88	6,292
1894	29	90	6,130
1895	27	94	6,550
1896	27	86	6,854
1897	27	92	6,951
1898	27	102	7,153
1899	27	104	7,352
1900	27	105	7,667
1901	26	105	7,976
1902	26	108	7,182
1903	26	108	8,237
1904	27	104	8,724
1905	27	111	8,877
1906	27	108	9,229

This increase in missions from 88 to 108, reflected the Church's enthusiastic response to the Bishop's challenge. A special booklet was prepared in 1906 by Miss Rosa Woodberry of Athens for the purpose of raising mission subscriptions elsewhere. Under the heading, "Some Facts about Mission Work in Georgia," these words appear: "Georgia is 90 per cent a Missionary Diocese, having but twenty-six [twenty-seven] Parishes, out of a total number of Stations of one hundred and thirty-eight. In fourteen years have been erected sixty-two church buildings, great and small; there are one hundred and twelve [108] Mission Stations, of which fifteen are partly sustained by local contributions in the cities where they are located; thirty-seven are partly sustained by the Diocesan Board of Missions, and sixteen colored, supported in the main by the General Board of Missions . . . ."

This special report offers some contrasting statistics concerning contributions toward missionary operations over the period 1892-1907. When Cleland K. Nelson became Bishop in 1892, parochial contributions for church extension for maintenance of the existing missions amounted to $4,744.40, while the missions themselves raised in that year $700.00 for their own support. But during the year 1905-1906 the contributions of parishes for the same purpose totalled only $3,789.16, while the missions managed to raise $20,729.08 for their maintenance and improvement. In the words of the report, "no better argument could be furnished for a continuation of our Missionary policy."

One of the Diocese's most active missions was St. Paul's in Atlanta. Its history extended back to 1880 when a group of Negro communicants organized a Sunday School and shortly thereafter entered into mission status in the Diocese. Church services and religious teaching at first were conducted upstairs over a drug store at the intersection of Lee and Gordon streets. Other moves took the little group to Pryor Hall at Peachtree and Auburn, and then to a building on Butler Street. In 1895 the Rev. William A. Green was named Minister-in-Charge of St. Paul's, and soon moved his church to a new building on Auburn Avenue. Within three years of his coming to St. Paul's, Mr. Green had begun another mission, St. Matthias' on Lawshe Street.

Another apparently flourishing mission during the same era was St. James' in Calhoun. Local Episcopalians had sought to have services in Calhoun since the early 1870's, and finally by 1898 a one-story wooden church had been erected and consecrated. Unfortunately, however, the little mission was short-lived. Gordon County's historian, Miss Lulie Pitts, gives this account of St. James' waxing and waning: "Surpliced clergymen intoned their rituals, troths were plighted at the little altar, and, unostentatiously, St. James' Episcopal Church . . .performed its mission of good. With the passage of years, however, members drifted away in search of new homes, the church no longer in use, was razed and the lot became a business site."

The Inman Park (Little Five Points) region of Atlanta was also the location of Episcopal missionary activity during the 1890's. Owing largely to the interest of Mr. and Mrs. D. P. Holland, several meetings and services were held in the locality during 1893 and 1894, conducted by various clergymen from St. Philip's and St. Luke's. Bishop Nelson encouraged the work, and suggested a church name: "Epiphany—for my own church in Bethlehem, Pennsylvania." In 1898 Epiphany moved into its new church building, constructed on a triangular lot between Euclid, Moreland and McLendon avenues.

One of the more recent missions to join the ranks of organized congregations in Georgia was St. John's in College Park. During the Summer of 1906 a group of Episcopalians met intermittently for services in a room over the local post office. In August St. John's was admitted to the Diocese as an organized mission, and in October Bishop Nelson laid the cornerstone of a new church building. Mr. Charles K. Weller served as principal Lay Reader until he left to enter Seminary. When he returned in 1912, he was Minister-in-Charge of St. John's.

The considerable expansion of the Diocese of Georgia which was so evident in the early years of the Twentieth Century made a division of the Diocese seem, to some Churchmen, a logical step. Particularly was this true of the Bishop.

At the eighty-first Convention in 1903, Bishop Nelson remarked on the "loneliness of the episcopate and the immense difficulties to be encountered by the man who should succeed to the mitre, the staff and the keys in the Diocese of Georgia." Two years later, the Bishop made even more specific reference to the problem.

During the eighty-third Convention in Macon in 1905, Bishop Nelson concluded his "Annual Address" by directing attention to the ardous nature of his office. "Since 1903," he said, he had "devoted all but fifteen or twenty days [each year] to the occupations of my office." A tremendous volume of business had fallen upon the Bishop's office with the doubling of mission stations and the near-doubling of communicants in the Diocese. Noting the peculiar status of the problem, the Bishop stated that "had we one hundred Parishes and fifty Missions the fulfillment of the task would be comparatively light, but under existing conditions one man is compelled to administer the affairs, temporal as well as spiritual, of more than one hundred churches." The administrative work of the Episcopate he termed "a perpetual grinding of the mills," and attributed to his "intelligent, quick and faithful clerk" the discharge of this work without undue delay.

Continuing in this vein, Bishop Nelson reiterated his opinion that the Diocese needed division of duties between two Bishops:

Observation and experience have convinced me that no arrangement of agent, Archdeacon or Coadjutor will ever satisfy the demands among these people who are most amenable when brought into direct touch with the authoritative head of affairs, but do not heed an intermediary. When, therefore, you proceed to secure additional Episcopal oversight and administration as well as ministration, there is but one way to effect it, that is, by division, upon which question my mind has undergone no change as to either its wisdom or practicability . . . . In ten years, this course would be abundantly justified by both the spiritual and financial results of what is simply the principle of concentration of effort.

Apparently the problems of financing had arisen as a possible block to Diocesan division. In his 1905 message, Bishop Nelson offered a possible solution: "a *modus vivendi* is open to you in the use of the entire amount yearly contributed for Diocesan Missions (with the consent, of course, of those who pledge it) than which no better application could be made in the interest of Diocesan Missions; while the three several trusts, for this same purpose, with specific gifts, can be relied upon for salaries of clergy and teachers."

Estimating the expenses at $5,000 each for the two Diocese, he proposed the following specific financing measures:

Source of money	For North-west Diocese	For South-east Diocese
From Permanent Fund	$ 900.00	$ 900.00
Assessments as per report of Finance Committee of 1904	2,508.00	2,499.00
Eight thousand Communicants at 15 cents per capita	600.00	600.00

From pledges to Diocesan Missions in the
        two sections respectively   1,868.00   1,355.00
                                                     ─────────   ─────────
                                                     $5,876.00 $5,354.00
Georgia Mission Fund   5,000.00
Clinch Fund and certain specified others   3,700.00
Remaining funds to be equally divided.

Following these clear-cut and specific proposals, the Convention of 1905 considered resolutions favoring the division which were drawn up by the Committee on the State of the Church. The committee argued that "no question of sentiment should be allowed to interfere with a matter of so great importance to the growth and welfare of the Church. If the proper divisional line can be selected, if the funds and assessments can be adjusted for this purpose, they believe the time is ripe for the carrying out of this long cherished project." These resolutions were then offered and unanimously accepted:

"*First,* it is the sense of this Convention that the Diocese of Georgia shall be divided into two new dioceses; and

"*Secondly,* (provided the first resolution is passed) The Bishop shall appoint a committee of four clergymen and four laymen to present a full and complete report to the next Diocesan Convention with all necessary details looking to the division of the Diocese."

The Bishop then appointed the following as the Committee on the Division of the Diocese: the Rev. Messrs. Charles H. Strong (St. John's, Savannah), Wyllys Rede (St. Mark's, Brunswick), C. T. A. Pise (Dean of the Cathedral, Atlanta), and John L. Scully (Trinity, Columbus); and Messrs. Luther Williams, (Christ Church, Macon), Wm. K. Miller (St. Paul's, Augusta), Wm. N. Hawks (St. Philip's, Atlanta), and Bryan H. Wright (St. Thomas', Thomasville).

Before the 1905 Convention adjourned, a map of Georgia was presented by the Bishop showing the existing parishes and missions, the seven Archdeaconaries, and a proposed division line. It was decided to print this map in the *Journal* of 1905 so that all Episcopalians in the state could have access to it in considering the topic of division of the Diocese.

By the time of the Convention the following year in Columbus, another committee had been created to deal with some of the technicalities of division: the Committee on Preliminaries to Division of the Diocese. Its members were the Rev. William B. Walker (Christ Church, Macon), Messrs. H. C. Cunningham (Savannah), and Z. D. Harrison (Atlanta). All three were members of the Standing Committee of the Diocese.

In his annual address to the Convention of 1906, Bishop Nelson referred again to the proposed separation. Following a brief summary of the amount of time devoted to his work in the preceding year, he remarked: "I am more than ever impressed with the economy to the Church which would result from a division of labor that would give me a part, at least, of the 65 days (of twenty-four hours each) spent on the cars and at railroad stations . . . . It is my solemn belief that no man reading these details [of my duties] would hesitate a moment in forming a conviction as to the necessity of erecting two Dioceses out of Georgia. I have been compelled to decline innumerable opportunities for good, both in neighboring and distant cities, because my time was already preoccupied."

In further justification of the separation, the Bishop offered some statistics comparing Georgia with other Dioceses. He pointed out that nine other Dioceses had half as many clergy as Georgia; that twenty-nine had half as many parishes and missions; that fourteen had half as many baptisms and confirmations; that eighteen had half as many communicants; and that twenty-one had half as much invested for benevolent purposes.

Bishop Nelson also called attention to certain other problems which the division would occasion, such as naming the new Dioceses. "I offer a consideration: That, by American precedent, the original title continues with the administrative center or see, whether that be the State Capital or otherwise." But regardless of the decisions to be made, the Bishop made two special pleas: "first, that nothing be done through partisanship for me; and, secondly, that nothing be said or done which will disturb the present harmonious condition of the Diocese."

Few who had listened to or read the Bishop's annual addresses for the past several years could doubt that Bishop Nelson ardently favored the separation. However, in an effort to avoid the impression that he was jamming the measure through the Convention, the Bishop offered these additional cautions: "While I realize, as no other man can, my inability to fulfill the demands of so great and increasing a territory, I would infinitely rather die struggling on with overwhelming obligations than disturb existing peace and unity, or be the cause of heart-burning and antagonisms." Characteristically, however, Bishop Nelson then said, "I can conceive how some may be yet unconvinced of the necessity of the proposed division, if local and parochial interests be placed above the extension of the Kingdom of God, but I cannot imagine how any one who really knows the Diocese can be otherwise than enthusiastic in this movement as offering a grand opportunity for advance."

A few hours thereafter the Chancellor of the Diocese, Frank H. Miller of St. Paul's in Augusta, gave his official recommendations for the division of certain funds, the duties of the Committee on Division, the corporate status of both proposed Dioceses, and proper notification to all parishes prior to making the decision. On the latter point, he reminded the Convention that a year ago it was agreed that parishes should receive a copy of the committee's report at least one month prior to the Convention; however, this was not complied with. Chancellor Miller expressed "grave doubts" that any transfer of trust funds created by the several parishes would be legal "except by the sanction of the parochial authorities respectively." He further observed that the action of the preceding year called for the establishment of "two *new* dioceses." In his opinion, this was impossible, and the word "new" should be struck from the minutes.

In response to a request from the Committee on Division as to how the dividing should take place, the Chancellor made a special report. Basing his opinions on Article 5 of the Constitution, and Canon 49, Mr. Miller argued that the Bishop's approval of the Committee's report on division should be obtained before the matter went to the Convention; that voting in the Convention should be by orders to determine "what portion is to be and constitute the new Diocese"; that sufficient evidence must be given to show that "the territory to be cut off and constitute the new Diocese is able and willing to suitably provide for the Episcopate thereof"; that trust funds be divided by application to a Court of

Equity so that legal problems involving property held under deeds or wills should be settled in a lawful manner; that following action by the Diocesan Convention ("which is final"), a petition should be presented to the next General Convention for approval of the division; that if the General Convention so approved, "then the Bishop of the Diocese must call a primary convention of the counties of the State comprising the new Diocese to meet at a point within its limits for the purpose of organization"; that at such a convention a name for the new Diocese should be selected and notice given to the Bishop of the old Diocese; and, finally, that a new Bishop be elected by whichever Diocese remained without a Bishop. The Chancellor then gave his opinion on the subject of which Diocese should retain the name "Diocese of Georgia": "The portion of the State of Georgia originally settled by the Church, in which is contained nearly all of the trusts, by deed or by will, which have been created, and in which the Diocesan Corporation was created, should . . . be and remain the old Diocese and retain its name."

By previous arrangement, the Convention adjourned into a Committee of the Whole on the afternoon of the second day in order to consider the proposed division. Judge George T. Cann, of St. John's, Savannah, presented the report of the Committee of the Whole. This report is of such significance to the history of the Episcopal Church in Georgia that it is given here in its entirety:

RESOLVED:

(1) That the present Diocese of Georgia be divided into two separate Dioceses, as follows: By a line beginning at the State line at Columbia County and running south and west from said junction of the State line and Columbia County and continuing north and west of the counties of Columbia, McDuffie, Glascock, Washington, Wilkinson, Twiggs, Pulaski, Dooly, Sumter, Webster and Stewart, and that the portion of the State lying north and west of these counties be formed and erected into a new Diocese.

(2) That the property of the Diocese of Georgia. viz.:
> The Widows' and Orphans' Fund,
> Permanent Fund for the Support of the Episcopate,
> Infirm and Disabled Clergy Fund, and
> Weston Bequest for the Education of Girls in the Diocese of Georgia,

be equally divided between the two Dioceses, and upon the organization of the new Diocese that this division be carried out by the present Bishop and the Board of Officers of the Diocese of Georgia, the same to be submitted to and confirmed by a proper Court of Equity in this State under the direction of the Chancellor of the Diocese.

But inasmuch as the Georgia Mission Fund, known as the Dodge Fund, must go to the Southeastern Diocese upon division, in order that this project of division be successfully carried out, the Clinch and Waldburg Funds for Missions be assigned to the Northwestern Diocese, provided that the division of the Diocese is conditional upon the legal division of the funds of this Diocese as provided herein.

In a vote by orders, this resolution was adopted unanimously by the Convention. It was then moved by William N. Hawks of St. Philip's Cathedral that "all preliminaries to the Division of the Diocese be referred to a Committee of three, to report to the Convention of 1907." This was adopted. On the following day, Bishop Nelson named one clergyman and two laymen to serve on this committee: The Rev. William Bohler Walker (Christ Church, Macon), H. C. Cunningham (Christ Church, Savannah), and Z. D. Harrison (St. Luke's, Atlanta).

The actual separation of the Episcopal organization of Georgia into two portions took place at the Diocesan Convention of 1907, held on May 15-17 in Savannah. In his opening address to the assembled clergy and lay representatives, Bishop Nelson issued an admonition against "prejudice," "contentions," and "partiality," reminding his audience that the question of the division of the Diocese was a "tempting field for dissension."

The Committee on the Division of the Diocese gave its report to the Convention, and it was ordered to be the special order of business for the noon session on the following day (May 16). Acting in accordance with the wishes of the Convention of the previous year, the Committee had prepared a careful report which showed the painstaking effort necessary to effectuate so important an act. Their summary included financial statements for the "Northwestern" and "Southeastern" Dioceses, showing the specific division of Diocesan funds, which in general followed the Bishop's recommendations. They also submitted "a list of parishes and missions which have with one or two exceptions (duly noted) sent in to us their affirmative action." In the Northwestern Diocese replies to the Committee's inquiry showed one hundred per cent agreement favoring the division. The twenty-eight churches and missions which would constitute this new diocese were:

Atlanta	St. Philip's	Ft. Valley	St. Andrew's
"	Incarnation	Greensboro	Redeemer
"	St. Luke's	Griffin	St. George's
"	St. Paul's	LaGrange	St. Mark's
"	All Saints	Macon	St. Paul's
Austell	Good Shepherd	"	Christ
Athens	Emmanuel	Milledgeville	St. Stephen's
College Park	St. John's	Marietta	St. James'
Columbus	St. Mary	Newnan	St. Paul's
	the Virgin	Norcross	(mission)
"	Trinity	Rome	St. Peter's
Carrollton	St. Margaret's	Tallapoosa	St. Ignatius'
Cedartown	St. James'	Washington	Mediator
Dalton	St. Mark's	West Point	Christ
Decatur	Holy Trinity		

Apparently the "one or two exceptions" not supporting the division of the Diocese were St. Luke's, Hawkinsville, and St. Andrew's at Darien. St. Luke's opposed the division outright, while the committee had not had a reply from St. Andrew's. Otherwise the Southeastern Diocese favored the move. Their twenty-four churches were:

Albany	St. Paul's	Frederica	Christ
Americus	Calvary	"	St. James'
Augusta	Atonement	Hawkinsville	St. Luke's
"	Christ	Savannah	Christ
"	Good Shepherd	"	St. Anne's
"	St. Paul's	"	St. John's
Bainbridge	St. John's	"	St. Paul's
Brunswick	St. Athanasius	"	St. Stephen's
"	St. Mark's	Tifton	St. Ann's
Cordele	Christ	Thomasville	St. Thomas'
Darien	St. Andrew's	Valdosta	Christ
"	St. Cyprian's	Waycross	Grace

Upon the arrival of the time set aside for consideration of the question of division, Bishop Nelson "spoke a few feeling and forcible words," and then led the Convention in prayer. The Rev. Charles H. Strong, Chairman of the Committee on Division, presented the report. H. C. Cunningham moved that the report be adopted. The motion was unanimously carried, "and the assembled Convention sang the Doxology." It is not difficult to imagine the fervent feelings with which this hymn was sung, climaxing as it did several years of planning and laborious action. The Bishop and his Diocese counted it one of the blessings which had flowed from above that the Episcopal Church in Georgia had grown to such population and numbers of churches and missions that two new Dioceses were to flourish where one had been before. As the one Churchman who knew better than any in the state what the new arrangement would mean to the future of the Church in Georgia, Bishop Nelson must have felt especial satisfaction and gratitude for the Convention's action.

During the next year or two intensive activity was carried on by various committees of the two new Dioceses to effectuate the separation. Each Diocese held its first new Convention, while at the same time a joint delegation representing the old Diocese made a report of the event to the General Convention. Constitutions and canons had to be adopted, monies apportioned, and the question of new episcopates resolved.

PART THREE

· ·

The Diocese of Georgia, 1907-1957

CHAPTER

❦ · X · ❦

THE DIOCESE OF GEORGIA CARRIES ON UNDER BISHOP REESE 1907-1936

BECAUSE it was continuing its honored name and traditions, although with reduced territories, the Diocese of Georgia's next annual convention carried on in the numerical sequence. Meeting in Augusta February 12-14, 1908, the convention was the eighty-sixth in the Diocese's history.

Urgent problems of readjustment faced the group. Probably none was of more immediate importance than the election of a new Bishop; for Bishop Nelson had chosen to go with the new Diocese. He sent a message to the Convention in which he described his last official actions before becoming Bishop of Atlanta. He also said that he had given to the Standing Committee of the old Diocese official notification of his decision to "administer said new Diocese"; and he described the transfers of funds and properties which had taken place.

The senior clergyman present in Augusta was the Rev. Charles H. Strong, D. D., rector of St. John's, Savannah, who was elected President of the Convention. Among several items of business discussed before the Convention moved to the election was the matter of the Bishop's remuneration. It was voted that the sum of $4,000 be set aside as annual salary for the Bishop. A substitute motion for $3,600 and a committee to provide in addition an Episcopal residence failed to carry.

At the hour appointed on the following day, the Convention proceeded to the election of a Bishop. By motion from the floor, the body met in closed session as a Committee of the Whole, during which nominations were presented. At 4:30 in the afternoon the Convention re-assembled, and seven nominations were laid before the house: Dr. Strong; the Rev. Shirley Carter Hughson; the Rev. Frederick F. Reese, D.D., rector of Christ Church, Nashville, Tennessee; the Rev. James R. Winchester, D.D., rector of Calvary Church, Memphis, Tennessee; the Very Rev. William T. Capers, of Lexington, Kentucky; the Rev. Robert S. Coupland, rector of the Church of the Ascension, Baltimore; and the Rev. Percy Gordon, rector of Grace Church, New Bedford, Massachusetts.

Because he was one of the nominees, Dr. Strong turned over the gavel of the Convention to the Rev. Charles T. Wright of St. Paul's, Albany. Mr. Wright announced voting regulations as follows: total number of clerical votes to be cast: 18; necessary to a choice: 10; total lay votes to be cast: 16 2/3; necessary to a choice: 8 2/3. Three lay ballots and four clerical ballots proved to be necessary before choices of both houses of the Convention would be determined. The first balloting showed Dr. Strong, Mr. Hughson, and Dr. Reese leading in both houses. In the second ballots in each order, Dr. Reese made some gains. By the third ballot, Dr. Reese was declared the choice of the Laity. The fourth vote of the Clergy gave Dr. Strong 6 votes, Dr. Reese 11, and Mr. Hughson 1, whereupon Dr. Reese was declared the Bishop-Elect of the Diocese of Georgia, subject to ratification by the Bishops of the Church and the Standing Committees of the Dioceses. By motion the voting for Dr. Reese was made unanimous. The Chair named the Rev. Francis A. Brown of Christ Church, Savannah, and Mr. William K. Miller, of St. Paul's, Augusta, as a committee to wait upon the Bishop-Elect and inform him of the action of the Convention.

Meanwhile, the Convention proceeded to the other affairs of the Diocese which needed urgent attention. William K. Miller, son of former long-time Chancellor Frank H. Miller, was elected Chancellor of the Diocese without opposition. Dr. Strong, the Rev. G. S. Whitney, the Rev. Charles T. Wright, and Messrs. E. S. Elliot, John A. Cobb, and H. C. Cunningham were elected to the Standing Committee. A few canons were appropriately altered in view of the division; other changes were recommended for the next convention's consideration. The Committee on the State of the Church urged that the Diocese give serious consideration to the needs and opportunities for expansion of the missionary work.

In this connection the detailed report of the Rev. D. Watson Winn, Missionary Archdeacon of Brunswick, offers interesting evidence of this concern on the part of the Committee on the State of the Church. Mr. Winn's statement covered operations at three missions: St. Jude's, Brunswick; St. Andrew's, near Brunswick; and St. Paul's, Jesup, during periods when they had no assigned missionary. Because of poor handling in the past, St. Jude's was "able to do but little for itself;" but with sympathetic encouragement he thought the mission could make much advancement. St. Jude's consisted of a church building, a rectory valued at $1,200 on which only $400 was owed, and a school valued at over $800. St. Andrew's, located three miles from Brunswick in a mill settlement, owed its origin and development largely to the work of its leading layman, Mr. James McRae. A new chapel was nearing completion, and Archdeacon Winn reported that the twenty communicants were anxious to use the new building. St. Paul's, Jesup, already was using a new chapel which featured folding doors dividing school room from chancel.

Concerning the total mission activity in the Diocese of Georgia, the Committee on Missions reported finances in "excellent" condition, depending, of course, on subsequent Diocesan contributions. The missions were listed as follows:

ORGANIZED MISSIONS, January 1, 1908

Augusta	St. Andrew's	7 communicants
Augusta	Christ	115
Augusta	St. Mary's (colored)	19
Bainbridge	St. John's	33
Brunswick	St. Anathasius' (col.)	201
Brunswick	St. Jude's	— (no report)
Belfast	(Not named)	15
Burroughs	St. Bartholomew's (col.)	95
Cordele	Christ	34
Darien	St. Cyprian's (col.)	109
Douglas	St. Andrew's	8

Fitzgerald	St. Matthew's	36
Hawkinsville	St. Luke's	—
Jesup	St. Paul's	—
Pennick	Good Shepherd (col.)	20
Pineora	Holy Trinity	20
St. Mary's	Our Savior (col.)	27
Sandersville	Grace	22
Savannah	St. Augustine (col.)	56
Tifton	St. Anne's	—
Valdosta	Christ	33
Vienna	Prince of Peace	9

Unorganized Missions

Abbeville		4
Albany	St. John's (col.)	—
Baxley		4
Blackshear	All Saints'	6
Grovetown	Heavenly Rest	4
Lumber City		4
McRae	St. Timothy's	9
Ocilla		1
Pooler	St. James'	17
Quitman	St. James'	10
Savannah	St. Andrew's	—
Savannah	St. Michael's	—
Waynesboro	St. Michael's	—

Fourteen Parishes comprised the backbone of the **Diocese** and served as nerve-centers for most missionary work.

Albany	St. Paul's (the Rev. Charles T. Wright)	237
Americus	Calvary (the Rev. James B. Lawrence)	66
Augusta	Atonement (the Rev. S. B. Carpenter)	91
Augusta	Good Shepherd (the Rev. Charles N. Tyndell)	240
Augusta	St. Paul's (the Rev. G. Sherwood Whitney)	465
Brunswick	St. Mark's (the Rev. R. E. Boykin)	306
Darien	St. Andrew's (the Rev. Francis M. Parsons)	84
Frederica	Christ Church (the Rev. D. Watson Winn)	94
Savannah	Christ Church (the Rev. Francis A. Brown)	698
Savannah	St. John's (the Rev. Charles H. Strong)	616
Savannah	St. Paul's (the Rev. Samuel B. McGlohon)	356
Savannah	St. Stephen's (the Rev. Richard Bright)	98
Thomasville	St. Thomas' (the Rev. Gerald A. Cornell)	95
Waycross	Grace (the Rev. Samuel J. French)	75

This, then, was the Diocese which the Rt. Rev. Frederick Focke Reese would direct in its years of regrouping, reorganizing, and rededication after the division. There were thirty-one clergymen in the Diocese and 4,439 communicants.

Frederick Focke Reese was consecrated as Bishop of Georgia in Christ Church, Savannah, on May 20, 1908. The Rt. Rev. Cleland Kinloch Nelson, Bishop of Atlanta, was Consecrator, with the assistance of Bishops Edwin G. Weed of Florida and Theodore D. Bratton of Mississippi. Bishop Thomas F. Gailor of Tennessee preached the sermon, and the new Bishop was presented by Bishop Albion W. Knight of Cuba and Bishop Coadjutor Beverly D. Tucker of Southern Virginia.

Frederick Focke Reese was born in Baltimore on October 23, 1854. After graduation from the University of Maryland, he entered Berkeley Theological Seminary and was ordained to the Priesthood in 1877. He served as priest in Baltimore, Virginia, Christ Church in Macon, and was rector of Christ Church in Nashville at the time of his election to the Episcopate in Georgia.

During the Spring of 1908 Bishop Reese was plagued by ill health, although he made some efforts toward meeting urgent Diocesan needs. During May the Standing Committee of the Diocese granted him a three-months leave of absence from active duties; however, as the Bishop's diary reveals, he continued in some of his regular duties—confirmations, conferences, and ordinations. On July fourth Bishop Reese entered the Savannah Hospital. Two days later he began convalescence at home; at the same time, he issued an authorization to the Standing Committee to carry on the necessary ecclesiastical business for him. Later in July Bishop Reese went to England for an extended stay. Upon returning in October, his physicians recommended that the Bishop remain free of Diocesan activity as much as possible; when the Standing Committee extended the leave of absence, Bishop Reese went upstate to Marietta, Georgia. As his health improved during the early spring of 1909, Bishop Reese increased his activities. On March 24 he felt strong enough to withdraw Diocesan control from the Standing Committee, and his diary entry for April 1 shows "On this day resumed Ecclesiastical Authority of the Diocese."

Because of the frequent interruptions to his work caused by illness, Bishop Reese was not able to complete a full year's activity in the Episcopate until 1910. During 1910 and the first four months of 1911, the Bishop confirmed 431 persons in 71 services. He performed altogether 227 services of various kinds in a total of 117 visits to 63 parishes and missions in the Diocese. Included among these services were 55 celebrations of Holy Communion, 8 baptisms, 1 wedding, and 1 ordination to the priesthood. The latter occurred on December 21, 1910, at St. Athanasius' Church, Brunswick, as Charles Benjamin Pritchett became a priest. Earlier (May 21, 1910), Bishop Reese had the pleasure of laying the cornerstone of St. Matthew's Church in Fitzgerald, just a few months after the Church of St. James', Quitman, was consecrated (February 15, 1910).

The Diocese's newest church building at Quitman brought the Diocesan total of such structures to 60. The oldest parish in the Diocese was, of course, Christ Church in Savannah. In 1910 Christ Church had 710 communicants, three parochial missions and 20 Sunday School classes with 250 pupils. The church building was valued at $75,000. The principal source of income for Christ Church Parish was the rental of pews, which in 1910 brought in $8,144.45. Other sources of income included: subscriptions and donations, $5,899.37; various guilds and societies, $1,898.17; collections in church, $977.09; Sunday School collections, $613.05; offerings at Holy Communion, $607.24; Woman's Auxiliary, $598.66; and money borrowed, $575.00.

The three missions operated by Christ Church were St. Michael's, St. Andrew's, and House of Prayer; the last-named was conducted by the Junior Auxiliary of St. Michael's Mission. At this time Christ Church was engaged in a fund-raising drive for the purpose of paying off a long-standing debt and also for securing a new organ. In 1912 the goal of $16,000 was reached and its objectives carried out.

Meanwhile, with the aid of the Standing Committee and Bishop Reese's occasional visits, the Diocese had made some progress. During these three years, the Diocese had increased by about six hundred communicants (4,439 to 5,037). While the number of parishes had remained constant (fourteen), some expansion and improvements had occurred in mission operations. New organized missions were The Messiah, St. Mary's; St. Mark's, Woodbine; Ceylon; Satilla Bluff; Christ Church, Dublin; St. Ignatius' (colored) and St. Perpetua's (colored), St. Simon's; St. James' (colored), Tarboro; and Good Shepherd (colored), Thomasville. The Ceylon Mission in Camden County was shown as a Proprietary Chapel; others in this special category were the Winter Chapel on Jekyl Island and a chapel in Belfast. On October 26, 1911, St. Michael's at Waynesboro celebrated the paying of its final church-building debts with a consecration ceremony. St. Michael's history dated back to 1889, when a devoted Churchwoman, Miss Lucy Blount, moved to Waynesboro and found no Episcopal work going on there. From the founding of the mission, it had been served by clergymen from Augusta.

New unorganized missions associated with existing churches in the Diocese were Redeemer, Bayvale (near Augusta); Epiphany, Cuthbert; St. Andrew's, Cypress Mills; Messiah, Owen's Ferry; and St. John's-in-the-Wood (colored), Darien. Other recently established unorganized missions listed simply as stations were Holy Trinity, Blakely; Calvary, Dawson; Lynwood (near Fitzgerald); Louisville; Maddox (in Sumter County); McIntyre; Perry's Mills (in Toombs County); Statesboro; Tennille; and Vidalia.

The small mission at Statesboro was served by the Rev. J. Herbert Woodward of Sandersville from 1907 to 1909, and by the Rev. H. L. Durrant of Sandersville for the next two years. Not until 1937 would this mission be assigned a name; the appellation, St. George's Church of Statesboro, would then last until 1953, at which time a new building was consecrated under the name of Trinity Episcopal Church.

Five of the new mission establishments were for Negro communicants. By 1910 there were fourteen congregations of colored people in the Diocese of Georgia. While there was but one Negro parish—St. Stephen's in Savannah—only two stations were listed as unorganized: St. John's in Albany and St. John's-in-the-Wood at Darien. The Colored Churchmen of the Diocese of Georgia assembled annually in separate council and were given support by the Diocese. A school for Negro youth was operated at Brunswick in connection with St. Athanasius' Mission. Bishop Reese reported in 1911 that he had affiliated this school with the American Church Institute for Negroes and had had it incorporated under the title, "St. Athanasius' School for Negro Youth." Association with the Institute would bring the Diocesan educational activity for Negro young people to the attention of "persons who are interested in the negro work of the Church, and also secure funds from these persons for its development and maintenance." Further additional financial support might be forthcoming from the Institute itself. Annual conferences at the school were planned, the Bishop announced, during which the Negro educational work of the Diocese might be studied and improved.

In his address to the Convention of 1911, Bishop Reese directed Diocesan attention to the entire problem of the "responsibility and opportunity" for spiritual and educational work among Negroes. In the Bishop's opinion,

every possible opportunity should be given this [Colored] Council and responsibility laid upon it for the direction and advancement of the work among their own people. . . . Brethren, the Southern white Churchmen must stand by the colored Churchmen and help them. They need it. In Christ's name they are entitled to it. We must rise above the prejudices and antipathies of the world. . . . I confidently appeal to your Christian sympathy with the weak and ignorant, and with those genuinely good and earnest colored people of whom there are more than you probably suspect, who are so pathetically and sincerely striving and hoping and praying for the elevation of their people. . . .

In connection with other problems facing the Diocese, Bishop Reese told the Council assembled at St. John's Church, Savannah, May 8-9, 1912, that a great need existed for reorganizing financial operations, especially in the area of parochial finances. "No other business," he said, "could be operated successfully on such methods." A few in each parish made regular contributions but many did not; giving by the latter was "either spasmodic or unintelligent and not cheerful." As a consequence, the parochial income was insufficient. Usually nothing was done about it until convention time drew near. Then the vestrymen awoke and appealed for a large Easter offering, or began to "scuffle around to collect the money to pay the assessments and apportionments . . . ." The end result, said Bishop Reese, was usually that a few parishioners carried the principal financial burdens of the parish, bills remained unpaid, Diocesan expenses suffered, and often rectors did not receive their entire income.

To rectify this unpleasant situation, Bishop Reese called upon each church to conduct a layman's canvass, covering every item of parochial financial obligations, "from the coal bill to the apportionment for General Missions." So that the new "Every Member Canvass" might be managed efficiently, the Bishop urged each clergyman and vestryman in the Diocese to order from the Board of Missions in New York a leaflet which thoroughly explained the canvassing system. Also, each parish should utilize the "Duplex Envelope" system. With proper use of envelope and canvass, "manifold more money" would result, not by a "miracle," but by "simply realizing on all the living assets, distributing the responsibility and privilege, resurrecting the dead and getting results from them."

Then, with the view that Diocesan fiscal affairs also needed overhauling, Bishop Reese directed that the Finance Committee make appropriate recommendations to the Convention along this line. The Finance Committee, after consideration of the Bishop's remarks, offered a resolution as follows:

RESOLVED that the Finance Committee report to this Convention assessments based on a small percentage for Parishes and Missions paying less than $1,000.00 for current expenses; between $1,000 and $2,000 a larger percentage; and those over $2,000 a still larger, the rate in each class to be fixed by the Committee; the current expenses to include salaries of clergy, organist, choir and sexton, and amount paid for fuel and lights.

This resolution was adopted, thereby implementing somewhat the Bishop's suggestions for more efficient financing to meet Diocesan expenses. A further step in this direction came with the adoption of an amendment to the Rules of Order authorizing the Bishop to appoint a permanent Committee on Finance consisting of five laymen; appointments were to be made at each Convention for the following year. The amendment would permit the committee to examine reports before convention time. Upon the passage of this measure, Bishop Reese appointed the following as members of the Diocese's first Permanent Finance Committee: Beirne Gordon and Charles Ellis, of Savannah, A. V. Wood of Brunswick, William K. Miller of Augusta, and Thomas Harrold of Americus.

At the following Annual Convention, held in the Church of the Good Shepherd, Augusta, May 14-16, 1913, Bishop Reese continued to chide his Churchmen for laxities in financial matters. This time he stressed the tardy submission of contributions for Diocesan Missions. Despite the apparent improvement on the part of a few parishes, the Bishop reported his feeling of dismay over conditions in this respect: "The fact remains that we have not done so well this year as last. . . ." Diocesan payment to the General Mission Fund for the year ending September 1, 1912, was $48 less than the previous year. "And now," complained the Bishop, "We are again behind. Are we indeed retrograding year by year?"

By 1915 the Diocese was feeling the effects of the recent fiscal improvements. Bishop Reese announced that "there is a growing sense of responsibility among our parishes in this respect. The more general experiments with the Duplex Envelope system are producing some results, not merely in securing more money, but in interesting more people."

As the major machinery of its domestic missionary enterprise, the Diocese of Georgia was continuing to use the convocations system. Four geographical areas had been organized: Augusta, Savannah, Brunswick, and Albany. The annual reports of the Archdeacons, as printed in the Diocesan *Journals,* offer valuable evidence of the intense interest of these missionary leaders, as well as substantial witness to expansion in the Diocese. During the ninety-third Annual Convention, held in Christ Church, Savannah, May 19-21, 1915, Bishop Reese commented specifically on mission increases. Referring with some pride to the completion of seven years in the Episcopate, the Bishop said "in all, we bear some witness in thirty-nine Counties out of the sixty-five Counties which comprise this Diocese." There were fifty-seven church buildings in twenty-six of these counties, and in seven counties regular services were held in other structures. In the remaining counties, "there are a few communicants known to reside for whom occasional services are held." In urging the Diocese to continue its missionary expansion, Bishop Reese encouraged further cooperation with the Archdeacons.

In their reports, the Archdeacons were generally optimistic. The Venerable James B. Lawrence, Archdeacon of Albany, reported that two conventions of his Archdeaconry were very successful in stimulating clergy and laymen to improve mission operations. He also stressed the efforts of his group in working with "our scattered Communicants." Archdeacon William Johnson, of the Augusta area, offered a report which he termed "of a routine character." Missions at Thomson and Harlem were still hurt by a continuing vacancy in the Church of the Atonement, whose Rector's assignments included those two missions. On the other hand, things were progressing smoothly at the Hawkinsville, Dublin, and Sandersville missions, which were "faithfully and efficiently cared for" by the Rev. H. W. Robinson. The Rev. D. Watson Winn reported that the Bishop's efforts to support most missions in the Archdeaconry of Brunswick left little for the Archdeacon to do. However, Mr. Winn reported this additional activity: two Sundays of each month were given personally to the Camden County Missions where he was Acting Vicar; on the second Sunday of each month he held services at the town of St. Mary's; and the five missions on the Satilla River were visited each month.

The Archdeacon of Savannah, the Rev. S. B. McGlohon, offered a brief report telling of efforts in behalf of St. Matthew's Mission at Fennel's Station, Thunderbolt. Weekly services were made possible there through the efforts of the Rev. Frederick North-Tummon and Lay Reader William Royal Sanderson.

Uniformly the four Archdeacons reported during most of this second decade of the twentieth century that great difficulties lay in seeking to expand the Church into the scattered rural areas. Bishop Reese discussed this problem at the 1913 Convention. He recognized that "Our Church has been too much a city Church, our clergy possibly are untrained and inexperienced in the methods of work suitable to the country." But nevertheless he encouraged Archdeacons, missionaries, and rectors to work in rural areas: "There is no reason why with wisdom and tact and zeal we should not be able to meet the issue. We can adapt our service to the requirements of those who are ignorant of it. . . . This sort of work must be done not with the sole and only motive to make Episcopalians or Churchmen; not merely fired with a proselyting motive of the zealot, but to preach God's blessed Gospel for the conversion of sinners, as we have learned it from our mother, the Church. . . . We must be wise enough to try to teach people those things which they can understand and not those things which they are totally unprepared to conceive."

Another phase of the same difficulty concerned small missions which had been abandoned. In 1913 the Diocese considered the case of the mission at Meldrim, where a small church was built in 1900. Shortly after the building was erected, the single family of communicants moved away. For nearly twelve years the Meldrim Mission had remained "almost entirely a silent church, with only occasional services." Bishop Reese told the 1913 Convention that an offer had been made to purchase the church from the Diocese. "I concluded that we were not selling churches." As justification for his decision, the Bishop announced that new communicants had moved into Meldrim and regular services were now being renewed.

One of the oldest churches in the Diocese was struck by a crippling disaster early in 1916. On March 16th, a large segment of downtown Augusta, including St. Paul's, was burned to the ground. A layman has left a vivid description of the holocaust:

When I arrived . . . the wind was blowing fifty miles an hour, and a great many sparks began to drop around in the Church yard. . . . In the course of time, everything was gotten out and removed, except the altar, which we left for the last, as we all had an idea the Church might be saved, although the wind was just one red hot volume. The Vason warehouse next door caught on fire, and then we realized we were in a very serious condition. In a little while the steeple caught. One paltry hose appeared on the scene, with which nothing could be done—it wasn't long enough. Men went up in the tower and on the roof, and time and again put out the fire. . . . It was not long before the Church steeple was one mass of flame. The beams of the building seemed to stand very well, but after a while some sparks lodged in the angle of a cornice at the back of the chancel . . . and there was no way to reach it. It burned rapidly, and in a little while the tower fell in.

The rector of St. Paul's, the Rev. George S. Whitney, found himself with a congregation of some six hundred and no church building. He held services for several weeks in the church yard, later in a large tent, and finally in the County Court House until a parish house was completed on April 8, 1917. In the meantime, the Church was being rebuilt and was ready for occupancy in September, 1918. Bishop Reese conducted the formal consecration of the new St. Paul's on May 7, 1919.

Much of the Diocese's mission activity concerned work among Negroes. In 1912 a proposal was received from the Diocese of South Carolina that the various southern Dioceses establish the post of joint Negro Suffragan Bishop to serve the entire region. The Diocese of Georgia established a committee to meet with a similar group from South Carolina to consider the proposal; the committee members were Bishop Reese, the Rev. G. S. Whitney, and Mr. W. K. Miller. This meeting took place in Augusta on February 9, 1912. The Georgia delegation, empowered only to confer, found the South Carolina committee prepared for more positive action, but torn by dissension within as to the proper course. The conclusions drawn by the group from the Diocese of Georgia, as reported to the Convention of 1913, seem to reflect the general trend in the Diocese as to the development of Church work among Negroes:

1. We see no reason due to racial disability why the negro should not be fully represented in the Church's Ministry so soon as men could be found upon whom the highest office can safely be bestowed. Whether there are at present any colored priests who would measure up to the standard required of the sober judgment of the Church is a matter that can only be determined by investigation.

2. We believe that there is a real necessity and a justifiable demand on the part of the negro Churchmen for authorized leaders of their own race if our Church is to command the allegiance of that race.

3. We believe that the Suffragan Bishop is the safest and most satisfactory plan by which the negro can be given such leadership, because it is the only plan by which complete control on the part of the white Bishop of the Diocese can still be maintained.

In the meantime, the National Church was considering a plan which would create special missionary districts for Negro work, with Negro Missionary Bishops named as leaders. The Georgia Convention of 1913 went on record as opposing such a plan, on the grounds that eventually a sizeable group of Negro Bishops sitting in the House of Bishops might lead a movement to detach Negro work from the main body and establish a separate Church. In 1914 Bishop Reese stated that in his opinion the national plan "would be disastrous for the Church and for the colored work. It would destroy the unity of each diocese as the jurisdiction of a single Bishop. . . . I am convinced that the hope of the colored people is in some sort of sympathetic relation with the Christian white people of the South. That contact in the Church is now secured by the fact that they are component parts of the same Ecclesiastical organism, the diocese, under one Bishop, the friend of both."

In 1913 the Diocese of Georgia admitted a Negro Church to parish standing. This was St. Athanasius' of Brunswick. The Rev. James J. N. Thompson was rector. St. Stephen's of Savannah was at that time the only other Negro parish in the Diocese. Negro missions were as follows:

Albany	St. John's	St. Mary's	Our Saviour
Augusta	St. Mary's	St. Simon's Island	St. Ignatius'
Burroughs	St. Bartholomew's	St. Simon's Island	St. Perpetua's
Darien	St. Cyprian's	Tarboro	St. James'
Darien (Inwood)	St. John's	Thomasville	Good Shepherd
Pennick	Good Shepherd	Waycross	St. Ambrose's
Savannah	St. Augustine's		

With this continued expansion of the Church through new missions for both white and Negro Episcopalians, and with enlargement of existing parishes, the Diocese of Georgia enjoyed satisfactory growth in the first ten years following the division of the state's Episcopal work. In 1918 Bishop Reese observed the tenth anniversary of his Consecration. While noting that the effects of the (First) World War had reduced the number of priests on duty in the Diocese to a ten-year low, the Bishop called attention to a 21% increase in communicants (4,439 in 1908, 5,376 in 1917) and a corresponding increase in missionary statistics. But, he remarked, "I have no talent for arrays of figures and I am not disposed to emphasize such facts as they would present. I hope and trust that in sight of God and according to the standards of His heavenly wisdom, we have both as individuals and as a Diocese grown in grace and wisdom and power." Turning to the broader areas of challenge which the Church would face after the war, Bishop Reese said, "The Church is on trial. . . . Are we capable of rising to the responsibilities of the hour? A complacent, comfortable religiousness is doomed. . . . When the war is ended . . . then the greater struggle will begin, to discipline into order the tremendous social forces which have been unloosed, to find a basis of sympathetic friendliness and understanding between the contending classes in society. We shall then probably face for the first time in history an unleashed democracy, world-wide in its sweep and aspiration." It would be the role of the church, he asserted, to move forward, to abandon aloofness, to rise to a position of leadership and unity. And, he added, "God save us from that . . . supercilious pride in our own fancied superiority and cynical contempt for the assumed inferiority of those who walk not with us in Church or society. . . ."

This broad approach, coupled with an intense interest in the expansion and growth of his own Diocese, would characterize his service as Bishop during the long incumbency of Frederick Focke Reese. For he too, like his distinguished predecessors, would live a long and full life and thereby give stability to a still-growing Diocese.

In the second year of post-war peace, during the ninety-eighth Annual Convention at Grace Church in Waycross, Bishop Reese offered evidence of a progressing Diocese. He welcomed the appearance of representatives from the Church of St. Michael and All Angels, Savannah, which was petitioning for recognition as a parish. Two years earlier, he related, the St. Michael's Mission in Savannah had re-located, and in a very short while an active congregation under the leadership of the Rev. J. D. Miller had shown such interest, membership increases, and financial strength that it was on the verge of parish status. Another new representative present came from St. James' Church in Quitman, which the Bishop had just elevated to the status of organized mission. As of January 1, 1920, all pews in the Diocese became free; on that date Christ Church of Savannah removed its rental system, the last one in the Diocese. The Rev. James B. Lawrence of Americus was given especial praise for his efforts in leading his congregation at Calvary Church to making the financial arrangements necessary to the erection of a new Church building. Another new church structure, St. John's in Moultrie, had been delayed owing to increased costs, but completion was soon expected.

The Bishop announced with pleasure that for the year 1919 the Diocese as a whole had generously oversubscribed its apportionment for General Missions, although the over-payment on the part of some churches was needed since several parishes were "badly deficient." In the area of Diocesan missions the picture was not as bright, for the number and amount of under-payments exceeded that of over-payments. A few other reports were cause for some disappointment, especially one which concerned a social characteristic of the 1920's also troubling other Dioceses. At Darien the railroad withdrew its facilities and some loss of population occurred. St. Andrew's in Darien suffered membership decreases in consequence, and had to fall back upon the Diocese for financial support. Also, the Bishop announced that Darien's "chapel-of-ease," St. Andrew's on-the-Ridge, had been de-consecrated and sold.

Late in 1922 one mission was able to capitalize upon a grant of land and take steps to erect a church building. The congregation on the Isle of Hope had been meeting intermittently since 1873 in various locations. In November, 1922, Miss Maria Henderson granted to the Episcopal Church in the Diocese of Georgia two parcels of land on the island. A few weeks later Bishop Reese attended a meeting at the island home of Mr. K. R. Bragg, and there St. Thomas' Mission was launched. On December 21, 1923, the new building was dedicated.

During 1922 the Diocese of Georgia entered upon its 100th

year. With the Centenary Observance scheduled for 1923, Bishop Reese asked that the anniversary be celebrated "with a becoming emphasis and dignity." Such was the character of the observance. The 101st Annual Convention of the Diocese of Georgia met for its centennial celebration on April 22, 1923, at St. Paul's in Augusta. The site was highly appropriate, for it was here in Augusta that the Diocese was first organized. In his message to the Convention, Bishop Reese, noting that "one hundred years of service and growth lie behind us," asked for Divine guidance to the Diocese as it sought to transmit this inheritance "enriched and enlarged by our labors to our posterity." Although the *Journal* labels this address an "Historical Sermon," most of its contents deal with current affairs of the Diocese. A "Georgia Centennial Pageant" was presented as a part of the observance.

Historical notes concerned with progress in his Diocese of more recent date appeared in the Bishop's remarks to the Convention of 1926. A source of concern ever since the division of the Diocese, he reminded the delegates, was the annual report of numbers confirmed. The average for each of the years since 1909 was only 257; but for 1925 it was 414. However, the pleasure which this report gave was offset by other figures: the average annual gain in communicants was only 60. "What became of the others?" he asked. Those moving away must have been balanced by those moving in. The distressing answer, the Bishop said, lay in losses suffered when members grew indifferent to reestablishment of church allegiance as they moved about *within* the Diocese. "That," he stated, "means sometimes to them the loss of any active interest in the Church or in religion. They are, so to speak, the waste product of the Church." Yet many businesses were making active use of their waste products—to many, it meant the difference between profit and loss. The Bishop called upon his brethren to concern themselves about these "waste products." "Every true churchman should be concerned . . . about the growth of the Church and the gaining and keeping of souls in its fold."

The twentieth anniversary of Frederick Focke Reese's Episcopate occurred in mid-1928, although the Bishop, in his message

to the next Convention, did not refer to the occasion in an
historic sense. In discussing again the question of the "disap-
pearing communicant," he remarked "There have been confirmed
in the twenty years of my Episcopate 5,190, an average of about
260 a year." Asking his hearers not to listen to him "with
genteel but unresponsive courtesy," Bishop Reese issued a challenging call to the clergy and laity of the Diocese of Georgia to
produce "a greater zeal and industry in Evangelism" in order to
show "a greater result in souls." "Are we," he cried, "so uncon-
cerned or so powerless that we can do nothing?. . . We must
be aggressively, though wisely, on the offensive." To the laity in
particular he urged an ardent "lay ministry of personal evangelism."

In 1929 the Diocese of Georgia accepted joint responsibility
with the Diocese of Atlanta for partial support of the Fort
Valley High and Industrial School. Earlier efforts of the Diocese
of Georgia to support education for Negroes were concentrated
in the St. Athanasius' School at Brunswick. Very substantial aid
came from the American Church Institute which was also assisting many other schools for Negroes. Eventually the Institute
decided to center its assistance upon fewer schools, and the
institution at Brunswick found itself totally dependent upon the
Diocese of Georgia. The effect was that the school had to be
suspended. Consequently when the offer came in 1928 from
the Diocese of Atlanta to share in the support of Fort Valley's
Negro school, Bishop Reese urged acceptance of the opportunity.
He reminded them that Fort Valley was located near the
boundary line of the two Dioceses, and stated that "a large
number of its pupils are from South Georgia." The Convention
resolved that the Diocese should undertake this support if possible, and authorized the Executive Council to proceed with
arrangements. The following year, the Council announced that
$200 had been secured for initial Diocesan subsidy to Fort Valley
School, that further financing was under study, and that the
Convention should elect Diocesan representatives to the School's
Board of Trustees. The body later named the Trustees as follows:
the Rev. Messrs. J. B. Lawrence and C. H. Lee, and Messrs.
J. A. Davis and F. P. Harrold.

Another eleemosynary enterprise of the Diocese of Georgia was undertaken in 1929. The Convention of that year voted to accept the Episcopal Orphans' Home of Chatham County as a Diocesan institution. This matter had been under consideration since 1927. A Visiting Committee of three members, to be appointed by the Convention, was to meet in conjunction with the home's Trustees to supervise and advise. Incorporated in 1853 in Chatham County under the title, The Orphans Home of the Protestant Episcopal Church, the home for orphan girls existed in several locations in Savannah until 1919, when its present site at 1010 East Duffy Street was purchased. Its Chapel of the Good Shepherd was consecrated in 1921.

Despite the effect of business and industrial growth in such urban centers as Savannah, Augusta, and Brunswick, the 1920's did not reflect throughout the Diocese of Georgia the general prosperity usually attributed to the nation as a whole during this era. The farmers of America did not share so abundantly in the financial and industrial boom; and throughout the Diocese of Georgia the farm economy continued to be the most important index to business conditions, particularly in the small towns where so many small parishes and missions existed. Some indication of the financial situation of the Diocese is reflected in the fiscal reports and arrangements made at the Convention of 1928, certainly a big year in the boom of the 1920's. The Treasurer was authorized to pay the Bishop's salary of $6,000, $5,400 of which was to be raised from assessments against the parishes and missions and $600 out of the income of the Episcopate Endowment Fund. A Diocesan expense budget of $3,100 was approved, including such items as Bishop's office expense and travel to General Conventions. This amount was to be raised by assessments of graduated ratios against parishes and organized missions as follows: those with expenses of $2,000 or over, 12 per cent; $1,000 to $2,000, 11 per cent; and under $1,000, 6 per cent. A total of $4,608.25 was expended during 1927 through the General Missions Fund; $3,172.40 of this amount was paid as salaries to six missionary clergymen. Altogether $18,925.20 was spent from all sources (Executive Council, Georgia Missionary Fund, and National Council), for salaries to 20 missionaries at some 30 locations. The Treasurer of the Corporation announced that during 1927 the loan on the Bishop's residence in Savannah was reduced from $7,000 to $6,000, and that the Diocesan equity in the property amounted to $8,000. For the year 1927, the Executive Council reported a total income of $19,593.21, from 40 parishes and missions and a few special collections.

The Depression of the Thirties was as keenly felt in the Diocese of Georgia as in its sister Diocese to the northwest. In 1932 Bishop Reese told the Annual Convention with "much regret and disappointment" that the Diocese had fallen far short in paying its quota to the National Council ($9,000 paid out of $12,200). The result of the Canvass of 1932 "was a still greater disappointment" to the Bishop and Executive Council: $28,652 had been requested, but only $20,575 was pledged; as a consequence, the Diocesan budget had been reduced to $12,675. Then the Bishop made a plea for greater sacrifices by all communicants in the Diocese so that a reduction in clerical salaries would not be necessary. In most instances, he remarked, the existing salaries "have not been more than enough to enable these men to live and support their families with great economy." Despite the seriousness of the national depression, the Bishop argued that "many people, probably the majority, are not suffering for the necessities and comforts, and in some cases, of the luxuries of life." Why then, he concluded, should not the laity of the Church fulfill parochial "obligations of noblesse oblige" to its clergymen?

The financial reports in the Diocesan *Journal* for 1932 illustrate some of the fiscal crises to which the Bishop referred. Concerning his own salary, the Bishop had already asked the Executive Council to release $1,000 for 1931 and to reduce the following year's salary a like amount. The Council replied by voting that the 1931 salary should be paid in full if possible, but agreed to propose to the next Convention the reduction for 1932. The Convention accepted this proposal "with deepest regret," although it also adopted a recommendation of the Finance Committee that for 1933 the Bishop's salary be restored to $6,000, ten per cent of which was to be paid out of the Episcopal Endowment Fund and the remainder through local assessments. Other Diocesan expenses reduced or eliminated in

1932 were these: *The Church in Georgia,* official Diocesan organ, was suspended; support of the Negro school at Fort Valley was reduced to $250; a committee was established to prune the compilation of the *Journal* so as to lower its printing cost; a budgeted item of $200 for the education of candidates was abandoned, as was a similar amount for repairs to the Bishop's house; and numerous other reductions were agreed upon. Altogether, the original operating budget for the Diocese was reduced from $16,465 to $12,675 in this manner.

In appreciation of the Bishop's remarks concerning a stepped-up support on the local levels, the Convention devoted part of its meeting time to the discussion of ways and means of improving the Every Member Canvass and of securing the best possible percentage of compliance with pledges. The Rev. Charles C. J. Carpenter of St. John's, Savannah, invited all canvass directors from every parish and mission to attend his sessions on training for canvassers, to be instructed by Miss Edith Johnston, "an expert in that work." A rising vote of thanks was given to Mr. Carpenter; and very shortly the Convention adopted a resolution endorsing the idea of a two-day institute at St. John's "in all things pertaining to the preparation for an Every Member Canvass and its proper conduct."

In the following year (1933) the depression was continuing, and again the Diocesan budget was reduced—this time from $12,512 to $9,865. Despite the good intentions of 1932, the Bishop's salary was again set at the reduced figure of $5,000. It was not until 1936 that the Diocesan budget could be set above $15,000, and the Bishop's salary of $6,000 was not restored until 1943.

1933 was a year of sentimental interest to Georgians generally, as the state marked the two hundredth anniversary of Oglethorpe's landing. For the Diocese of Georgia, the date had double significance. Not only was it the bicentennial of the founding of the Church in Georgia, but it was also the twenty-fifth anniversary of the Episcopate of Frederick Focke Reese. The 111th Annual Convention of the Diocese met at Christ Church in Savannah on February 12, 1933. Special ceremonies commemorating the respective anniversaries included a joint meeting with the Young People's Service Leagues of the Dioceses of Georgia and Atlanta, the preaching of "an historical sermon" by Bishop Mikell of Atlanta, and a patriotic service conducted jointly by the Church leaders and the Georgia Society of the Colonial Dames of America.

Within the next twelve months the Diocese of Georgia faced the possible loss of its Bishop. During the latter part of his annual address in 1934, Bishop Reese said: ". . . It is not improbable that this will be the last Convention address that I shall be permitted to make to you. . . ." Later, in the sessions of the Convention, Bishop Reese issued this statement:

My conviction has been growing for sometime that it was becoming increasingly difficult for me to carry on the work of the Diocese as it ought to be done. And I have now come to the conclusion that the time has arrived when I must be relieved and the Diocese also relieved and permitted to secure the leadership of a younger and more active Bishop. I can no longer bear the burden of responsibility nor endure the labor of travel necessarily incident to my office . . . due to my age and . . . physical infirmities.

Bishop Reese gave the Convention his official "consent to the election and consecration of a Bishop Coadjutor for the Diocese," if they chose to do so. If, however, no such action would be taken, then he announced that he intended very shortly to submit to the Presiding Bishop of the House of Bishops his resignation of jurisdiction as Bishop of Georgia, and thereby "retire on pension from the active exercise of my ministry."

Immediately the Convention resolved that "every effort be made to avoid the resignation of our beloved Bishop;" and it put the Bishop's message into the consideration of the Standing Committee. On August 30, 1934, the Standing Committee and the Bishop issued a call to the Diocese to assemble in a special meeting at Grace Church, Waycross, on November 8, "for the purpose of electing a Bishop Coadjutor . . . and to make financial provisions in connection therewith." Again Bishop Reese issued his official consent to the election of a Bishop Coadjutor. The delegates then established the Bishop Coadjutor's salary at $5,000; and provided that Bishop Reese should have the use of "the Episcopal Residence" in Savannah "for the remaining years of his life free of expense and without any embarrassment."

Then the Special Convention entered upon the election. Bishop Reese asked the President of the Standing Committee, the Rev. David Cady Wright of Christ Church, Savannah, to take the chair, and the Bishop left the assembly. The following clergymen were nominated: The Rev. C. C. J. Carpenter (St. John's, Savannah), Dr. Henry D. Phillips (Trinity, Columbia, S.C.), Dr. James B. Lawrence (Calvary, Americus), the Rev. John Moore Walker (St. Luke's, Atlanta), Missionary Bishop William P. Remington of Oregon, Missionary Bishop Elmer N. Schmuck of Wyoming, and Missionary Bishop Middleton S. Barnwell of Idaho. To be elected, nominees must receive thirteen clerical and nine lay votes. Twelve ballots were taken and counted without both these majorities being received for any one nominee; although Dr. Phillips led in votes among the clergy, often with more than enough, Mr. Carpenter usually led among the laity. Upon the failure of the twelfth ballot to elect a Bishop, the Special Convention adjourned to reconvene later.

The Second Session of the Special Convention met at St. Paul's Church in Augusta on January 15, 1935. Dr. Phillips, Mr. Carpenter, and Dr. Lawrence were renominated and balloting began anew. Again Dr. Phillips led the clergy and Mr. Carpenter the laity in four ballots. (During the second and fourth, the names of Bishop Remington and Bishop Barnwell appeared). Then Mr. W. W. Douglas, lay delegate from Christ Church, Savannah, moved that the convention adjourn into separate bodies, that each order elect three representatives, and that the six representatives meet and make a report to the Convention. This was adopted; and later that day the Joint Committee reported as follows: (1) "one reason for the deadlock . . . is because the Clergy have not given a sufficiently preponderant vote in favor of any one candidate to impress the Laymen with any sense of the advisability of accepting their vote;" and (2) that voting be upon the names of the three leading candidates of the fourth ballot (Phillips, Carpenter, and Lawrence), and that if a sixth

ballot be required, the candidate receiving the lowest vote in
the fifth voting should be dropped. The Convention adopted
these proposals and voted again. Among the clergy it was Phillips, Carpenter, and Lawrence; and among laymen Carpenter,
Phillips, and Lawrence. Thereupon Lawrence's name was
dropped, and a sixth ballot occurred. Again Phillips won in the
clergy and Carpenter in the laity. After the seventh ballot
revealed similar voting sentiments, the Rev. Mr. Joseph Burton
of St. Michael and All Angels in Savannah moved that the
names of Phillips and Carpenter be removed from further consideration and that new nominations be received. This was carried.

Bishops Remington, Schmuck, and Barnwell, along with
Dr. Lawrence and Dr. Wright, were nominated; before balloting began, however, Dr. Wright withdrew his name. Although
none of these candidates received a sufficient vote in either house,
Bishop Barnwell's name led each group. On the ninth ballot,
Bishop Barnwell received substantial majorities in both orders
and was declared the duly elected Bishop Coadjutor of Georgia.

When the next regular Convention of the Diocese of Georgia
assembled at St. Paul's, Albany, in May, 1935, Bishop Reese
gave his last formal address to the Diocesan conclave. He
happily welcomed the presence of Bishop Coadjutor-elect Barnwell, and looked forward "with eager anticipation" to his joining
the Diocese permanently. "My own poor health," Bishop Reese
noted, had prevented the usual amount of visitations, and
this lent further weight to the wisdom of the Diocese in naming
a Bishop Coadjutor.

At St. Paul's in Savannah, the Rev. Geoffrey M. Horsfield had
recently become rector, replacing the Rev. W. W. Ware, who
had resigned owing to ill health. The Rev. John B. Walthour
(later to become the fourth Bishop of Atlanta) had resigned at
Grace Church, Waycross, to accept a call out of the Diocese,
and this position was still vacant. Other vacancies were yet
unfilled in the churches at Douglas and Fitzgerald and in the
colored missions at Albany and Hawkinsville. Fitzgerald was
being served monthly by Dr. Lawrence of Americus, while the
two colored missions were being aided "without compensation"
by the Rev. Messrs. Cobey of Albany and Skottowe of Hawkins-

ville. During 1934 the number of confirmations was one of the largest in Diocesan history, being 319. Bishop Reese expressed his thanks to the Bishops of Upper South Carolina, Atlanta, and Eastern Oregon and to Bishop Coadjutor Barnwell "for assisting me in holding confirmations which I was unable to do." Despite his poor health, the Bishop was able to make 54 visits to 31 parishes and missions, hold 30 confirmations, celebrate Holy Communion 23 times, participate in 56 services, and deliver 52 sermons and addresses. In fiscal affairs, "the tide seems to have turned." 90 per cent of the pledges for the Diocesan program had been collected, as compared with 70 per cent in 1933. The year ended with about a thousand dollars more on hand than at the beginning of the year ($1,370 compared with $334). A bank loan of $750 was paid off, clearing a note which had been carried for several years.

Bishop Reese did not attend the Annual Convention of 1936, for he was in very poor health, and since October 1, 1935, Bishop Barnwell had assumed the working leadership of the Diocese. Fourteen months later, on December 22, 1936, Frederick Focke Reese died in Savannah. In eulogizing his predecessor, Bishop Barnwell wrote,

He was a preacher of great power and fearlessness. He had an abiding faith in God and his fellow men. His sphere of influence went far beyond the limits of this Church. He was a stalwart champion of the religion of Christ as this Church hath received it. This world is the richer for his life and the Church Triumphant is richer for his entrance into it. Long will his shining light remain an example to those of us who are left to carry on his work. . . .

CHAPTER
✻ · XI · ✻

BISHOPS BARNWELL AND STUART

Upon THE death of Bishop Reese, Bishop Coadjutor Middleton Stuart Barnwell became the fifth Bishop of the Diocese of Georgia. Although he had assumed active leadership of the Diocese in the preceding year, 1937 constituted his first full year in activity. At that time, the white members of the Diocese were organized in fourteen parishes, twelve organized missions, eleven unorganized missions with church buildings, five mission stations, four parochial missions, and one proprietary chapel; while among colored Churchmen there were two parishes, nine organized missions, two unorganized missions, and one parochial mission.

White Parishes
(listed in order of union with the Diocese)

Location	Name	Date of Union	Rector
Savannah	Christ Church	1823	the Rev. David C. Wright
Augusta	St. Paul's	1823	_____ (vacant)
Frederica	Christ Church	1823	the Rev. Charles H. Lee
Savannah	St. John's	1841	the Rev. Ernest Risley
Darien	St. Andrew's	1843	the Rev. Frederick Cousins
Augusta	Atonement	1851	the Rev. Jackson H. Harris
Brunswick	St. Mark's	1851	the Rev. Royal K. Tucker
Albany	St. Paul's	1852	the Rev. Harry S. Cobey
Americus	Calvary	1865	the Rev. James B. Lawrence
Thomasville	St. Thomas'	1868	the Rev. Robb White, Jr.
Augusta	Good Shepherd	1869	the Rev. Lawrence M. Fenwick
Savannah	St. Paul's	1892	the Rev. Geoffrey M. Horsfield
Waycross	Grace	1906	the Rev. Howard V. Harper
Savannah	St. Michael and All Angels	1920	the Rev. Joseph Burton

ORGANIZED MISSIONS
(alphabetically)

Location	Name	Rector
Augusta	Christ Church	the Rev. Jackson H. Harris
Bainbridge	St. John's	the Rev. Herbert Scott-Smith
Cordele	Christ Church	the Rev. F. J. Wilson
Douglas	St. Andrew's	the Rev. Stephen E. Barnwell
Dublin	Christ Church	
Fitzgerald	St. Matthew's	the Rev. Stephen E. Barnwell
Hawkinsville	St. Luke's	
Jesup	St. Paul's	the Rev. Frederick Cousins
Sandersville	Grace	
Tifton	St. Anne's	the Rev. F. J. Wilson
Valdosta	Christ Church	the Rev. Thomas G. Mundy
Woodbine	St. Mark's	the Rev. Charles H. Lee

UNORGANIZED MISSIONS
(with church building)

Location	Name	Rector
Blakely	Holy Trinity	the Rev. H. Scott-Smith
Cuthbert	Epiphany	the Rev. James B. Lawrence
Isle of Hope	St. Thomas'	the Rev. Robert H. Daniell
Meldrim	St. Andrew's	the Rev. Robert H. Daniell
Moultrie	St. John's	the Rev. F. J. Wilson
Pennington	St. James'	the Rev. James B. Lawrence
Pooler	St. James'	the Rev. Robert H. Daniell
Quitman	St. James'	the Rev. Thomas G. Mundy
St. Mary's	Christ Church	the Rev. Charles H. Lee
Vienna	Prince of Peace	the Rev. James B. Lawrence
Waynesboro	St. Michael's	the Rev. Jackson H. Harris

MISSION STATIONS

Location	Name	Rector
Blackshear	All Saints'	the Rev. Howard V. Harper
Benevolence		the Rev. James B. Lawrence
Dawson	Calvary	the Rev. James B. Lawrence
McRae	St. Timothy's	
Waverly		the Rev. Charles H. Lee

PAROCHIAL MISSIONS

Location	Name	Rector
Brunswick	St. Jude's	the Rev. Royal K. Tucker
Brunswick	St. Paul's Chapel	the Rev. Royal K. Tucker
Savannah	St. Andrew's Chapel	the Rev. David C. Wright
Waycross		the Rev. Howard V. Harper

PROPRIETARY CHAPEL

Savannah   Good Shepherd   Episcopal Orphans' Home

COLORED CHURCHES
PARISHES

Location	Name	Rector
Brunswick	St. Athanasius'	the Rev. J. Clyde Perry
Savannah	St. Stephen's (later St. Matthew's)	the Rev. Gustave H. Caution

ORGANIZED MISSIONS

Location	Name	Rector
Albany	St. John's	the Rev. Harry S. Cobey
Augusta	St. Mary's	the Rev. Charles H. Dukes
Burroughs	St. Bartholomew's	the Rev. J. H. Brown
Darien	St. Cyprian's	the Rev. Frederick Cousins
Pennick	Good Shepherd	the Rev. J. Clyde Perry
Savannah	St. Augustine's (later combined with St. Stephen's to form St. Matthew's)	the Rev. J. H. Brown
St. Mary's	Our Saviour	the Rev. Charles B. Pritchett
Thomasville	Good Shepherd	the Rev. Robert N. Perry
Waycross	St. Ambrose's	the Rev. Charles B. Pritchett

UNORGANIZED MISSIONS

Location	Name	Rector
Darien	St. John's Chapel, Inwood	the Rev. Frederick Cousins
Hawkinsville	St. Phillip's	

PAROCHIAL MISSION

St. Simon's   St. Ignatius' Chapel   the Rev. Charles D. Lee
   Island

The Diocese in 1937 numbered 5,391 white and 1,029 colored communicants. 344 white and 50 colored officers and teachers served 2,569 white and 530 colored Sunday School members.

For eighteen years (1936-1954) Bishop Middleton Stuart Barnwell administered his Diocese, bringing an active and vigorous leadership to a lengthy period of service. In this respect he followed in the tradition of the four Bishops who preceded him, each of whom served more than twenty years. His period included the late Depression years, the prosperity of the late Thirties and early Forties, World War II, and the post-war era down to the mid-Fifties, during which the Church was enjoying its most substantial growth.

By the end of 1953, Diocesan statistics showed the following developments:

Number of parishes—increase of two: (Christ Church, Augusta, 1951; St. Alban's, Fleming Heights, Augusta, 1953)
Number of missions (organized and unorganized)—decrease of four.
Parochial and proprietary mission chapels—decrease of three.

However, during the era the total number of communicants increased to 8,156, with 469 officers and teachers serving 3,814 church school members.

On the fifth anniversary of his jurisdiction in Georgia, Bishop Barnwell urged Churchmen to look deeply into the intense problems of world affairs existing in 1941—a fateful year. Calling specific attention to the Forward in Service program recently launched by the Presiding Bishop, Barnwell noted that it was but an extension of the previous Forward Movement, but with the emphasis on outward signs. The earlier movement produced a substantial increase in daily Bible reading and prayer; but "this is not enough." The goodness of Churchmen, he said, "must flow forth in Christian service, witness bearing and Gospel preaching" to the rest of the state, nation, and world. With great emphasis the Bishop said "we have the finest Church in the world and do less with it than almost any other group of Christians that I know." He asked all delegates to the Convention to work within their parishes and missions to implement the Forward in Service program.

The continued expansion of the Church into promising domestic missionary areas seemed to Bishop Barnwell a logical step for the Diocese, both to carry out the new Forward in Service program, and to justify the continued existence of missions. Yet, he pointed out in 1941, "we are concerned with the shrinkage in missionary *giving*." With such reductions occurring in the midst of a new prosperity, the answer semed to lie in more and better missionary education—that is, informing communicants about the crisis and the needs for expansion. At the present, he mourned, "we are being forced to the unhappy policy of leaving certain mission stations unfilled for the time being."

The report of the Department of Missions for the following year (1942), reflects this concern on the part of the Bishop. Only five missions had resident clergy: Bainbridge (whose missionary also served Blakely), Darien (also serving Jesup), Tifton (also serving Fitzgerald), Hawkinsville (also serving McRae), and Valdosta (also serving Quitman). The remainder were being handled as follows:

Atonement, Augusta	—Rector of St. Paul's, Augusta
Waynesboro	—Rector of St. Paul's, Augusta
Christ Church, Augusta	—Rector of Good Shepherd, Augusta
Cordele	—Occasional services by nearby clergy
Douglas	—Rector of Grace Church, Waycross
Dublin-Sandersville	—To be combined into a new field
Woodbine	—Rector of St. Mark's, Brunswick
Cuthbert	—Archdeacon of Albany
Pennington	—Archdeacon of Albany
Vienna	—Archdeacon of Albany
Benevolence	—Archdeacon of Albany
Dawson	—Archdeacon of Albany
Isle of Hope	—Rector of St. Michael's, Savannah
Pooler	—Rector of St. John's, Savannah
Moultrie	—Rector of St. Thomas', Thomasville

This report covered white missions, and that for colored missions was equally critical.

The Archdeacon of Albany, mentioned above, was one of but two Archdeacons then active in the Diocese. Previously the Diocese had utilized five or six such officials to supervise and coordinate mission activities in the scattered parts of the Diocese. The Ven. James B. Lawrence, rector of Calvary Church of Americus, was the sole white Archdeacon in 1942; supervising Negro missions was Archdeacon Robert N. Perry of Thomasville. In 1947 when Mr. Lawrence retired from active service, Bishop Barnwell commented on the Archdeacon's forty-three years of faithful duty: "So far as my knowledge of the record goes, this is the longest period of service rendered by any man in the history of the Diocese." How long he had been attending conventions, or even serving as Secretary of the Diocese, the Bishop did not know. "Dr. Lawrence is still a missionary," said the Bishop, "and he comes to this convention with a request that we designate our offerings toward a new roof on the Church of the Prince of Peace at Vienna."

In his annual address to the Convention of 1944, Bishop Barnwell urged the Diocese to adopt a plan which would implement the mission expansion program without increasing Diocesan budgets. A well-organized system of securing local voluntary contributions among the six thousand communicants should, he said, produce a sufficient amount of money to get the program underway; and thus stimulated by voluntary gifts, members of the Diocese should then be willing to increase their regular missionary giving so that these new stations could be continued and others launched. Such a collection would make possible the construction of new buildings much needed at stations like Jesup, Christ Church in Augusta, Moultrie, and Bainbridge. The "Tifton Plan" should be studied for utilization elsewhere, for as the plan developed, it provided for a single-unit construction of a combination parish house and rectory and cost but six thousand dollars.

The Committee on the Bishop's Address introduced a resolution which the Convention adopted:

RESOLVED, that this Convention approve in principle the raising of twenty-five thousand dollars by voluntary contributions only, without resort to quotas or assessments, for the advance building program of the missionary work in the Diocese, especially in Christ Church, Augusta, St. Paul's, Jesup, and the combined negro churches in Savannah. This convention commits this task to the Executive Council, and calls upon every communicant of the Diocese for active support over and above his local building program.

During the following year, thousands of pieces of literature were dispatched to some two thousand selected communicants of the Diocese, along with blank checks and return envelopes. At the Convention of 1945, Bishop Barnwell announced that he was "greatly disappointed" over the response to this appeal for the new Forward Movement in the Diocesan mission fields. His office had borne the brunt of the labor and expenses involved in such mailings, and the receipt of "considerably less than three thousand dollars" seemed to be a poor return. He suggested that some other machinery be adopted for the drive's continuance. The Convention's action was to resolve that "the Executive Council be instructed to prosecute to a successful conclusion the Diocesan Campaign to raise $25,000 for forward work in the Diocese."

The Diocesan Reconstruction and Advance Fund Campaign —as it was now called—was merged with a drive conducted in answer to the National Church's appeal for Forward Movement funds. Following the Convention of 1945, the Executive Council decided to seek a minimum goal in the Diocese of $50,000; the first $30,000 would be sent to the National Church; the next $20,000 applied to the Diocesan program; and all amounts received above that to be equally divided between the two. In 1946 the Executive Council reported its "utmost satisfaction" with the response. To date some $24,000 had been forwarded to the National Church, and the Council expected to obtain much of the remainder in the coming year. An outstanding example of another type of giving occurred in 1945. In this year Mr. Robert W. Groves made a gift of his home on Victory Drive, Savannah, to the Diocese for the Bishop's residence.

Bishop Barnwell's address to the Convention of 1945 afforded him an opportunity to observe his tenth anniversary as a Bishop in the Diocese of Georgia and the twentieth anniversary of his Consecration to the Episcopate (he was Missionary Bishop of Idaho for ten years before coming to Georgia). He addressed the delegates "My Dear Friends," and emphasized that the phrase exemplified "the relationship which I have sought to build between myself and my people during the past ten years. . . . The happiest and most useful relationship for Bishop or Priest is that of Friend to his people. It means trust—and service—and love. And beyond this there is nothing else."

The larger portion of his address, however, concerned the war situation, with a considerable emphasis on hopes for the peace which would follow. The Convention adopted a resolution endorsing the program of the Dumbarton Oaks Conference, and authorized the Bishop to send this telegram to Secretary of State Edward R. Stettinius:

The following resolution was passed at the annual Convention of the Episcopal Diocese of Georgia, April 19, 1945.

The Dumbarton Oaks proposals seem to us the first step toward a just and durable peace. We therefore endorse these proposals and commend them to our fellow churchmen for study and we urge that as citizens they support the basic principles outlined. We request further that special services of prayer be held within the Diocese during the San Francisco Conference and that the members of our Church be encouraged to continue steadfast in prayer throughout the Conference Period.

Within a few weeks the war ended in Europe, and by mid-August the Japanese phase was concluded. Speaking to the Convention in 1946, Bishop Barnwell commented that "the war has ended, but peace has not come." He referred to the problems of hunger and political unrest in Europe and Asia. He saw these as the inevitable result of war, which "is human hatreds raised to their highest earthly power." Hatreds always bring death and suffering. "We continue to flout God's Laws, and inevitably God mows us down! . . . We asked for it—and we got it!"

Although no new parishes applied for admission to the Diocese during the immediate post-war years, mission work prospered. In 1947 Bishop Barnwell seemed pleased to report the varied activities of many parish priests who were demonstrating a "splendid missionary spirit." As examples, he listed the Rev. Messrs. Hamilton West of Augusta who served Waynesboro; Edward M. Claytor of Augusta who tended to Atonement in that city; Savannah's William H. Brady who was taking care of Pooler and the Isle of Hope; Charles Wyatt-Brown of Waycross who was serving St. Mary's and Woodbine; G. Ralph Madson of Albany, in charge of the colored mission there also; and William C. Baxter of Americus who was taking over part of the mission work (specifically Blakely, Cuthbert, Pennington, Vienna, Benevolence, and Dawson) formerly done by Dr. Lawrence. He had special praise for the Rev. George W. Shirley of Thomasville who "has for years been an unpaid missionary." Mr. Shirley's work at Moultrie was so successful that they began to support a resident missionary; while Bainbridge and Cairo were now receiving his attention.

In 1947 the Diocese of Georgia took steps to end distinctions between white and colored Churchmen in the constitution, canons, and in official references. This action was in line with trends in the other southern dioceses. In the Diocese of Georgia colored Episopalians had been meeting in a separate Council, presided over by the Bishop of Georgia. In 1947 this procedure was terminated, and the constitution and canons amended so that in the future representatives of both races would attend the same assembly and have the same voting privileges.

A continual heightening of interest in laymen's activities produced by 1949 an official organization of The Episcopal Churchmen of the Diocese of Georgia, which would sponsor, promote, and conduct the annual Diocesan Layman's Conference. Further, the new group was charged with responsibility for serving as the official channel for dissemination of information pertinent to responsibilities and interests of the laity.

Much of this lay interest in the Church had been engendered over the years at special conferences and retreats at the Diocesan assembly, Camp Reese, which in 1949, celebrated its twenty-fifth anniversary. Its location on St. Simon's Island dated from 1932 with a gift of $7,500 from Mr. and Mrs. Charles Chapin of Thomasville, $1,000 from the Executive Council, and $1,300 from the Diocesan Building Fund. Chapin Hall at the Camp was constructed and also ten lots were purchased from these funds. In succeeding years eleven additional lots were secured and buildings given as follows: Jonnard Cottage (1933), by St. John's Church, Savannah; Wright Cottage (1934), by Christ Church, Savannah; Augusta Cottage (1936), by St. Paul's and Good Shepherd, Augusta; Alexander Cottage (1938), by the Young People's Service League; and Aiken Cottage (1938), from miscellaneous gifts.

But despite these and other signs of general Diocesan prosperity, Bishop Barnwell waged an unceasing struggle to obtain a sounder financial structure for Diocese and parish. Commenting on his fifteen years as Bishop in 1950, he quoted Biblical passages to justify his efforts. "If you reluctant, doubting business men," he said, "will apply these Christ-given principles to your own program of parish finance, you will find that they work out." He recognized the profit-making spirit of the free enterprise system in "these highly competitive days;" but he reminded laymen that two spirits had to co-exist, with different principles: "If a Christian went into business and tried to apply the laws of selflessness, he would probably go broke financially . . . and when a business man goes into . . . religion as a vestryman . . . and tries to apply the law of . . . business, he is going to go broke spiritually."

In 1950, one of the missions in the Diocese celebrated the fiftieth anniversary of the consecration of its Church building. This was Grace Church at Sandersville, which was undergoing a period of renewed vigor under the leadership of the priest-in-charge assigned a year earlier, the Rev. N. Chafee Croft of Augusta. One of Mr. Croft's needed innovations was regular worship, which had not been conducted in Sandersville for some thirty years.

A mission which was enjoying the benefits of a recently completed new building was Christ Church in Valdosta. On February 20, 1949, the first service was held in the mission's new location at Patterson and College streets; and by 1954 its membership and local activity had grown so well that Christ Church was admitted to the Diocese as a parish, with the Rev. Michael J. Kippenbrock, its Vicar since 1953, assigned as rector.

At Sylvania, a sixty-year lapse in regular Church work ended in February, 1951 when the Rev. James C. Caley of St. Michael's in Waynesboro presented two Sylvanians to Bishop Barnwell for confirmation. This was followed by a meeting during which the Church of the Epiphany was organized as a mission in Sylvania, and it was admitted to the Diocese at the next Council.

One of the "most-traveled" churches in the Diocese was Christ Church in Cordele. Its building was transplanted in 1952 to a third location, this time at 1st Street and 15th Avenue, where it was re-dedicated by Bishop Barnwell on May 10, 1953.

A new mission in the Diocese was Trinity Church in Cochran. Admitted to the Diocese as a mission on May 21, 1950, the new

congregation held its early meetings in the Community House
and later in the Methodist Church. In June of 1951, however, a
prominent Baptist layman, Mr. J. T. Edmondson, donated a plot
of land to the Episcopalians; and from this beginning a church
structure was ready for use by May 10, 1953.

In 1949 the Rev. Harcourt E. Waller, Jr., of St. John's in
Bainbridge, began conducting services for communicants in
Cairo. This work accelerated Episcopal activity in Cairo which
had previously been dormant from 1931 until revived in 1948
by the Rev. George W. Shirley of Thomasville. In 1950 the
Cairo congregation was received into the Diocese as the Grace
Church Mission, with Mr. Waller in charge. A new church
building was consecrated by Bishop Barnwell on October 21,
1951.

In 1954, at the age of 72, Middleton Stuart Barnwell retired.
During the Convention of the preceding year, he told the delegates of his impending retirement in accordance with the canons
of the Church. His address for 1953 contains interesting highlights of his varied experience in the work of the Church, and
also of the history and condition of the Diocese of Georgia.
"As Field Secretary and Missionary Bishop," he said, "I have
worked in this country from Southern Florida to Seattle, and
from Kennebunkport, Maine, to San Diego, California. . . . It
has been a full life and a happy life, and life owes me nothing."
With retirement impending, he intended to rest; and, he added,
"I think I shall go fishing, of which I have always talked a lot,
but of which I have done very little." In discussing the required
characteristics of a Bishop, he commented that it did not demand
"the highest grade of mentality" or "pulpit eloquence." Instead,
"slow, steady, plodding and patient work" was the one element
which would build and maintain the Diocese. And "robust
health and good driving ability" should not be ignored. In a
diocese like Georgia, he rather wryly noted that a Bishop should
be "either a celibate, or a man who is very unhappily married
. . . for he will live on the highway." The Bishop spoke of
"relentless weekends" on the road visiting the scattered churches
of the Diocese, and added, "in between he tries to make friends
with his wife and others who live in his home town."

With his retirement immediately on the horizon, Bishop Barnwell in this same address urged the Diocese to avoid "caucusing and electioneering" as the time drew near for the election of his successor. He reminded the delegates that eighteen years ago the Convention twice dead-locked on two men, "either one of whom would have made you a better bishop than you got." As for his own election, he said it was "not because anyone in particular wanted me, but because none of you were able to get the man you DID want, and I was already a bishop, and the cost of consecrating a new one would run to . . . two thousand dollars." He recommended obtaining information about as many eligible men as possible, but cautioned against trying to commit votes in advance. The divided sentiment existing when he first came to the Diocese of Georgia took a long time to heal.

Bishop Barnwell announced in 1953 that he intended to have the Chancellor (Judge W. Walter Douglas of Savannah) study the canons and draw up a plan by which the election should be conducted. At the Convention of 1954, the Chancellor's plan was presented and adopted, and a most harmonious election took place. Seventeen nominations were received, without speeches in accordance with previous agreement: the Rev. George M. Alexander, rector, Trinity Church, Columbia, S.C.; the Rev. William C. Baxter, rector, St. Alban's, Fleming Heights; the Rev. William S. Brace, rector, Grace Church, Waycross; the Rev. Allen G. Clarkson, rector, Good Shepherd, Augusta; the Rev. Harry L. Doll, D.D., rector, St. Paul's, Baltimore; the Very Rev. Clarence R. Haden, Dean, Grace and Holy Trinity Cathedral, Kansas City, Missouri; the Rev. Lawrence H. Hall, Canon, Trinity Cathedral, Cleveland, Ohio; the Rev. Henry B. Hodgkins, D.D., rector, Christ Church, Pensacola; the Rev. G. Ralph Madson, rector, St. Paul's, Albany; the Rt. Rev. Louis C. Melcher, D.D., Missionary Bishop of Central Brazil; the Rev. George H. Murphy, Canon Pastor, St. Philip's Cathedral, Atlanta; the Rt. Rev. Iveson B. Noland, D.D., Suffragan Bishop, Louisiana; the Rev. John A. Pinckney, rector, St. James', Greenville, S.C.; the Very Rev. J. Milton Richardson, Dean, Christ Church Cathedral, Houston, Texas; the Rev. Ernest Risley, rector, St. John's, Savannah (withdrawn before balloting); the Rev.

Charles F. Schilling, rector, St. Paul's, Augusta; the Very Rev. Albert R. Stuart, D.D., Dean, Christ Church Cathedral, New Orleans; and the Rev. Harcourt E. Waller, Jr., priest-in-charge, St. John's, Bainbridge, Holy Trinity, Blakely, Grace Church, Cairo (withdrawn before balloting).

The first ballot showed each candidate receiving at least one vote in either order but the second ballot found the clergy voting 15-10 for Dean Stuart over Dr. Doll; while the laity voted 19-2/3 for Dean Stuart, 5-1/3 for Dr. Doll, and 1 for Canon Murphy. By motion, the lay delegates then voted to cast a unanimous ballot for Dean Stuart; and upon learning this, the clergy did likewise. Within a few days the Diocese received word of Dean Stuart's acceptance. The new Bishop of Georgia brought to the Episcopate a distinguished heritage dating from ancient Scottish kings through the early history of South Carolina. A contemporary among his fellow Bishops has termed Bishop Stuart "a man of learning and of good taste . . . a scholar, a gentleman, and a saint."

The consecration of Albert Rhett Stuart as the sixth Bishop of Georgia took place on October 20th, 1954 in St. Paul's Church, Augusta. Since this was the first consecration in the Diocese in many years, there was great interest manifested in this event and it received wide newspaper coverage and television publicity.

The Reverend Charles Schilling, Rector of St. Paul's Church, Augusta, served as Master of Ceremonies. The Consecrator was the Presiding Bishop, the Most Reverend Henry Knox Sherrill, D.D., whose Chaplain was the Rev. F. Bland Tucker of Christ Church, Savannah. The co-Consecrators were the Rt. Rev. Middleton S. Barnwell, retired Bishop of Georgia, and the Rt. Rev. Girault Jones, Bishop of Louisiana. The Preacher was the Rt. Rev. Noble C. Powell, Bishop of Maryland. Attending Presbyters for the Bishop-elect were the Rev. Allen Clarkson, rector of the Church of the Good Shepherd, Augusta, and the Rev. Porter Ball, rector of St. Paul's Church, Savannah. The Bishop-elect was presented for Consecration by the Rt. Rev. Randolph R. Claiborne, Jr., Bishop of Atlanta, and Rt. Rev. Iveson Noland, Suffragan Bishop of Louisiana. Besides these Bishops officiating, there were six Bishops from neighboring dioceses present. The Church of England was represented by the Bishop of New Guinea.

The year of Bishop Barnwell's retirement (on October 1, 1954) and Bishop Stuart's accession (October 20) was a very significant one for the Diocese. Bishop Barnwell expressed genuine pleasure over the recent upsurge in missionary interest, especially singling out the developments at St. Alban's Church of Fleming Heights (near Augusta), which was admitted to the Diocese as a new parish in 1954. Other new parishes admitted that year were St. Thomas', Isle of Hope; Christ Church, Valdosta; and St. John's, Bainbridge.

In the following year St. Paul's of Jesup was admitted as a parish, thereby bringing to fulfillment a mission begun more than fifty years earlier. Late in December, 1953, a new mission was launched at Harlem (near Augusta) in an effort to bring Episcopal services to Columbia and McDuffie counties on the border of the Diocese. By November of 1955, Trinity Church of Harlem was consecrated by Bishop Stuart. The Diocesan *Journal* for 1955 shows six convocations active under the following Archdeacons: Savannah, the Ven. T. Porter Ball; Augusta, the Ven. Allen B. Clarkson; Dublin, the Ven. William F. Bassill; Albany, the Ven. G. Ralph Madson; Thomasville, the Ven. Michael J. Kippenbrock; and Waycross, the Ven. William S. Brace. Reporting for the Executive Council's Department of Missions, Chairman Clarkson stated that "most all of the regular work of the Diocese is well covered . . . and new fields and new arrangements are in the process of being made."

The efforts in these "new fields and new arrangements" were very evident by the mid-Fifties, and reflect both the cumulative effect of Bishop Barnwell's interest and the new enthusiasms generated by Bishop Stuart. One of the "new arrangements" adopted in 1955-56 was enlargement of the Department of Missions of the Executive Council. In addition to regular members of the Council, the group now included the Diocesan Archdeacons, the District Chairmen and the President of the Woman's Auxiliary, the Area Keymen of the Laymen's League, and other interested laymen. In 1956 the Chairman of the Department of Missions, the Rev. William C. Baxter, reported the inauguration of special visits to the department's meetings by missionary clergymen from the Diocese who gave first-hand accounts of their own problems and thus stimulated specific interest and attention. According to Chairman Baxter, the principal difficulty still was lack of funds for expansion. However, when asked to increase their own support by ten per cent, nine missions responded favorably, and more were expected to join their ranks. The Department asked the Diocese to accept these new organized missions: Church of the Holy Apostles, Savannah; Church of the Annunciation, Vidalia; and St. Francis', Pelham. On the other hand, they asked that St. Andrew's parish in Darien, whose membership had dwindled drastically, be reverted to mission status. Finally, the 1956 report asked the Finance Department for $41,000 in the Executive Council's budget.

A better centralized management of Diocesan affairs became possible during 1957. In March of that year the newly acquired Diocesan House on East Bay Street in Savannah was dedicated as Diocesan Headquarters, with offices, conference room, and chapel.

The experience of the Annunciation Mission in Vidalia reflected the twentieth-century pioneering on which Bishop Barnwell had commented from time to time. In December, 1954, the Rev. J. N. Reid of Savannah addressed the Vidalia Woman's Club and remained through the evening to celebrate Holy Communion at the Presbyterian Church building for twenty-seven persons. This beginning stimulated a series of visits by Bishop Stuart and local activity by some twelve communicants in Toombs county. Early in February, 1955, the Rev. Peter Fleming of St. Paul's in Jesup initiated a series of bi-weekly Sunday evening services which, by mid-summer, were being conducted in a former library of the Community House. During the following spring official petition to the Diocese for recognition as an organized mission was granted.

Something of Albert Rhett Stuart's approach to his responsibilities and analysis of his opportunities as the sixth Bishop of the Diocese of Georgia is revealed in his address to the Convention which met at St. Thomas' Parish in Thomasville, May 8-9, 1956, approximately eighteen months after he had succeeded Bishop Barnwell. The new Bishop outlined six steps which he deemed necessary if the Church was to "fulfill her responsibility in this generation and improve her evangelistic witness." In the first place, there must be a "renewal of confidence and conviction" that it was the mission of the Church "to proclaim her Lord as the Way, the Truth, and the Life for all Mankind." This involved a concentrated program of work and education in every parish and mission. He particularly recommended year-round use of Church Schools; continual instruction for confirmation, marriage, and baptism; attitudes of study within every parish organization—vestry, Woman's Auxiliary, choir, guilds, men's clubs, etc.; "Quiet Days of Prayer" for adults and young people; a Diocesan retreat and conference center to augment local efforts; and "preaching missions in our congregations."

Secondly, it was necessary that the Church "appreciate the magnitude of her present opportunity." An all-out effort should be made by every member of every congregation to create "a welcoming fellowship" by direct evangelistic effort aimed at increasing the ranks by baptism and confirmation. Many people were troubled by the times, by materialism, by some of the unpleasant characteristics of the new era. "People are discovering that a life full of gadgets is no satisfactory substitute for a life lived in the power and presence of God." Members were urged to adopt a program of personal evangelism: "It is high time the Episcopal Church rose from her dignified posture of waiting to be discovered . . . and went out into the byways and hedges seeking the souls for whom her Lord died."

The third necessity logically stemmed from those previously listed. New congregations must be established in areas where the Church had no work and in newly developing urban communities. The Bishop offered statistics comparing county populations with Church memberships to show that "it is obvious our people have not been taught the meaning of evangelism. . . ." A concomitant improvement lay in increased contributions, in abandoning practices of "casual giving": "We cannot teach people to give for the work of the Kingdom of God by Bazaars, fairs, suppers and such like."

A fourth and very specific need lay in an accelerated support of the Church's University of the South at Sewanee. In general, the members of the Diocese were responding favorably to the regular needs of the university. However, the Bishop pointed out, "the immediate opportunity before us is to join with the other owning dioceses of the University in completing All Saints Chapel." He announced that the Executive Council had agreed to his recommendation that the Diocese accept a responsibility of $17,200 to help complete the Chapel, and he hoped that the offerings would surpass this amount.

"The Witness of the Christian Home and Family" was the topic of his fifth point. The Bishop expressed sharp concern over mounting divorce rates, and urged consideration of the sanctity of the Christian marriage partnership as a basic factor in this problem "of human relationships."

The question of "human relationships" led Bishop Stuart into his sixth area of responsibility—the racial problem. His concern over "hysterical fear and political opportunism" led him to urge Churchmen to be vigilant "lest the fear and prejudice surrounding us infiltrate our thinking and confuse us as to our clear duty. . . ." He reminded the Diocese of the many years during which white and colored Churchmen had known "their unity in Christ and have labored together in one fold under one shepherd to bring other sheep of the Good Shepherd into it." He earnestly advocated policies of "reason in the midst of hysteria," "patience and charity in the midst of prejudice," "fellowships between the races in prayer, worship, and work," and recognition of the fact that "the solution of the problem of our society lies not in the realm of law but in the realm of faith and grace."

The general progress of the Diocese of Georgia after three years under Bishop Stuart is revealed in the statistics for 1957:

Communicants	9,976
Sunday School—pupils	4,151
adults	786
staff	570
Confirmations	591

PARISHES

Location	Name	Rector
Albany	St. Paul's	the Rev. G. Ralph Madson
Americus	Calvary	the Rev. Paul L. Ritch
Augusta	Christ Church	the Rev. Robert E. Wilcox
Augusta	Good Shepherd	the Rev. Allen B. Clarkson
Augusta	St. Alban's	the Rev. Alfred Mead
Augusta	St. Paul's	the Rev. Charles F. Schilling
Bainbridge	St. John's	the Rev. John Paul Jones
Brunswick	St. Mark's	the Rev. Talbert Morgan
Isle of Hope, Savannah	St. Thomas'	the Rev. G. Edward Haynsworth
Jesup	St. Paul's	the Rev. Peter W. Fleming
Moultrie	St. John's	the Rev. Kenneth M. Gearhart
St. Simon's Island	Christ Church	the Rev. Junius J. Martin
Savannah	Christ Church	the Rev. F. Bland Tucker
Savannah	St. John's	the Rev. Ernest Risley
Savannah	St. Matthew's	the Rev. Gustave H. Caution
Savannah	St. Michael's	the Rev. Pearson H. Sloan
Savannah	St. Paul's	the Rev. T. Porter Ball
Thomasville	St. Thomas'	the Rev. George W. Shirley
Tifton	St. Anne's	the Rev. Charles C. Demere
Valdosta	Christ Church	the Rev. Michael J. Kippenbrock
Waycross	Grace	the Rev. Hallie D. Warren, Jr.

MISSIONS

Location	Name	Rector
Albany	St. John's	the Rev. O. E. Primo
Albany	St. Mark's	the Rev. John R. Wooley
Augusta	Atonement	the Rev. N. Chafee Croft
Augusta	St. Mary's	(vacant)
Blakely	Holy Trinity	the Rev. John Paul Jones
Brunswick	St. Athanasius'	the Rev. Thaddeus P. Martin
Burroughs	St. Bartholomew's	the Rev. Gustave H. Caution
Cairo	Grace	the Rev. Ben A. English
Cochran	Trinity	the Rev. John O. Ford
Cordele	Christ Church	the Rev. Robert L. Nichols
Cuthbert	Epiphany	the Rev. George V. Johnson
Darien	St. Andrew's	the Rev. W. Birt Sams
Darien	St. Cyprian's	the Rev. Thaddeus P. Martin
Dawson	Holy Spirit	the Rev. George V. Johnson
Douglas	St. Andrew's	the Rev. Herman B. Huff
Dublin	Christ Church	the Rev. John O. Ford

Fitzgerald	St. Matthew's	the Rev. Herman B. Huff
Harlem	Trinity	the Rev. Joseph L. Peacock
Hawkinsville	St. Luke's	the Rev. Robert L. Nichols
Hawkinsville	St. Philip's	the Rev. Robert L. Nichols
Pelham	St. Francis'	the Rev. John R. Wooley
Pennick	Good Shepherd	the Rev. Thaddeus P. Martin
Pooler	St. James'	the Rev. T. Porter Ball
Quitman	St. James'	the Rev. Michael J. Kippenbrock
St. Mary's	Christ Church	the Rev. Albert H. Hatch
Sandersville	Grace	the Rev. John L. Kelly
Savannah	Holy Apostles	the Rev. J. Bryan Griswold
Sav. Beach	All Saints	the Rev. Albert H. Hatch
Statesboro	Trinity	the Rev. Robert E. H. Peeples
Swainsboro	Good Shepherd	the Rev. James P. Crowther
Sylvania	Epiphany	the Rev. Robert E. H. Peeples
Thomasville	Good Shepherd	(vacant)
Vidalia	Annunciation	the Rev. James P. Crowther
Waynesboro	St. Michael's	the Rev. Holland B. Clark
Woodbine	St. Mark's	the Rev. Albert H. Hatch

PAROCHIAL MISSION CHAPELS

Brunswick:　St. Paul's Chapel. Parochial mission of St. Mark's Parish. The Rev. Talbert Morgan

St. Simon's:　St. Ignatius' Church. Parochial mission of Christ Church. The Rev. Junius J. Martin

PROPRIETARY CHAPELS

Savannah:　Chapel of the Good Shepherd, Episcopal Home for Girls. The Rev. Thomas L. Hastings, Chaplain

Savannah:　St. George's Chapel, Diocesan House, 611 East Bay St. The Bishop

The Rt. Rev. Middleton Stuart Barnwell died in Savannah on May 6, 1957, having had three years to observe the continued progress and spiritual growth of the Diocese of Georgia. His successor, Bishop Albert Rhett Stuart, was proving not merely adequate to the challenge, but, in the true spirit of his predecessors and his contemporary in the Diocese of Atlanta, abundant with wisdom and inspiration for the era of growth which the Episcopal Church in Georgia was facing in the late Fifties.

PART FOUR

· ✷ ·

The Diocese of Atlanta, 1907-1957

THE RT. REV. CLELAND KINLOCH NELSON, D. D.
Bishop of Georgia 1892-1907
Bishop of Atlanta 1907-1917

CHAPTER

✦ · XII · ✦

THE DIOCESE OF ATLANTA IN
THE FORMATIVE YEARS

THE NEWLY created Northwestern Diocese held its "Primary Convention" on December 4, 1907 in that Diocese's oldest parish, Christ Church of Macon. First order of business was an address by Bishop Nelson. He told the assembled delegates that a historic moment lay before them: "This is the beginning of history. . . . [For] every new Diocese is an entity, and should have its identity . . . by which it will be distinguished from its sisters." On the question of a name for the new Diocese, he suggested that while "geographical divisions, mountains and rivers" might be utilized, a better choice might be made by choosing one of the names of several cities, "all dignified by a Church constituency, by history and life and endeavor, as centres." Specifically, he mentioned Athens, Atlanta, Columbus, Macon, and Rome. Concerning constitution and canons, Bishop Nelson urged that the Convention agree to get along with as many existing laws which governed the old Diocese as possible. This assembly, he argued, was present on a dedicated task— "let us not dull their enthusiasm by that most wearisome of tasks—tinkering Canons."

In the first message to the new Diocese, Bishop Nelson went beyond the organizational problems. He chided North Georgia Episcopalians for failures to participate actively in the church service. "The music of the Church," he said, "has degenerated into a concert of the Choir. . . . Let us not rest until we get the people to raise their voices to read and to sing." Sunday Schools

201

also needed attention. The Bishop asked his parishes to make determined efforts to expand and improve the instruction. Often, he remarked, "while we have been discussing Sunday School systems and methods the children have been staying at home or running the streets." Finally, Bishop Nelson urged his people to adopt a realistic attitude toward the Church's missionary work both domestic and foreign, "to touch the sources of supply" so that the expansion of the Church could be accomplished without overworking a few missionaries.

After the election of a secretary of the Convention, and the naming of an assistant secretary and nine committees, the group turned to the question of its Episcopate. With Bishop Nelson out of the room, a resolution praising his work and qualifications and naming him as Bishop of the new Diocese passed unanimously. When the Bishop returned, this resolution was read to him and he accepted the appointment with a short inspirational talk.

The next important order of business in this historic session was an announcement that the General Convention of the United States Church had approved the petition of the Diocese of Georgia for the division of its territory into two Dioceses. The organized missions of the new Diocese were listed as follows: Atlanta: Holy Comforter, St. Paul's, and Epiphany; Cartersville: Ascension; College Park: St. John's; Columbus: St. Mary the Virgin; Fort Valley: St. Andrew's; Dalton: St. Mark's; Decatur: Holy Trinity; West Point: Christ Church; Macon: St. Mark's; Kirkwood: St. Timothy's.

The question of new constitution and canons was, by vote of the Convention, referred to a committee of five, who were charged to meet during the recess between Conventions and to make a report to the next gathering. Another committee of five was created to suggest a name for the new Diocese for current consideration. A similar committee was created to nominate persons for these positions: Treasurer of Diocesan Missions, Delegates to the Missionary Council and Alternates, Members of Court of Array, Trustees of the University of the South, Trustees of the Appleton Church Home, Treasurer of the Appleton

Church Home, Deputies to the General Convention and alternates, and Trustees of the Weston Bequest Fund.

At the beginning of the afternoon session, the Rev. Troy Beatty, chairman of the committee appointed to consider a name for the Diocese, came into the convention hall and reported his group's failure to concur, and added that he had not been able to assemble the entire committee. The Convention promptly voted that the matter should be deferred until a full committee could consider the matter. About an hour later, Mr. Beatty returned with a majority and a minority report. Three committeemen, he said, preferred the name "Diocese of Atlanta," while the other two wanted "Northern Diocese of Georgia." The Convention voted upon the report and adopted the name "Diocese of Atlanta" by a two-thirds majority (36-18).

Mr. Beatty then introduced a resolution from the committee, to the effect that the name which was adopted should be substituted for the name "Diocese of Georgia" wherever it occurred in the constitution and canons of the old Diocese. This was approved by the assembly.

The question of constitution and canons was a knotty one. Before a title for the Diocese was decided upon, the Convention had already debated the correctness of adopting a resolution which would permit the old constitution and canons to serve except for name and geographic boundaries until new or amended regulations could be approved. After some discussion it was felt that this could not be done by the Convention—despite the fact that until such regulations could be adopted, old procedures would have to be used! Several canonical amendments were offered, two of which pertained to procedure in the Diocesan missionary work. The Convention referred all of these to a Committee on Constitution and Canons; concerning the important subject of missionary work the delegates voted that the Bishop should take such matters directly under his jurisdiction until appropriate procedures should be adopted. Before the end of the meeting, however, the delegates did adopt a constitution for the Diocese of Atlanta. Canons would have to be written later, and a committee of five was named by the

Bishop to make a report on canons at the next Convention:
Rev. Troy Beatty, Rev. S. Alston Wragg, Judge William H. Felton
of Macon, and Messrs. Z. D. Harrison and Thomas Egleston.

Legal matters were next attended to. The Standing Committee
was named as the group to apply for and accept the charter for
the new Diocese, which would grant the rights to own real estate
and personal property, to acquire property by purchase, and to
receive property by gift or bequest. A resolution verifying
previous arrangements for the division of Diocesan funds was
adopted.

New Diocesan lay officials were named as follows: Chanc-
cellor, Robert C. Alston; Treasurer, Rhodes Browne; Registrar,
W. N. Hawks. The Diocese's very important Standing Committee
was to consist of the Rev. Messrs. C. B. Wilmer, C. T. A. Pise
and Troy Beatty; and Messrs. Z. D. Harrison, Luther Williams,
and T. D. Tinsley. By the time of the next Convention (1908),
the Rev. J. S. Bunting and Mr. T. H. Nickerson were serving on
this committee in lieu of the Rev. Mr. Wilmer and Mr. Williams.
Upon the shoulders of these several church workers fell the
bulky burden of effectuating the operation of the new Diocese
during the next dozen months.

One of the principal arguments for division of the Diocese
had been that it would be the most effective way to extend the
Church's home missionary work. In the 1907 Convention of
the new Diocese, the problems of mission activity came up
several times. The Committee on Missions told the Convention
that the parishes and missions already established should make
an all-out effort in the coming year in contributions for mission
extension during the first year of the new Diocese. The Woman's
Auxiliary, they reported with some pride, had already created a
fund to support a "Woman's Auxiliary Missionary." The committee reminded the Convention of several promising areas for
new missions, and suggested that, "having organized our forces,
polished our armor and prepared for battle, we do go forth and
take this great territory for Christ and His Church."

These early months in the history of Georgia's second Diocese
saw continued efforts to put the new organization on a sound
basis. During the period between the "First" Convention in

December, 1907, and the "First Annual" Convention in May, 1908, many committee meetings were held and innumerable details disposed of. Financial matters, such as division of funds belonging to the old single Diocese and the determination of amounts of assessments on various parishes and missions for Diocesan expenses, were some of the difficult problems which had to be solved. While the Committee on Canons was thrashing out a set of by-laws to present to the next Convention, the Committee on Missions was working with the Bishop and clergy to survey the Diocese's progress and needs. Lay lawyers were applying for the Charter of the Diocese, while others conferred on tax problems. And still the Church's work went on. The Bishop traveled about the Diocese preaching, baptizing, confirming, conferring with his clergy, consecrating new churches and re-examining old ones.

From a standpoint of service in Georgia, the senior clergyman in the new Diocese of Atlanta was the Rev. Charles B. Hudgins of St. Peter's, Rome, whose work in the state began in 1887. Next in seniority were the Rev. J. J. P. Perry, Commissary to the Bishop (in Georgia since 1890), and the Very Rev. C. T. A. Pise, Dean of the Cathedral in Atlanta (1891). Bishop Nelson had come to the state to assume the Episcopate in 1892, the same year that Good Shepherd's rector at Cave Spring, the Rev. George E. Benedict, commenced his ministry in Georgia. Another clergyman who began his Georgia work in the early 1890's was the Rev. Troy Beatty of Emmanuel, Athens (1893). In 1898 the Rev. John J. Lanier and the Rev. Thomas Burry initiated their Georgia service. By 1908, Lanier was stationed at Mediator in Washington, and serving as missionary to Greensboro, Madison, and Union Point, while Burry was at Grace Church in Gainesville, and serving as missionary to Norcross and Winder. The remaining clergy on duty in the new Diocese of Atlanta during its first year of existence are listed below, with earliest dates in Georgia, and locations as of 1908:

the Rev. Tullius C. Tupper	1900	Chaplain, U. S. Penitentiary, Atlanta
the Rev. C. B. Wilmer	1900	St. Luke's, Atlanta
the Rev. R. F. DeBelle (Deacon)	1900	Missionary, Atlanta

the Rev. Albert E. Day	1902	St. Paul's, Atlanta
the Rev. S. Alston Wragg	1903	Trinity, Columbus
the Rev. Z. S. Farland	1903	All Saints, Atlanta
the Rev. D. F. Hoke	1904	St. George's, Griffin
the Rev. Gilbert Higgs	1905	Holy Comforter, Atlanta, and Missionary
the Rev. Harris B. Thomas	1906	St. James', Cedartown, and Missionary
the Rev. Henry D. Phillips	1907	St. Mark's, LaGrange, and Missionary
the Rev. E. Leon Henderson	1907	Archdeacon for work among colored, Atlanta
the Rev. H. Baldwin Dean	1907	St. Mary the Virgin, Columbus
the Rev. John S. Bunting	1908	Christ Church, Macon
the Rev. Luther G. M. Williams	1908	St. Andrew's, Fort Valley, and Missionary
the Rev. W. J. Page	1908	Holy Trinity, Decatur, and Missionary
the Rev. Charles N. Tyndell	1908	St. James', Marietta
the Rev. Robert W. Patton	1908	Secretary, 4th Missionary Department, Atlanta
the Rev. William Scarritt	1908	St. Stephen's, Milledgeville, and Missionary
the Rev. G. L. L. Gordon	1908	Ascension, Cartersville, and Missionary
the Rev. Thomas Duck	1908	St. Matthias', Toccoa, and Missionary

As may be noted from the list above, seven churches had just undergone a change in rectors. St. Paul's, in Macon, had none. This situation reflects the somewhat unusual period of flux in which the new Diocese found itself during the beginning years. At the Annual Convention in 1908, Bishop Nelson commented on these difficulties which expressed themselves in the mission picture as well. Principally responsible for mission problems, he said, was the "migratory character of the population in our smaller towns chiefly under the influence of the centralizing trend toward larger towns and cities." Such developments had in the recent past rendered almost dormant missions at Atlanta (Epiphany and Good Shepherd), Norcross, Macon (St. Mark's), LaGrange, Buford, Athens (St. Mary's), Austin (St. Paul's), Clarkesville (Holy Cross), Elberton (Holy Apostles'), Kingston

(St. Andrew's), and Marshallville (St. Mary's). Yet the Bishop noted that "a return wave" of communicants "brings about a condition which fully justifies the efforts put forth to plant a station wherever a nucleus of earnest people can be secured." One of these evidences of "a nucleus of earnest people" joined with a "return wave" was Epiphany Mission in the Inman Park section of Atlanta. Once considered a "suspended" mission, Epiphany in 1908 applied to the Diocese for admission as a parish, and at the Convention of that year this was approved.

Continuing his address, Bishop Nelson deplored the lack of a regular minister at St. Paul's in Macon, as well as the fact that no new church buildings as such had been erected in the new Diocese. But great indeed was his gratification and pleasure in the over-all progress which his new Episcopate had made since its inception. "In the aggregate," he said, with hyperbole not typical of Bishop Nelson, the Northwest Georgia Episcopal Churches had produced "a record unequalled in the history of the Diocese before or since the division of Georgia" (!). He detailed some of the progress. Despite a "greatly diminished force," he said, the Cathedral in Atlanta had prospered significantly. St. Luke's in Atlanta had raised "the almost incredible sum of $40,000" for a new building and other expenses. Its neighbor, the Church of the Incarnation, boasted a new parish house. Bishop Nelson paid especial tribute to a fourth Atlanta church, All Saints', which, although organized but six years earlier, had paid off its debt entirely, had given $11,000 for city missions, $40,000 for Diocesan missions, and had raised even more for general missions. In the suburbs of Atlanta other cheerful signs existed. St. John's, College Park, showed "the largest per capita offerings of any Church in the Diocese," and was making plans to free itself of debt before the next Convention; and "Decatur and Kirkwood are taking on new life."

Outside of Atlanta, the Bishop continued, progress was equally pleasing. At LaGrange, "the Rev. Mr. [Henry] Phillips is applying himself with energy and judgment to the expressed interest and approbation of the citizens of that rapidly increasing town." Fort Valley was accumulating a respectable fund for a church building; Milledgeville was "enthusiastic" over its new rector; Cedartown, Dalton, and Cartersville were doubling their pledges to the Diocese; and so the Bishop's summary went.

As might be expected, the report of the Diocesan Board of Missions for the same year was more specific than the Bishop's remarks. Yet the same spirit of pride in accomplishments is reflected in the Board's summary, although not expressed in such glowing words. "Your Board finds itself somewhat encouraged in its review of the year's endeavors," they said. Indeed, considering that this report covered the first year of independent Diocesan existence, there were grounds for this encouragement. On income for missionary work, the Board expected "no considerable default" for 1908-1909. They reported many specific items, of which these samples are representative: the Rev. W. J. Page had been placed in charge of the "suburban missions" at Decatur, Kirkwood, and College Park; services had been resumed in Hapeville and Newnan after "a silence of about eighteen months"; Norcross had secured a building for church use, and "a cheery, industrious little band" constituted its congregation; Eatonton had been reopened, and the Milledgeville rector assigned to it and to Sparta; the Rev. L. G. H. Williams of Fort Valley had been especially active in bringing new life to the missions at Barnesville and Talbotton, and he had also instituted new missions in Butler and Montezuma; and the Rev. G. L. L. Gordon was serving well in Kingston, Dalton, and Calhoun, in addition to his regular assignment at the Church of the Ascension in Cartersville.

Overall, continued the report of the Board of Missions, the most important factor in the success which was being experienced in Diocesan expansion was the decision of the previous Convention to order a direct assessment upon all the parishes and missions for the Diocese's own work. "This act of courage," in the opinion of the Board, "has resulted . . . in a new realization on the part of the Parishes and Missions of a responsibility as well as a privilege" to provide for the growth of the Church. Then the Board asked the Convention to provide five thousand dollars for domestic missions in the coming year by assessment of the various units of the Diocese. In so doing, the Board noted with gratitude that the Rev. Z. S. Farland of All Saints' in

Atlanta had assumed for his parish the raising of one-fourth of the five thousand. When All Saints' was consecrated by Bishop Nelson late in 1907, he paid tribute to this missionary zeal: "This Parish has boldly announced as its watchword 'The World for Christ,' has adopted as its platform 'no progress without Missions,' [and] has justified in practice through its brief history of six years the principles which I have advocated."

The Committee on the State of the Church offered statistical justification of the previous remarks by the Bishop and the report of the Board of Missions. Thirteen parishes, eighteen organized and twenty-one unorganized missions had submitted reports to the Committee. The overall number of communicants in the Diocese had risen from 3,968 to 4,318. The populous counties of Fulton, Cobb, and DeKalb accounted for 2,410 of these church members. Five of the largest cities of the Diocese (Atlanta, Macon, Columbus, Rome, and Athens) had 3,774 communicants. "From these figures," summarized the Committee, "the steady drift of population into the larger centers puts upon the city parishes the obligation of grateful generosity towards the Missions and weaker Parishes in the country and smaller towns."

Later in the convention the Committee on the State of the Church issued a warning concerning the Diocese's support of this promising missionary work and other church-supported activity. "Only one Parish, Emmanuel Church, Athens, and one Mission Station, St. Andrew's Church, Fort Valley," they pointed out, "have made all of these offerings." They urged that all conscientious Episcopalians return to their parishes resolved to bring them into line with the only two who were faithful, or all the glorious plans of the Diocese might come to disaster.

Some indication of Bishop Nelson's zeal in the first year of his new Diocese can be taken from his diary for that period. In twenty-two churches he had confirmed ninety-six persons. He visited as many as possible of the new mission stations, preaching, baptising, confirming, and dedicating. He appeared frequently in services at the Cathedral, sometimes jointly with such distinguished clergymen as the Bishop of Cuba and the Bishop of Southern Brazil. Bishop Nelson even conferred a degree during this period, that of Doctor of Music to J. Fowler Richardson.

On May 20, 1908, in Savannah, in company with seven other Bishops, Nelson participated in the consecration ceremonies of Frederick F. Reese, the new Bishop of the Diocese of Georgia.

The Bishop's diary also reveals that he spent a good bit of time with the thorny but necessary problems of the division of funds and properties resulting from the creation of the new Diocese. For example: on Dec. 13, 1907, he spent the day in Brunswick "attending to matters involving the transfer of property to my successor." Three weeks later he spent another entire day with a committee from the Diocese of Georgia "checking off securities and transferring interests." Deeds, journals, policies, and other papers were dispatched to Savannah on January 18, 1908. Frequently thereafter, other conferences were necessary for the proper settlement of these matters.

One of the most difficult problems pertained to the Waldburg Fund, which was an endowment fund from the interest of which postulants for Holy Orders were given scholarships at Sewanee. Chancellor Alston reported to the Diocese of Atlanta in the 1908 Convention that the new Diocese should have equal powers to determine the disposition of these assets, which then amounted to some $15,000. Apparently, he said, "a satisfactory settlement seems probable."

A "satisfactory settlement" was reached on a local problem, according to another item in the Chancellor's report. In March, 1908, the city of Atlanta sought to increase the taxes of the Diocese on a basis of higher assessments than the Church authorities thought proper. Chancellor Alston and other officers of the Corporation arranged a compromise, under the terms of which the property taxable in Atlanta was assessed at $20,000.

In the year that followed, the Diocese of Atlanta continued with its efforts to become a creditable organization. In the trend suggested by earlier developments, the city churches showed encouraging progress. At the next convention, which they called "the Second annual meeting of the Council" (Atlanta, 1909) the Bishop particularly praised Trinity Church, Columbus, which had "secured a valuable rectory"; Christ Church, Macon, whose improvements were "excellent;" St. James', Marietta, which was showing "encouraging growth;" Holy Trinity, Decatur, soon to build a rectory; and the LaGrange Mission, which "challenges your inspection and admiration and makes loud appeal for your generous aid that this may be a centre of training for expansive movement." Bishop Nelson confirmed more than three times as many as in the previous year; and had the pleasure of launching a long-desired project.

For some years Bishop Nelson had wanted to establish a Diocesan school for girls, to continue in the same spirit as Bishop Elliott's Montpelier Institute. He told the 1909 council that he had purchased a lot in Atlanta, organized a Board of Trustees, and with them had made plans for "financing this effort to erect and equip a commodious and complete building as soon as practicable." The charter for Nelson Hall, as the school was named, was presented to the Trustees on July 28. He called on the delegates to support this educational project both to evidence the Church's civic interest and to support "our position in this State as an agency for a broad and liberal culture." Nelson's philosophy of church-sponsored education was interestingly expressed:

One of the most important missions of the Church today is to combine faith and education in proper and harmonious proportions. Learning does sometimes nurture pride of intellect with its consequences, but ignorance, the twin-sister of conceit, is the mother of a brood which can not be estimated for danger and wrong. If the offspring be in one age superstition, it is fanaticism in another, in yet another intolerance, and again stupid opposition to progress, fear of truth and preference for inherited prejudices and theories worn thread-bare by unreasoning and unhistorical use.

Church and press also came in for some discussion at the 1909 Council. The Rev. Cary B. Wilmer raised the question in referring to statements attributed to him in both the Atlanta *Constitution* and the Atlanta *Journal*, pertaining to differences between the Roman Catholic and Protestant Episcopal Churches. Dr. Wilmer said that he was completely misquoted in both instances, and the Convention upheld him by vote. Then the Rev. Thomas Duck introduced a motion that future Conventions have a Committee on Press Reports. This effort in the area of public relations was adopted.

Chancellor Alston had an interesting if somewhat exasperated report to make in 1909 on the continuing problem of the Waldburg Fund. The Diocese of Georgia, he announced, had decided that under the terms by which the fund was originally established, the right of nominating recipients of the scholarship money was a "personal right appertaining to the office of Bishop of that Diocese." Therefore, the Diocese of Georgia had withdrawn its original expression of willingness to arrange for joint or equal nominations between the two Dioceses, or even to submit the problem to Judge J. R. Lamar of Augusta who had agreed to act as arbitrator. Arguing that the Bishop of Atlanta was a successor to the Bishop in office at the time the fund was created (1891-92), and therefore equally eligible to participate in the nominations, Chancellor Alston remarked that "it is now necessary to institute a friendly litigation to test the questions of law involved."

Meanwhile, the Diocese of Atlanta had adopted the canons necessary to the proper operation of its business. Most of these were replicas of those used in the old Diocese, including one which provided for the convocations system of mission supervision. These territorial areas centered around Athens, Atlanta, Columbus, Macon, and Rome. Bishop Nelson again warned his churchmen to be wary of extending missions into areas which might not be able to support them over a long period. He did not urge that they cease to establish new Episcopal locations in areas of small population—far from it. He did suggest that such openings be considered "experimental . . . for the reason that changes in our semi-rural population present a condition to be reckoned with."

These early years of the new Diocese continued to be a time of change and reaction to new conditions. The Council of 1910 was the last one regularly scheduled for December. In that year the Diocesan representatives voted to change the meeting date to May, thus returning to the traditional post-Easter period so long used in the old Diocese. Further, they decided to eliminate the meeting altogether in 1911 and to reconvene in May of 1912, preferring to wait eighteen months rather than meet again after only six months. The gathering which met at Trinity Church in Columbus on December 7 and 8, 1910, was termed the "Third Annual Council." However, it was determined to adjust the numbering so that the gap in 1911 would be taken care of, and also to include the so-called "First" Convention of 1907 which had laid the foundation of the Diocese. Therefore the gathering of May 22 and 23, 1912, at Christ Church in Macon was referred to as the "Fifth Annual Council;" and all subsequent annual meetings of the Diocese of Atlanta have been consecutively numbered from that point.

In 1910, at the conclusion of the Diocese's third year of separate existence, fifteen parishes made up the basic organization:

Athens	Emmanuel	Columbus	Trinity
Atlanta	St. Philip's Cathedral	Griffin	St. George's
Atlanta	St. Luke's	Macon	Christ Church
Atlanta	Incarnation	Macon	St. Paul's
Atlanta	All Saints'	Marietta	St. James'
Atlanta	Holy Comforter	Milledgeville	St. Stephen's
Atlanta	Epiphany	Rome	St. Peter's
Cedartown	St. James'		

One of the most prospering of these parishes, although one of the newest, was All Saints' of Atlanta. The enthusiasm for missionary contributions shown by this church (previously noted) was matched by the spirit of its parishioners in supporting the parish itself. One of the leading sources of this effort was Mrs. Mary J. Peters. Called by Bishop Nelson "for many years the patroness and helper of all Church Works," Mrs. Peters in 1910 supplemented previous land gifts (now the sites of Church and Sunday School) by donating a large lot on West Peachtree Street for continued Church expansion. Strongly commending Mrs. Peters at the Council in 1910, Bishop Nelson argued that "such noble deeds demand of us more than passing notice or a record in a current report."

The newest parish in 1910 was Holy Comforter, also of Atlanta. Named as rector of that Church in the same year was the Rev. John D. Wing, who, after leaving Holy Comforter in 1912 served at the Church of the Incarnation in Atlanta; Grace Church in Anniston, Alabama; Christ Church, Savannah; and St. Paul's Church, Chattanooga, Tennessee. In 1925 Mr. Wing was made Bishop Coadjutor of Southern Florida, and seven years later became Bishop of that Diocese.

Twenty-three organized missions were listed:

Athens	St. Timothy's	Gainesville	Grace
Atlanta	St. Paul's	Greensboro	Redeemer
Atlanta	St. Andrew's	Kirkwood	St. Timothy's
Atlanta	St. Matthias'	LaGrange	St. Mark's
Austell	Good Shepherd	Macon	St. Mark's
Cartersville	Ascension	Madison	Advent
Clarkesville	Holy Cross	Newnan	St. Paul's
College Park	St. John's	Talbotton	Zion
Columbus	St. Mary the Virgin	Toccoa	St. Matthias'
Dalton	St. Mark's	Washington	Mediator
Decatur	Holy Trinity	West Point	Christ Church
Fort Valley	St. Andrew's		

Unorganized missions in 1910 were these:

Barnesville	All Saints'	LaGrange	Good Shepherd
Calhoun	St. James'	Marietta	St. Barnabas'
Carrollton	St. Margaret's	Mount Airy	Calvary
Cave Spring	Good Shepherd	Norcross	St. John's
Clarkesville	Grace	Sparta	Ascension
Columbus	St. Christopher's	Tallulah Falls	St. James'
East Point	St. Paul's	Tallapoosa	St. Ignatius'
Eatonton	All Angels'		

St. James' Parish in Marietta boasted two parochial missions: Kirk's Chapel and Union Chapel. Ten establishments in the Diocese were listed merely as "Stations:"

College Park, Gate City Mills Station
Columbus, North Highlands Station
Cornelia Station
Elberton, Holy Apostles' Station
Lindale Station
Manchester Station
Montezuma Station
Rockmart Station
Union Point Station
Winder Station

These lists bore ample testimony to the trends in the Diocese's development which the Bishop, the Board of Missions, and various committees had discussed at earlier Councils. There seemed to be a definite tendency for strengthening of missionary work in the populous centers. Atlanta and suburbs, for example, contained six organized missions, one unorganized mission, and one station, in addition to its six well-established parishes. Several once-promising almost-rural parishes had by 1910 become reduced in status, such as Zion in Talbotton and Grace in Clarkesville. Equally disturbing were the reports on four establishments which were listed as "dormant:"

Austin, St. Paul's	Kingston, St. Andrew's
Hapeville, Christ Church	Marshallville, St. Mary's

One drawback in the expansion of missionary work at this time was the slow progress of the convocations system. Of the five established in the new Diocese, only two had a report to make to the 1910 Council: Macon and Atlanta. The Rev. John S. Bunting, Dean of the Macon Convocation, stated that his group had held one meeting since December, 1909, attended by four clergymen and three laymen, and a delegate of the Woman's Auxiliary. As to the accomplishments of the meeting, Dean Bunting reported: "The proposed work of starting a [new] mission at Macon, the needs of Barnesville and of Sparta were considered and the entire meeting was pervaded by a good spirit, but there was no distinct and important business transacted beyond this." Although listing a few more meetings, the report from the Atlanta Convocation was hardly more reassuring; it concluded with this sentence: "The Society was ultimately organized, but so far as the Dean knows, has not yet been launched."

During the next eighteen months the mission situation in the Diocese of Atlanta continued in a state of flux. When the Council met again in 1912, seven missions listed previously as organized were now in the unorganized status; four had changed from unorganized to organized; one mission had become dormant and one dormant station became an organized mission; three new establishments were listed (Holy Innocents', in Atlanta; St. John's and St. James', in Macon); and six locations were dropped from the list altogether (North Highlands in Columbus, Lindale, Manchester, Kirk's Chapel in Marietta, Montezuma, and Rockmart).

Once again the Committee on the State of the Church warned the Diocese of the serious consequences to its mission program if extremely careful planning were not used in proposed expenditures for the missionary work. The various mission stations receiving aid from Diocesan funds over a lengthy period should be required to "make good, in some measure, at least, as the price of continued assistance." Also, the "limited means at our disposal" should be put to work in "strategic" locations of best advantage where "there are signs of most vigorous growth." The Committee recognized the difficulty of securing good personnel for missionaries and regular rectors, and gave a report on prevalent salary ranges in the Diocese. Seven received salaries ranging from $2,000 to $3,600; three were paid $1,500; ten were in the $1,000 to $1,200 bracket; "and one Priest serves without any stipend at all." As a fringe benefit for the clergymen, the committee urged that rectories be provided wherever possible, for they felt that a "permanent home for the rector or missionary is a spiritual asset of decided value."

One of the missions listed as new in 1912 was St. James' in Macon, which had begun a few months earlier under the auspices of Christ Church. The first service for St. James' was conducted by the Rev. John S. Bunting, rector of Christ Church. A legal charter was issued to the new Church on March 9, 1915; and shortly thereafter a "little box of a building," containing "a most cantankerous and temperamental stove" and a "funny little pipe organ," became the Church building. By the following year the mission had grown to such proportions that St. James' was admitted to the Diocese as a parish. Later, the Rev. William C. White accepted a call as rector.

Despite the peculiarities of the mission situation, and the recurrent problems of shifting populations in his Diocese, Bishop Cleland Kinloch Nelson must have enjoyed the Council of 1912 with particular pleasure. Many were the congratulations entered in the official minutes, for Bishop Nelson was in his twentieth year as Bishop. His address to the Council reflects some of his warmth. He commented on the gloomy side rather briefly, and then elaborated on what he termed "abundant reason for encouragement." Material evidence of progress, he said, was often lacking when actually "some of the most devoted service" was being performed. "We must beware of relying upon the physical test as either sufficient or satisfactory, and look closely at the spiritual results which are vouchsafed to our prayers." He cited the example of the missionary activity in and near Toccoa where, despite "difficult connections," diligent and persevering labors were being performed by a missionary "of godliness, energy, and aptness." (The Bishop was praising the work of the Reverend Thomas Duck.)

At the previous Council meeting (in 1910), a resolution had been adopted which established a committee to consider the establishment of a regular periodical to be published by the Diocese. This had been one of Bishop Nelson's long-desired projects, and at the 1912 Council he showed a sample copy of a publication called "The Atlanta Churchman." He recommended that such a journal be published monthly by the Diocese, at a cost of $30.00 per issue. Later in the meeting, a resolution from the Woman's Auxiliary approving such a paper was introduced and passed, and the Diocese set aside $360.00 annually for this purpose.

Another favored project of Bishop Nelson's was not progressing so well. This was Nelson Hall, the educational institute for young women. The Bishop's disappointment over the situation is clearly revealed in the brief remarks on the subject in his address to the Council: "I should like once more to direct your attention to the proposed School for Girls in Atlanta which has a claim not as yet met either by expression of interest or bestowal of gifts."

The subject of education did receive strong consideration in the Council in connection with another matter. This had to do with certain "false and misleading statements" in a number of textbooks in English history concerning the Reformation period. Objection was raised to the suggestion in these works that the Protestant Episcopal Church was a "recently founded sect." Apparently a strong case against the textbooks was presented to

the Council in 1912, for they adopted a resolution disapproving
of such "misrepresentation" which was "making its impress upon
the minds of our own Church children as well as others." The
resolution authorized the Bishop to appoint a commission to
examine the situation "and proceed in the way wisest in their
judgment to discover and correct such teachings in the public
and other schools in this Diocese." In addition, they were to consult with similar committees in other Dioceses "in an effort to
induce authors and publishers of English histories to correct such
mistakes." The Bishop later appointed the Rev. Messrs. S. Alton
Wragg and C. T. A. Pise to the Commission, along with
Mr. O. A. Coleman.

But the more pressing matters of the status of parish and missionary operations continued to be of major concern to the
Diocese. This is reflected in the challenging report of the Committee on the State of the Church, made at the sixth annual
meeting of the Council, held on May 28-29, 1913, at Emmanuel
Church in Athens. The Committee lashed out vigorously at
those parishes and missions which failed to submit reports for
the previous year's work. Without complete reports, they
argued, their statistics on the state of the Diocese were invalid.
For example, the 1913 summary showed 249 less communicants
than in 1912 (4,795 compared to 5,044), even though Bishop
Nelson's diary for the same period indicated that he had confirmed 304! The committee said that the "falling off" would
probably be offset by data in the mission reports; if not, it probably meant "that some of the clergy are attempting to prune
their communicant lists of dead material."

The Bishop had taken some definite steps to "prune" some
"dead material." The mission operations at Kingston and Newnan were abandoned because "every effort to secure a congregation has proven vain." The decaying mission buildings in those
towns were sold by the Bishop and the Church Corporation. Also
seeking to improve the missionary operations, Bishop Nelson
advocated the combining of the convocations of Macon and
Columbus, and this was done by the Council.

Often Bishop Nelson gave vent to strong feelings in his annual
addresses, and that of 1913 was no exception. On this occasion

he voiced sharp criticism of conditions of untidiness and disre-
pair which he found all too prevalent in his visits around the
Diocese. He cited without location such instances as these: "an
old cushion" which for ten years had been used by one church to
fill a hole in the wall; "a broken door latch" which had long
been a source of annoyance in a parish until the Bishop himself
had it repaired; "rubbish of all kinds" piled up behind churches
for fifteen years; and "germ-laden objects" left lying around in
dark corners. He urged the creation of parish committees to
police the church areas, so that "the house devoted to the
worship of Almighty God should have lavished upon it the same
consideration for neatness and appropriateness as the best of our
homes."

One of the canons adopted by the Diocese shortly after the
division was number 23, which established "The Cathedral of
the Diocese of Atlanta." The several sections of this canon principally entitled the Bishop to select his Cathedral Church;
created a General Chapter to consist of the Board of Missions;
and named a Minor Chapter comprised of the Bishop, Dean, and
ten members of the laity to be elected in the same manner and
to have the same functions as parish vestrymen. In 1914 steps
were taken to reorganize this arrangement. By resolution, the
Diocesan Council abolished the General and Minor Chapters as
such and created a Cathedral Chapter to govern the Cathedral's
local affairs. Membership and duties of the Cathedral Chapter were
similar to that of the old Minor Chapter. With reference to the
Cathedral's relationship with the Diocese, a Cathedral Board of
Trustees was established as a corporation, to be composed of
three ministers and three laymen chosen at large from the
Diocese, and six laymen from St. Philip's. Presiding officer of the
Cathedral Chapter was to be the Dean, chosen by the Chapter on
the Bishop's nomination, having the same relationship to the
Cathedral as a rector to his parish. The Bishop was named as
Chief Minister-in-charge, with the Cathedral serving as his ad-
ministrative headquarters. Further, the resolution specifically
provided that St. Philip's continue as the Cathedral Church under
this name: "The Cathedral of St. Philip in the Diocese of
Atlanta."

Another change in arrangements occurred in 1915. One of the most important committees in the Diocese was the Committee on the State of the Church. This group, named at each meeting of the Council, examined yearly reports of all other committees, officials, and agencies of the Diocese and gave a combined report to the Council on current conditions and problems. Its recommendations were usually important to the future of the Episcopal Church in Northwest Georgia, but they were often quickly conceived. It would seem obvious that such significant reports and recommendations should be more carefully prepared.

Apparently with such reasoning in mind, the current Chairman of the Committee, the Rev. Charles H. Lee of St. Paul's Parish, Macon, presented a resolution at the 1915 Council which would make the Committee on the State of the Church a "standing committee." Three clergymen and two laymen, to be named annually by the Bishop, would comprise the committee which was to meet and report at least quarterly and travel about the Diocese if need be. Lee's resolution authorized the committee not only to take up such matters as the Bishop should refer to it, but also to consider questions "on its own initiative, especially as to how to make the Church more of a power in the life of today." The resolution was adopted and was made a canon the following year. In addition to Mr. Lee, the other members of this committee in 1915 were the Rev. Messrs. Thomas Duck and J. R. Atkinson, and laymen E. C. Peters and R. W. Graves.

During this period the quick devastation of fire wrought havoc among two Georgia churches. The first of these occurred in 1916 and destroyed St. Paul's in Augusta. The second fire gutted another St. Paul's in Georgia, this time the very active organized mission for Negroes in Atlanta—a disastrous fire in 1917 took the entire church plant. St. Paul's Vicar, the Rev. A. A. Hewitt, obtained an old Sunday School building from St. Philip's Cathedral and had it moved to the Auburn Avenue location of the burned building. Services were conducted in the transported structure until a new church was completed in 1924.

The year 1917 marked the twenty-fifth year of Cleland Kinloch Nelson's episcopate in Georgia and more especially his tenth year as head of a new diocese. The ninth annual meeting of the Council of the Diocese was held at St. Peter's Church in Rome. Perhaps conscious of his long service, the Bishop told this Council that he was "profoundly grateful" that his "health and strength" were well preserved. He felt especially proud of "a record of service unexcelled in most respects by any year of my episcopate." Much of this success, he thought, was due to his work with the "church at large" on such assignments as the Board of Missions, the Commission on the Revision and Enrichment of the Prayer Book, the American Church Building Fund Commission, and a number of committees of the General Convention. In such work, he remarked, "I have followed the godly advice of the Committee on the State of the Church 'to serve tables less,' with corresponding attention to weightier matters."

Despite or because of the upheaval then going on in Europe, Bishop Nelson continued, "the church year has been a good one for the parishes and for some of the missions." The Bishop's diary revealed that 338 persons had been confirmed that year. He was pleased to note signs of "a spiritual uplift" among the clergy and "increased interest" among the laity. "No Bishop," he said proudly, "was ever blessed with a more loyal body of clergymen and laymen." Nelson noted a difference between loyalty and blind obedience. He would not "compel obedience" of anyone in the Diocese; what he had always asked for had been "acquiescence to lawfully constituted authority, even if inconvenient; and to obey the Bishop chiefly because and when he demonstrates that having due consideration for all, and in the exercise of his best judgment he fulfills his responsibility. . . . Obedience should be a privilege, not an obligation."

In line with this train of thought, Nelson went on to discourage practices of deviation from church ritual. He reverted to the kind of admonitions of the clergy so typical of his long episcopate. He charged his ministers to make no abbreviations in the service except among such non-essentials as "hymns, anthems and *long* discourses." The Bishop pronounced his disapproval of "omissions of or interpolations into the prescribed order." He seemed displeased with certain practices which had developed in the marriage service, particularly the use of

Lohengrin for the wedding march. The laity of his Diocese also came in for criticism in this address. He seemed to sense a feeling of hostility or, at least, coldness toward strangers in some churches. Nelson suggested that "more and better-instructed ushers" be provided; that Prayer Books opened to the correct pages should be given to visitors; and that special efforts should be made to make them feel at home "in their Father's house and yours." Surely some of his audience must have flushed with embarrassment when Nelson ordered, "Do not block the alley, as street car conductors generally do, but make way and [give them] a welcome."

Bishop Nelson took time out from ecclesiastical matters to warn his Diocese about what seemed to him "disregard of justice and indifference to the value of human life" then extant in Georgia. He was evidently referring to the lynching of Leo M. Frank during the previous August. Frank was convicted and sentenced to death for the slaying of Miss Mary Phagan. Later his sentence was commuted to life imprisonment. Inflamed in part by anti-Semitic articles in the publications of Georgian Thomas E. Watson, a mob stormed the state penitentiary and took Frank nearly two hundred miles away before hanging him on a tree. North Georgia's Episcopal Bishop spoke of his distress that men were "so lost to sense of right and of the sacredness of law as to conceal the perpetrators of crime." Such acts, he felt, would "undermine the very foundations of human society." In characteristically strong terms he appealed to his ministers to "eradicate crime and vice out of the hearts of your people, to stand and to speak as one voice in condemning all violations of law and order; to get lynching and the causes which produce it out of your heart and mind." In a ringing challenge to the laity he expressed this wish: "that you will not sully your religion or imperil your own hope of salvation by contenancing as admissible or even thinkable the taking of human life except by the authority which wields the sword of justice, if such power be given to any court or class of persons."

This was Bishop Nelson's last Diocesan Council meeting. On February 12, 1917, Cleland Kinloch Nelson died at the age of sixty-five. He had been a priest of the Church for forty-one years, the last twenty-five of which were as Bishop. His great contributions to the Church in Georgia lay in the evidence of two flourishing Dioceses where one had existed before. Like Bishops Elliott and Beckwith before him, longevity of devoted service had aided the cause to a large degree. All in the Diocese mourned his passing, especially the parishioners of the Cathedral of St. Philip. The Cathedral's official historian records this tribute to the head of their church: "His death marked a loss to the Cathedral . . . which can never be fully estimated or stated. By his quarter-century of unceasing efforts he had transformed a discouraged, diminishing Parish, burdened with debt, torn by internal discord, and defiant toward authority as a result of years of unreasonable oppression, into the Cathedral of the Diocese, extremely harmonious in its external and internal relations, free of debt, with the largest property holdings and the third largest congregations in the Diocese."

CHAPTER
❧ · XIII · ❧

BISHOP MIKELL'S EPISCOPATE
1917-1942

FACED once again with the necessity of selecting a new Bishop, the Diocese of Atlanta held its annual Council somewhat earlier in 1917 than was customary. Meeting at St. Paul's Church, Macon, on April 18-20, some two months after Nelson's death, the Council received nominations for the vacant episcopate. Seven clergymen were voted upon in the first six ballots. Leading but without the necessary majority was the rector of St. Luke's Church in Atlanta, the Rev. Cary B. Wilmer, D.D. Other nominees, listed in order of total votes in the first ballot, were the Rev. Messrs. H. D. Phillips, H. J. Mikell, S. A. Wragg, Troy Beatty, C. E. Wheat, and J. S. Bunting. On the seventh ballot the name of the Rev. R. S. Coupland, (rector of Trinity Church, New Orleans), was introduced, and on the ninth, the name of the Rev. C. W. Whittaker. By the twelfth ballot only Wilmer and Coupland were still in the running; Wilmer then was polling sixteen clerical and six-and-one-third lay votes, while Coupland had twelve and fourteen respectively. Four more ballots were taken with this identical result. Finally, just before the seventeenth voting, Dr. Wilmer seconded the nomination of Dr. Coupland and requested those who had voted for him to support Coupland. On the eighteenth ballot, Wilmer received the votes of three clergymen, while Coupland's totals soared to twenty-six and eighteen-and-one-third respectively. Upon a motion, the election of Dr. Robert S. Coupland as second Bishop of the Diocese of Atlanta was made unanimous, and a committee was named to call upon him and issue the invitation.

The Council took no action on the question of a salary for the Bishop other than to accept the Diocesan budget from the Finance Committee. This called for a continuance of the former salary of $4,000 per annum and made no provision for the Bishop's living quarters. Apparently the relatively low salary and lack of expense emoluments were at least partly responsible for the fact that in May Dr. Coupland declined the invitation. The committee which had discussed matters with him reported that in the discussion of salary they expressed their view that the Diocese intended to improve the arrangements for financial remuneration to the Bishop, but of course they could not give him any specific promises. Following receipt of Coupland's refusal, the chairman of the committee, Dr. Wilmer, sent a telegram urging reconsideration, but this too was declined.

Promptly the Standing Committee of the Diocese decided to recall the Council for an adjourned meeting on June 20, 1917, to conduct another election. The notice to the Diocese listed other items of business as well, principally that "of fixing the salary of the Bishop." The Council met at St. Philip's Cathedral in Atlanta on June 26 (the meeting had been postponed a week owing to a conflict with the convention of Rotary International in Atlanta). Before the election began, steps were taken to improve financial management in the Diocese. By amendment to the canons, a new Diocesan Finance Committee was created to consist of four ministers, four laymen, and the Bishop. Of more immediate importance to the business at hand, the Council voted to raise the Bishop's salary to $5,000, with an additional $1200 for living expenses.

The following clergymen were nominated for Bishop: the Rev. Henry J. Mikell, D.D., the Rev. W. A. R. Goodwin, D.D., the Rev. H. D. Phillips, and the Rev. Cary B. Wilmer, D.D. On the first ballot Dr. Mikell was one vote shy of election. His nearest runner-up was Dr. Wilmer. The second voting made Dr. Mikell the new Bishop by an overwhelming majority, and Dr. Wilmer's motion that the election be made unanimous was carried.

The new Bishop was consecrated at St. Philip's Cathedral on November 1, 1917. Bishop William A. Guerry of South Carolina was the preacher; Bishops Charles E. Woodcock of Kentucky and Frederick F. Reese of Georgia presented the Bishop-elect; and Bishops Thomas F. Gailor of Tennessee and Edwin G. Weed of Florida performed the consecrating rites. The Master of Ceremonies for the entire occasion was the Dean of the Cathedral, the Very Rev. Thomas H. Johnston.

Bishop Mikell's new Diocese consisted of fifteen parishes, twenty-four organized missions, eighteen unorganized missions, and ten dormant stations. The parishes and their priests were as follows:

Athens	Emmanuel	the Rev. A. G. Richards
Atlanta	All Saints'	the Rev. W. W. Memminger
Atlanta	Cathedral	the Very Rev. Thos. H. Johnston
Atlanta	Epiphany	the Rev. Russell K. Smith
Atlanta	Holy Comforter	Bernard Suttler, Sr. Wdn.
Atlanta	Incarnation	the Rev. Israel H. Noe
Atlanta	St. Luke's	the Rev. Cary B. Wilmer
Columbus	Trinity	the Rev. S. Alton Wragg
Griffin	St. George's	the Rev. Percy W. Jones
Macon	Christ	the Rev. R. F. Gibson
Macon	St. James'	the Rev. J. Francis McCloud
Macon	St. Paul's	the Rev. Charles H. Lee
Marietta	St. James'	the Rev. Randolph R. Claiborne
Milledgeville	St. Stephen's	the Rev. J. H. Flye
Rome	St. Peter's	the Rev. H. F. Saumenig

The organized missions were these:

Alto	(unnamed)	the Rev. Thomas Duck
Atlanta	St. Mary's	the Rev. G. I. Hiller
Atlanta	St. Matthias'	W. Q. Rogers, Lay Reader
Atlanta	St. Paul's	the Rev. A. A. Hewitt
Barnesville	All Saints'	H. R. Chase, Lay Reader
Carrollton	St. Margaret's	
Cartersville	Ascension	
College Park	St. John's	W. J. Mills, Lay Reader
Columbus	St. Christopher's	the Rev. J. S. Braithwaite
Dalton	St. Mark's	
Decatur	Holy Trinity	the Rev. V. C. Lacey
Elberton	Holy Apostles	the Rev. Thomas Duck
Fort Valley	St. Andrew's	the Rev. W. P. Browne
Gainesville	Grace	the Rev. I. M. Merlinjones
Griffin	St. Stephen's	the Rev. E. L. Braithwaite

Kirkwood	St. Timothy's	the Rev. Russell K. Smith
LaGrange	Good Shepherd	
LaGrange	St. Elizabeth's	the Rev. A. A. Hewitt
LaGrange	St. Mark's	the Rev. R. T. Phillips
Macon	St. Mark's	the Rev. J. R. Brooks
Madison	Advent	E. L. Pennington, Lay Reader
Manchester	St. Paul's	the Rev. W. P. Browne
Talbotton	Zion	the Rev. W. P. Browne
Toccoa	St. Matthias'	the Rev. Thomas Duck
West Point	Christ Church	the Rev. Robt. T. Phillips

Unorganized missions were:

Atlanta	Holy Innocents	the Rev. W. W. Memminger
Atlanta	St. Andrew's	
Austell	Good Shepherd	A. H. Irvine, Sr. Wdn.
Cave Springs	Good Shepherd	
Clarkesville	Grace	the Rev. Thomas Duck
Dahlonega		the Rev. C. A. F. Ruge
East Point	St. Paul's	H. J. Fear, Lay Reader
Greensboro	Redeemer	
Hapeville	Christ Church	
LaGrange	Holy Comforter	the Rev. R. T. Phillips
Macon	St. Stephen's	the Rev. Chas. H. Lee
Marietta	St. Barnabas'	the Rev. A. A. Hewitt
Marietta	Union Chapel	the Rev. R. R. Claiborne
Mt. Airy	Calvary	the Rev. Thomas Duck
Roswell		
Sparta	Ascension	the Rev. J. H. Flye
Tallulah Falls	St. James'	the Rev. Thomas Duck
Washington	Mediator	

Listed as "dormant" were these stations:

Athens	St. Mary's
Austin	St. Paul's
Calhoun	St. James'
Clarkesville	Holy Cross
Columbus	St. Mary the Virgin
Eatonton	All Angels'
Helen	Transfiguration
Marshallville	St. Mary's
Norcross	St. John's
Tallapoosa	St. Ignatius'

At his first Diocesan Council Bishop Mikell properly addressed clergy and laymen on what appeared to be a critical

condition in the Diocese: there had been no increase in the number of parishes since the separation of the two Dioceses. Furthermore, the number of organized missions had increased but one, although there had been some shifting about in status from organized to unorganized and vice versa. But the number of dormant stations had increased to ten and there seemed to be every likelihood that this trend might continue. Bishop Mikell called upon Churchmen to be ready to sacrifice time and money in this crisis. The Board of Missions, he pointed out, needed funds to provide missionaries for the smaller stations; also, volunteer workers from larger churches were needed to assist in planting the stations more firmly into the Diocesan picture. "We cannot suffer the Church to die in these towns," he exclaimed. "Our Churchmanship means something more Christian [than refusals to assist small missions]. . . ."

One method he suggested for strengthening the Church in small Georgia towns was to work with students at the various colleges in the Diocese. Many of these boys and girls, he pointed out, "have never heard of the Episcopal Church. The Church ought to be so represented in these places that it will commend itself to the students. While they are getting an education along other lines, it will not be amiss to add to their education some knowledge of the Church and the things for which the Church stands." Implicit in this suggestion is Bishop Mikell's own long-standing personal interest in church work among college students, a project which would shape up in future activity of the Diocese of Atlanta.

Apparently the convocation system was not functioning, judging both from the condition of the missions and from the recommendations of the Board of Missions. This group reported to the Diocesan Council their decision taken the previous year to establish four groups of missions, each under a missionary priest. These would include specific areas in geographic proximity. Thus far only one of these groups was operative, although the other three contained missions which were being served variously by the rectors of nearby parishes who were "partially supported by the Board, either for doing missionary work in connection with their parochial cures, or else as a partial support for weaker parishes unable to pay the full stipend of the minister." The Rev. Thomas Duck was in charge of the one successful group. He was serving organized missions at Alto, Elberton, and Toccoa; and unorganized missions in Clarkesville, Mt. Airy, and Tallulah Falls. The Board urged the Council to give serious consideration to the support of this entire project.

The Committee on the State of the Church again raised the issue of poor reporting from the mission stations, which made it difficult for the Diocese to evaluate this work and also to plan the necessary expenditures. On the brighter side, two churches in Atlanta came in for especial praise from the committee. These were St. Luke's, which had paid off a $10,500 mortgage, and All Saints', which had expended $36,592 for improvements. Overall, summarized the committee, Church property in the Diocese was valued at a minimum of $400,400, plus whatever values might be possessed by the mission stations which failed to file reports.

One concern of prime importance to the new Bishop and his Diocese was World War I in which Georgians were then engaged. Part of Bishop Mikell's first address was devoted to problems and opportunities in church work which the war had begotten. He reminded the Council that the General Convention of the Protestant Episcopal Church had created a war commission whose duties were "to coordinate and stimulate spiritual work and to assist the Dioceses in whose borders the Camps are situated, to keep the soldier in touch with his Church and carry the Church to the soldier." The commission sought to place an Episcopal minister in each such camp. Bishop Mikell reported that with the help of the commission the Diocese of Georgia had taken just such action. At Camp Gordon a Mr. Hiller was on duty as civilian chaplain; at Camp Wheeler was a Mr. McCallum, on loan from the Diocese of Georgia; in Atlanta, Incarnation's rector, the Rev. Israel Noe, was serving at Fort McPherson as well; and Fort Oglethorpe, in the northwest corner of the state, was being attended to by clergymen from Chattanooga. The war commission asked the Diocese of Atlanta for $1,500 to further this work, and Bishop Mikell had evidently forwarded this request to his people with enthusiasm, for the report of contributions showed $1,641.71 given.

Members of the Council were imbued with a full measure of patriotism in 1918. The Rev. I. M. Merlinjones of Grace Church, Gainesville, placed a resolution before the Council which would authorize the Bishop to convey to President Wilson by telegraph an expression of "the united support and hearty co-operation of the Diocese of Atlanta." The resolution was carried by unanimous and rising vote. Before the Council adjourned, Bishop Mikell read to the assembly the following message.

> The President is in receipt of your. . .kind telegram of April 19th and he asks me to tell you and the members of the Annual Council of the Episcopal Church of the Diocese of Atlanta that he is grateful for your heartening pledges. With an expression of his warm thanks for your support, I am
>
> Sincerely yours,
> J. P. TUMULTY
> Secretary to the President

During his first Diocesan address Bishop Mikell expressed warm praise for two phases of activity in the Diocese. The first of these was church work among Negroes: "We are doing fairly efficient work among the colored people and contributing to that work as generously as any other Southern Diocese. . . . In some places the outlook is especially encouraging." The Bishop noted that there were five colored clergymen and one postulant, "all of whom are doing faithful work."

The report of the Board of Missions on Negro work seemed to justify the Bishop's praise. In addition to the five colored ministers at work, eighteen Negro lay workers and a total of 820 children in Negro parochial schools made this activity in the Diocese seem very promising. Athens, Marietta, LaGrange, Macon, Griffin, Columbus, and Atlanta were very active in this respect, and a wider scope of activity seemed only dependent on further financial support.

The other particular work singled out by Bishop Mikell for special attention was the LaGrange Social Settlement which he termed "one of the outstanding social service works in the whole

American Church." Along with its support from the General Board of Missions, this mission activity among white mill operatives was explained and praised by the Bishop. His additional comment offered an interesting statement of the Church's role in labor problems: "Greater than the problem of this war is the problem of the adjustment when the war is over of the relationship between the laborer and the employer, between organized labor and the country at large. Surely the part of the Church is to teach the employer that the man employed does not exist only to make profits for him, but that every man is entitled to a fair chance in life, a fair amount of comfort and leisure . . . and to teach the workman that physical comforts are not the whole of life, but that he owes a duty of loyalty and efficient service to the man who employs him."

The omni-topical address of Bishop Mikell to his first Council in 1918 also included reference to an often unsung but nonetheless dedicated part of church activity: the Woman's Auxiliary. In his opinion the Auxiliary had three duties. The first was to assist the parish in raising money necessary to meet obligations to the General and the Diocesan Board of Missions. Next, "because they are especially interested, to undertake to contribute to some special work; third, through their United [Thank] Offering, to contribute once every three years in a large way to the advance work of the Church." Too few women seemed to display the "missionary, outward-looking spirit" which was so necessary to this work, said the Bishop. He suggested that clergymen encourage and enlarge the active Auxiliary, and that laymen support the hard and dedicated work of their wives.

Bishop Mikell also took up three of his predecessor's pet projects. Some time earlier Bishop Nelson had suggested a Diocesan conference to supplement the Annual Council and to improve generally the education of Episcopalians. This was supported by the Diocese to the extent that a canon was adopted which would give such a conference legal existence. However, little else had been done about it. Bishop Mikell was of the opinion that Nelson's idea was an excellent one and deserved the attention of everyone in the Diocese. At such conferences "matters of interest in the Church" could be discussed much more fully and by a larger group than the exigencies of the Annual Council would permit. He commented that the need was not only for "a working Laity"—there must also be "a studying Laity." Bishop Mikell felt that Episcopalians should address themselves frequently to the Church's history and progress, to its role in current life and in the American scene. "A man is not going to be a thoroughly loyal Churchman," he added, "until he is a thoroughly informed Churchman."

A second proposal of Bishop Nelson's which Bishop Mikell mentioned was the Church Club of the Diocese of Atlanta. Planned as a laymen's organization by Nelson, the club was to be centered in Atlanta with vice-presidents in Athens, Columbus, Macon, and Rome. Having been advised by some of its officers that the club was hopelessly moribund, Bishop Mikell told his 'assembly that it reminded him of a reference by the German poet Heine to a famous horse: "a splendid animal, well-groomed, beautifully caparisoned; it had but one defect—it was dead."

The third item mentioned by Bishop Mikell pertaining to pet projects of the former Bishop was the idea of a Diocesan periodical. Bishop Mikell said that he too thought it very worthwhile, for "corporate consciousness" would improve if an adequate organ of communication existed. He suggested a new plan to provide a Diocesan paper. Why not take advantage of *The Witness,* a weekly national Church publication which offered to publish local news of interest to a particular Diocese once a month in issues circulated only to that Diocese? The Diocesan charge for this, reported the Bishop, would be only one hundred dollars a year. Individual subscribers would pay a dollar a year; "by paying that subscription a person would get a general Church paper every week and once a month it would contain matters of local Diocesan interest." The Bishop said that the plan was already working very successfully in many Dioceses. As an editor for news about the Diocese of Atlanta, the Bishop was appointing the Rev. R. R. Claiborne of St. James', Marietta.

Two additional actions of the 1918 Council should be mentioned here. The Committee on Episcopal Residence introduced a resolution which would empower the Diocese to raise money for the purpose of securing a house for the Bishop. Unanimous

THE RT. REV. HENRY JUDAH MIKELL, D. D.
1917-1942

THE RT. REV. JOHN MOORE WALKER, D. D.
1942-1951

THE RT. REV. JOHN BUCKMAN WALTHOUR, D. D.
1952

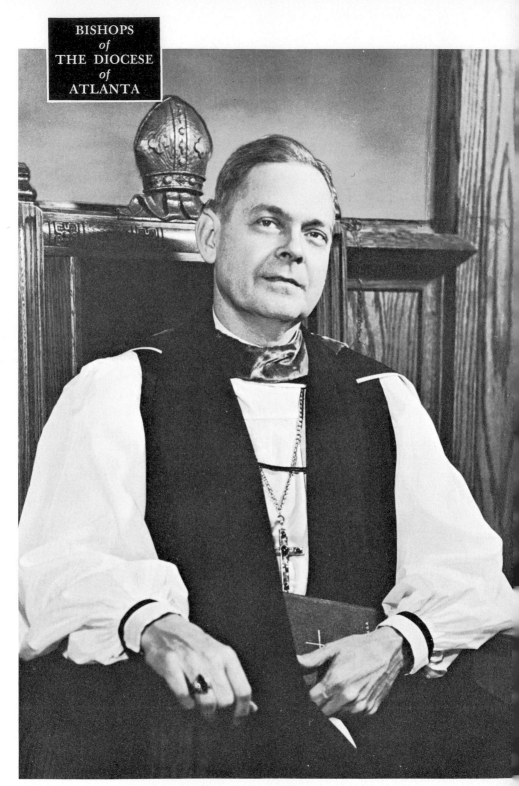

BISHOPS
of
THE DIOCESE
of
ATLANTA

The Rt. Rev. Randolph Royall Claiborne, Jr., D. D.
1953-

passage of this proposal by the Council indicated an awareness of a long-standing deficiency in their physical support of the Episcopate. Also, in order to improve the financial status of all the clergymen, steps were taken in 1918 to bring the Diocese into association with the Church Pension Fund of the General Convention. Since the Diocese of Atlanta had had some difficulty supplying funds enough for its own pension system, it gladly joined the national system.

The Diocese of Atlanta had chosen for its Bishop a man with wide interests and a strong determination to consider all phases of its operation so that weaknesses, such as the inadequacy of mission activity, could be improved. Of course, Bishop Mikell could not know that his greatest ally would be time. For he too, like three great Bishops before him, would serve his Diocese for more than twenty years. Longevity of leadership by a man of vision and action would once again prove invaluable. A clergyman who knew Bishop Mikell well has since described the impact of Mikell's work: "He was a man of impeccable appearance and of unforgettable ecclesiastical bearing who, with his incomparable preaching lifted men to high vision in the ceaseless quest for abundant living."

The Episcopalians of his Diocese were soon to discover that Henry Judah Mikell was a man of forthright principle who did not hesitate to speak his mind even on touchy issues. For example, during the twelfth Annual Council meeting at All Saints' in Atlanta, May 7-8, 1919, Bishop Mikell used a considerable part of his address to criticize both clergy and laity for indifference and selfishness which he thought all too prevalent in the Diocese. The discipline of the laity seemed to him a very serious problem, caused in part by "the disunity and divisions of Christianity." A member of one denomination who was disinclined to obey rules and regulations of that order could too easily transfer to another faith. Indeed, the Bishop noted with concern that there were cases where Episcopalians had transferred from one parish to another simply because of desires to escape church discipline.

But even worse were those laymen who "very cheerfully excommunicate themselves." Bishop Mikell quoted canon 45:

"All persons within this Church shall celebrate and keep the Lord's Day, commonly called Sunday, by regular participation in the public worship of the Church, by hearing the Word of God read and taught, and by other acts of devotion and works of charity, using all godly and sober conversation." With wry humor, the Bishop remarked, "Too many persons within this Church seem to consider that the said 'works of charity' begin at home." Unfortunately, he pointed out, no penalties were attached to the breaking of the canon. Small wonder, he said, that the Committee on the State of the Church cried out, "How about the army whose names fill our Parish registers yet are absent from the Parish Treasurer's records, and their persons from God's house and table?"

This led the Bishop into a sharp attack on "our too many utterly indifferent Church members," of which he quoted an outsider's remark that the Episcopal Church seemed willing to carry the world's largest burden. Such outsiders, he said, too often judge all Episcopalians by the indifferent ones. Lent, for example, seemed to be a "sham and a show" in the Episcopal Church because some members gave it lip service only.

Bishop Mikell suggested three possible uses of discipline to combat such indifference and selfishness. Most important, he hoped that these members could learn to discipline themselves. Secondly, if a "sense of loyalty and responsibility" did not soon manifest itself in members needing such discipline, the clergy should take a hand not only from the pulpit, but through "fearless and straight talking" in personal visits; although Mikell regretted that this was "something we clergy sometimes refrain from doing for fear of giving offense." The third proposal to exert influence on wayward members was that loyal Churchmen should be encouraged "to visit their displeasure on indifferent fellow-members, showing them plainly that they disapprove of their selfish disregard of the Church and religion."

Portions of Bishop Mikell's address and diary for the period 1918-1919 show the effects on the Diocese of Atlanta of the dreadful influenza epidemic which swept the United States during and just after World War I. On October 20, 1918 (less than a month before the Armistice), he noted in his Diary that "this is the second Sunday on which practically every church in the Diocese has been closed on account of the epidemic of influenza." The 1919 meeting of the Council had been scheduled for January but was postponed to May. He told this assembly that the postponement had been caused by the continued prevalence of the disease.

One development during his first full year in the Episcopate was evidently very pleasing to the Bishop. This was the decision taken on November 11, 1918, by the Trustees of the Fort Valley High and Industrial School to place the school under the auspices of the Diocese of Atlanta. The Fort Valley institution, where young Negroes received industrial and some academic training, was reported by the Bishop as "the most important work among colored people in the Diocese." Support for its activity previously came entirely from the General Board of Missions and the American Church Institute for Work among Negroes. Now the Diocese of Atlanta was involved spiritually and financially—the latter to the extent of two thousand dollars a year. A majority of the Trustees were Episcopalians, and an Episcopal clergyman was to become the school's resident chaplain. Bishop Mikell told the Council of 1919 that "There could not be a more opportune time than the present for the Church to take a further interest in Negro education. This war, which Negro people have loyally supported, where Negro troops have fought valiantly, has given to the Negro a new idea of development, a new desire for citizenship. The best and most highminded leadership must come to his aid, sane and spiritual influences must be thrown about him, a right direction given to his training and education. The Church School is the most effective way for accomplishing this."

One of the Diocese's smaller organized missions was Christ Church in West Point, centered around a small wooden Chapel. In 1920 a tornado blew into West Point and demolished the building. The effect was demolition of the mission also, for despite the continued interest of its mother parish, St. Mark's in LaGrange, only a few communicants in West Point remained interested, and soon the mission was abandoned. Various efforts to revive it would not be successful until the 1950's, and then under a new name—St. John's.

The period between World War I and the Depression Era saw a continued growth in the Diocese of Atlanta under Bishop Mikell's leadership. The year 1922 marked the fifteenth year of the new Diocese. During this period the number of clergy had grown from twenty-nine to forty-one. The fourteen parishes and nineteen organized missions of 1907 increased to seventeen and thirty respectively, while the total number of communicants rose from 4,988 to 6,000. Bishop Mikell's reports for the period 1921-1929 show a total of 2,694 confirmations.

In 1925 the Committee on the State of the Church reported 8,666 baptized persons and 6,710 communicants. While the latter figure represents a respectable gain over a three-year period, the committee stated that it felt there were even more in the Diocese, but—the age-old complaint—inadequate reporting made it impossible to give any higher figure. Indeed, throughout the decade this and other Diocesan committees cried out constantly for more thorough reporting by parishes and missions. In 1924, for example, the Committee on the State of the Church complained that "the figures given for baptized persons or total membership . . . are made by the different rectors upon so many different bases, or else represent mere guesswork, that these figures are totally unreliable. . . ." Three years later this same committee announced their belief that "a decided advance" was taking place in the Church, but if one were to examine the parochial reports, "this conclusion could never be reached."

The complaints about reporting usually centered around several deficiencies: some parishes and missions submitted no reports at all, some waited about five years to "clean out the dead wood" and make their records reasonably accurate, some turned in summaries based on estimates or "use of round numbers," and a few consistently waited until the meeting of the Council to submit reports. Concerning this last point, the Committee on the State of the Church told the 1919 meeting that this practice made their report to the Council often so late on the agenda that it therefore became "wasted labor to prepare a report to be read in the closing hours of the Council to an attendance dwindled to an impatient handful, said report then to be embalmed in the ink of the Journal's appendix like a fly in amber."

In a concerted effort to improve the situation, the Council of 1925 adopted a canonical amendment on reporting. Canon 10 was changed to require that rector and wardens utilize specially prepared blanks to report to the Bishop and Council the "spiritual and temporal conditions" of each parish. The Diocesan Secretary was to send out the blank forms each January 1st and the reports were due in by February 15. Although reports for the following year seemed to improve, by 1928 the Committee on the State of the Church was again lamenting: "Your committee thinks it quite futile to give an entire resume of each item in these reports because there are many of us who fail to give all the information the form asks presented." Apparently this problem would remain as long as churches were organized —despite the resulting dissatisfaction to summarizers of the times and present-day historians alike.

One definite improvement was evident by the middle of the decade. The *Journal* for 1925 gave, for the first time, a combined listing which showed parishes and missions alphabetically by location; the names of the rectors; the numbers of baptized persons and of communicants; the size, amount, and value of church property (including church seating capacity); the amount of insurance carried on the property; the total of indebtedness, if any; the number of baptisms during the year; and other statistics.

Relative sizes of the seventeen parishes in 1925 were as follows:

Parish	Location	Number of Communicants
St. Luke's	Atlanta	932
St. Philip's	Atlanta	811
All Saints'	Atlanta	795
Trinity	Columbus	632
Christ	Macon	438
St. Paul's	Macon	340
Epiphany	Atlanta	328
St. James'	Marietta	275

Emmanuel	Athens	263
Incarnation	Atlanta	190
St. Peter's	Rome	184
Holy Trinity	Decatur	176
St. George's	Griffin	150
Our Saviour	Atlanta	110
St. James'	Macon	100
St. James'	Cedartown	54
St. Stephen's	Milledgeville	35

Standing in twelfth position in the list is Holy Trinity, Decatur. This parish, under the leadership of the Rev. Harry F. Kellar, had joined the Diocese in 1920. Its wardens were F. H. Wilkie and D. C. Lawton, while vestrymen were Donald Donaldson, H. L. Parry, Louis Estes, R. P. Christian, J. Skinner, and H. Young. Nearby, one of the newer churches in Atlanta, Epiphany, was enjoying considerable growth. In 1923 a new church was constructed, along with a parish house. The newest parish in 1925 was the Church of Our Saviour in Atlanta, whose petition was accepted by the Council that year. Bishop Mikell commended the "intensely interested" congregation of Our Saviour and predicted a bright future for the new church.

The prosperity of the 1920's resulted in a respectable number of new-building projects in the Diocese of Atlanta. For example, new parish houses were constructed by Trinity Church, Columbus; Christ Church, Macon; and St. Luke's, Atlanta. St. Stephen's, Milledgeville, and St. James', Cedartown, built new rectories. At Emmanuel Church, Athens, a new Chapel was dedicated to a former rector.

Two churches celebrated important anniversaries during the decade. Christ Church, Macon, marked its centennial with services which evoked from Bishop Mikell warm praise for the church's one hundred years of activity. "Christ Church," he told the Council of 1925, "has grown stronger with the years and is a leading influence, not only in the city of Macon, but in our Diocesan life, responding generously to every call." In 1923 St. Philip's Parish of Atlanta (the Cathedral Church) celebrated its seventy-fifth anniversary. Only a little younger than Atlanta itself, St. Philip's also was a church of steadily increasing influence and prestige.

The second smallest church in the Diocese was St. James', in Cedartown. In 1927, this church for the first time was the site of Council sessions. Bishop Mikell expressed his appreciation to the host parish, and in elaborating on the problems of St. James' he gave some indication of the difficulties of all small parishes and missions: "The condition of our Churches in the smaller cities sometimes gives us great anxiety. For the present the problem has been solved here [at Cedartown]—and the solution is for a talented and devoted Clergyman to take charge, and in spite of temptations to move elsewhere, remain with the smaller Parish, gaining the love of his own people and the confidence and respect of the community."

Three years later Bishop Mikell had almost identical comments to make about the work of the Rev. Edward N. McKinley at the Church of the Mediator in Washington, Georgia. Energetic and dedicated young men of McKinley's type were needed for these smaller missions, said Bishop Mikell, but, "the trouble is that their work attracts the attention of larger Parishes and they are enticed away."

The problem of the smaller parishes and missions continued to be a vexing one, especially in areas where the number of communicants dropped to pitifully small congregations or in some cases none at all. In 1920 the churches at Eatonton and Tallapoosa were sold by the Bishop, while in Calhoun the church lot was disposed of. Some clergymen in the Diocese felt that there was little point in trying to resuscitate such helpless missions. In 1919 the Committee on the State of the Church asserted that it was the duty of the small bands of Episcopalians in the smaller communities to be missionaries themselves, "to seek to establish the Kingdom of God where they are, and to make to the church a return in prayer and labor that . . . [would] make the expenditure of time and effort in their neighborhood justifiable." Unless they did so, the committee stated, the Diocese was not justified in providing more than an occasional service for them.

One approach to the problem was a possible reorganization of the mission-and-missionary arrangement. While at Christ Church, Macon, for the thirteenth Council in 1920, the Diocesan representatives created a new body to govern mission activities. Called the Executive Board, and given broad powers to supervise and administer missionary, educational, and social work, this group replaced the Diocesan Board of Missions. The new Board was to consist of the Bishop, six clergymen, six laymen, and three women. The first members of this board were: the Rev. Messrs. Oliver J. Hart, H. Fields Saumenig, R. R. Claiborne, H. A. Wiley, S. A. Wragg, and A. G. Richards; Messrs. N. K. Smith, H. V. Kell, David Woodward, F. F. Baker, C. L. Bunting, and A. H. Sterne; and Mrs. E. B. Harrold, Miss Rosa Woodberry, and Mrs. C. L. Pettigrew.

One of the Executive Board's responsibilities was to appoint missionaries and to determine their salaries and allowances. The budget for 1921 shows eleven such appointments:

> the Rev. Thomas Duck, $2,000 and expenses
> the Rev. H. F. Kellar (Kirkwood), $100
> the Rev. I. H. Noe (College Park), $100
> the Rev. J. F. McCloud (Fort Valley), $200
> the Rev. G. I. Hiller, $1,400
> the Rev. A. H. Marshall (St. Mark's, LaGrange), $1,860
>   ($1,500 and $360 for rectory)
> the Rev. H. S. Cobey (Gainesville) $1,800 ($1,500 and $300 for
>   rectory)
> the Rev. G. W. Gasque, $1,700, and expense account of $318.96
> the Rev. H. R. Chase, $1,800
> Miss Steele (LaGrange), $1,000
> Miss Forman (LaGrange), $300

One of these missionaries, the Rev. H. R. Chase, reported considerable success in a special enterprise with which he assisted the rector of Trinity Church in Columbus. This concerned work "of great importance" done at nearby Fort Benning, where a "gratifying number" of army personnel were confirmed.

In 1925 another change was introduced in further efforts to improve the domestic mission situation. A special Diocesan Committee on Evangelism, with Bishop Mikell's endorsement, called upon each minister to meet with his vestry and congregation and lay before them the great need for capable volunteers in the mission fields. If clergymen had "fitness for preaching Missions," they should ask the Bishop for an assignment. Likewise, if there were laymen "who are interested and have fitness for the work" they should be utilized. Finally, the committee asked that rectors who were then planning to begin a mission which would need aid should make it known. Only six responses came from the Diocese to all of these requests. Two clergymen volunteered their services and another announced that he was beginning a mission.

Apparently this lack of interest continued through the decade. In 1929, during the Council sessions at Christ Church in Macon, the Committee on Evangelism commented on indifference to mission problems in the Diocese. Not more than three parishes, they said, usually responded regularly to the committee's appeals for information or suggestions. Despite frequent correspondence, telephone calls, and personal interviews, "only a negative interest" existed among the majority of churches. The committee offered praise for the results attained by the three cooperating parishes (not specifically named) who as a result had enjoyed exceptionally large confirmation classes.

Another recurring suggestion to assist mission work was that a Diocesan Missionary be secured. Bishop Mikell called a special meeting of the Executive Board to discuss this in 1925, but it was the consensus of the members that the necessary financial expenditure would make the project impossible. Despite the general prosperity of the 1920's, and a certain amount of new building around the Diocese, the general financial structure remained in a shaky condition. Early in the decade the Diocese of Atlanta joined others in the United States in cooperation with a regular annual drive for funds called the Nation-Wide Campaign. Using a now-commonplace method called the Every Member Canvass, pledges were obtained for the entire area of church financing—parochial, missions domestic and foreign, Diocesan expenses, and support of the General Convention. At most of the Council meetings after the adoption of this system, Bishop Mikell deplored the inadequacy of the pledges reported. Particularly in the support of missions were the pledged amounts insufficient, and in some cases less than half the communicants pledged at all. The Executive Board in 1925 instructed its treasurer to borrow money to pay the expenses of continuing missionary enterprise. This the Bishop characterized as "admirable faith, but very poor business." He saw only one way to combat it, and that was a real effort on the part of Council delegates to return home and persuade their colleagues of the necessity of making—and paying—larger pledges. In addition, the Executive Board recommended to all parishes that the duplex envelope be adopted, along with a plan of "individual apportionment" in mapping out their work.

Providing an adequate parochial salary for rectors was a major difficulty. In 1919 the Council adopted a resolution that each parish make an effort to pay its minister at least $1,800 per annum "or its equal." This latter phrase referred to living expenses, furnishing rectories, and the like. The Bishop's salary was also a matter of concern, especially since it had been an item of considerable importance in the efforts to secure a successor to Bishop Nelson. By the end of the decade Bishop Mikell's salary was listed at $7,000, with an additional $1,200 for expenses; and he had been provided with a house on Seventeenth Street in Atlanta.

Another dwelling close to the hearts of many in the Diocese was the Appleton Church Home. During the 1920's this institution was moved four miles out of Macon to a larger location on Forest Hill Avenue in order to provide improved, enlarged, and more sanitary quarters for the girls. Although a report on the school in 1921 indicated that the girls appeared "rosy, plump and well cared for," the desire to move was based on conditions which could not be improved at the Macon site except through means more expensive than moving. This proposal was discussed considerably. On August 2, 1922, Bishop Mikell's diary records the official decision to move the Home, and a special committee was appointed at the next Diocesan Council to solicit subscriptions for $50,000 in order to purchase new property and construct the new institution. Apparently the appeal was touching and effective, for within sixty days the committee reported that enough pledges had been received.

The contract for the new home was let in 1923, but an unusually bad winter prevented completion of the operations until nearly a year later. Altogether, the construction and outside improvements cost $61,677.07. The Trustees of the Home named the Rev. Oliver J. Hart, Mrs. Marshall J. Ellis, and Mr. W. Andrew Taylor as an Executive Committee to govern affairs at Appleton. The children were moved in on August 1, 1924, and in September all those of school age were enrolled in the public schools of Macon. This constituted a departure from previous arrangements, for formerly only those of high school grades went to the Macon schools.

On January 1, 1925, the Executive Committee hired Miss M. Agnes Treat to serve as Superintendent of the Appleton Church Home at a salary of $100 per month. The committee instructed the Treasurer of the Diocese to give Miss Treat a monthly allowance of $350 with which to operate. At the annual Trustees meeting a few months later, Superintendent Treat asked for and received an additional $100 monthly to improve the children's diet. In order to give Episcopalians of the Diocese an opportunity to see what was being done at Appleton, May 10 was declared as a Diocesan Visitation Day, and some 250 visitors came, most of whom registered as from Macon, Griffin, Milledgeville, and Fort Valley. In the hope that a wider representation of parishes might come next time, the second Sunday in May was set aside for an annual Diocesan Pilgrimage to the Appleton Church Home.

In this and similar aspects of Diocesan problems, Bishop Mikell took an active interst. Like his predecessors, he travelled a good bit. In addition to the normal demands on his time for visiting in the Diocese, in 1920 he went overseas with other American bishops to attend the Lambeth Conference. On July 11 he preached at the Lambeth Parish Church and at St. Augustine's Church in Kilburn. His public speaking ability earned him frequent invitations to speak at commencements, civic luncheons, and such special occasions as the Kappa Alpha Banquet on January 19, 1922, where he spoke about Robert E. Lee. Apparently he was deeply interested in the Lost Cause, for he gave talks on Lee and related subjects a number of times in the 1920's. On April 9, 1928, when the statue of Lee on the side of Stone Mountain was unveiled, it was Bishop Mikell who gave the invocation. One of his more bizarre duties occurred on

August 11, 1922, when in the Fulton County jail he "confirmed one person under sentence of death."

The frequent references to commencement addresses in Bishop Mikell's diary reflect his particular interest in the spiritual development of young people. During his address to the Sixteenth Annual Council in 1923 at St. Luke's in Atlanta Bishop Mikell challenged the parishes to participate actively in the recently established Young People's Service League. Already, he stated, successful chapters existed at All Saints' in Atlanta, Christ Church and St. Paul's in Macon, and St. James' in Marietta. The interest demonstrated by these young people seemed to him to be "one of the encouraging signs of our Church life today," and he felt that there should be a chapter of the League in every church in the Diocese.

While there seemed to be general approval in the Diocese concerning these remarks, some of Bishop Mikell's outspoken opinions on other subjects must have made Episcopalians squirm. For example, in discussing the Nation Wide Campaign during the 1920 Council he remarked that he hoped enthusiasm would accompany the drive. Then he added somewhat bitterly "but one trouble with this Church is that there are too many Protestants in it—too many people who protest against any plan which their own wisdom has not conceived. . . . There are still people in the Church who distrust anything that demands enthusiasm."

Often the Bishop spoke about the Episcopal Church as a part of the American scene. His comments to the Council in 1929 are typical of his opinions on this subject. Reporting on the recent General Convention, he said that the national Church represented every state in the Union and American soil beyond. "We may be small and weak in many places, but we are there bearing our witness of Christian faith and practice. And who shall say that American religious life, with its narrow-minded intolerance, its ignorant prejudices, its strange vagaries, its warfare of sects, and American anti-religious life with its increasing attacks on Christian morals and the Christian home, does not need our witness of sane, temperate, tolerant, cultured Christian truth?"

The materialism to which the Bishop referred in these remarks, and which is usually considered a characteristic of the

United States in the Twenties, was a matter of some concern to Diocesan leaders. The Committee on the State of the Church emphasized this point in 1922: "The industrial discontent of the working classes is intensified by their knowledge of the wasteful and wanton irresponsibility of so many of the wealthy today. . . . The truth is that Christian people must take a stand and uphold earnestly the decencies and moralities and honesties of life. Failure here imperils the whole social fabric."

One area of the "social fabric" in which the Diocese sought to "uphold the decencies and moralities of life" was among poorer classes in Georgia. Just after World War I the Council created a Diocesan Commission on Social Service, "the duty of which shall be to promote the cause of Social Service," and the Commission was authorized to work with a similar body in the National Church. In 1920 the work of this Commission was absorbed into the duties of the newly established Executive Board of the Diocese. Until 1921 the most outstanding social service work in the Diocese centered in the mill village activity at LaGrange, which had been going on for fifteen years. The two churches there, Good Shepherd and Holy Comforter, were under the guidance of the Rev. J. W. Fulford. Originally, when the work was begun, the Church and the mill owners shared equally in building and maintenance costs. Unfortunately, however, as the work continued the Diocese found itself unable to keep up with its share of the expense, and the manufacturers took on more and more of the financial responsibility. Although the Bishop felt that the Church was putting in an equal share in terms of "the character and self-sacrifice" of the mission workers and "the up-lifting influence" of the Church's spiritual activity, the Diocese lost its partnership control. Bishop Mikell told the Council meeting at St. George's in Griffin in 1921 that "gradually the party that was putting in the most money began to desire the larger share of control and the time came during the past year when it seemed wise for the Church to withdraw from the larger share of the welfare work it had been conducting and to confine itself to religious, pastoral, and catechetical activities."

Another direction in which the Diocese's interest in social service led, combined with an expanding mission and parochial program, concerned the work among Negroes. On June 27, 1918, Bishop Mikell appointed the Rev. E. L. Braithwaite as the Diocese's first Archdeacon for Colored Work. A few years later the Bishop reported to the Council that Negro communicants in the Diocese numbered 250. Far greater numbers, he noted, were recipients of the Church's influence through the education program. Six schools for colored children were operated by the Diocese, the largest of which, at Fort Valley, had 674 pupils. Students at the five others aggregated 612.

Frequently Bishop Mikell expressed his opinions as to the type and nature which the Diocesan work among the colored should assume. "Our church is the only church doing any considerable work among our colored people which is not divided according to color into two organizations," he told Episcopalian clergymen and laymen in 1921. "We recognize that we are brothers in Christ, and we must therefore, act on the fundamental principles of Christ which are peace and not strife, forgiveness and not revenge, self repression and not passion uncontrolled, justice toward the weak and ignorant and not a hideous oppression." His references to "passion uncontrolled" and "hideous oppression" concerned recent anti-Negro demonstrations by the Ku Klux Klan. The Bishop expressed harsh criticism of such "appalling acts of injustice," and asserted that "God has never yet given any race permanent power unless it has shown itself morally equal to the trust. If the white race in the South is to maintain its control it must show that it is the superior race, not by force, not by secret organization and deeds of midnight cruelty, but by an even-handed dispensing of justice, by forbearance and tolerance and kindness. The white race . . . must show . . . to God and man that the two races can live side by side, socially separate, but each enjoying equal protection under the law. . . ."

The Committee on the State of the Church reported in somewhat similar vein: "We shall continue [to stand] against separate church organizations for the Negro. He has his spiritual privileges with us, thank God, and a JIM CROW church government is not to be thought of. . . . Whatever the difficulties and discouragements of the situation, we know that violence and distrust will never mend it, that the weapon is education of the mind and spirit, and that the way out is by patience with a race whose development is generations behind our own. . . ."

The most promising Negro church mission in the mid-Twenties was St. Paul's in Atlanta. Convinced that it was "the most important work among our Colored Churchmen," Bishop Mikell felt that it should have an adequate church building. He therefore raised $25,000 by mortgaging certain property on Auburn Avenue for which he was trustee for St. Paul's. The congregation contributed to the building and equipment, and the Bishop reported that they had pledged themselves to pay the interest and establish a sinking fund on the principal. Unfortunately, however, the year 1925 saw the failure of one of the most important businesses among the Atlanta Negro community, and many influential members of St. Paul's congregation suffered heavy financial loss; some were even forced by the circumstances to move out of Atlanta. Bishop Mikell called upon the delegates at the 1925 Council to aid St. Paul's in this time of crisis.

The Bishop also called upon the Diocese to assist with another Negro activity: the Church High and Industrial School at Fort Valley. Throughout the Twenties, although the school grew in program and number of students enrolled, the Diocese's support dwindled. In vain did Bishop Mikell exhort his Churchmen to increase their giving to support this important project. Most of the donations for Fort Valley came from the outside. In 1925 George Foster Peabody and the Carnegie Foundation gave money for a new library building. Mrs. Royal C. Peabody donated a new trade school building. At the same time, when an appeal was made in the Diocese for help, only two thousand dollars a year was voted for maintenance. By 1929 the school had two additional buildings, one for high school academics and the other a combination auditorium and elementary training school. Both of these were donated by outsiders; while the Diocese managed to raise only $3,000 for the school, half of which came from one donor.

In an effort to increase Episcopal support for the school in 1929 the Diocese of Georgia was invited to join in its support, and the Board of Trustees was reorganized to include representation from that Diocese; however, a stipulation of the new arrangement was that the Bishop of Atlanta was always to be Chairman of the Board.

Diocesan reaction to this and similar projects was disappointing to Bishop Mikell. But despite the materialistic concepts of the age, and notwithstanding the greatly increased cost of Church living with the inflation of the late Twenties, there was much for the Diocese to be proud of as the decade drew to a close. At the Twenty-First Annual Council of 1928 which met at St. Peter's in Rome, Bishop Mikell reviewed the accomplishments and progress of the Diocese's first twenty years, and, more particularly, the developments in the ten years of his Episcopate. He issued these comparative financial statistics:

	1917	1927
Value of church property	$1,125,750	$2,033,650
Receipts of parishes & missions	103,757	323,684
Contributions to Diocesan missions	4,839	
Budget to Diocesan expenses		35,778
Contributions to General Church missions	4,497	16,200
Contributions by Woman's Auxiliary	6,899	11,333

Perhaps less encouraging than these expressions of growth was the comparison of numbers of communicants. This total was 5,644 in 1916, while ten years later there were 7,203, or approximately 28% increase. In this connection, Bishop Mikell expressed concern over the decrease in mission stations during the decade. However, he said, "I found some of them dead, and it did not seem necessary to keep their names on longer on our roll, and some of them were struggling so hopelessly, with only two or three communicants, that it seemed wiser to give them up and concentrate on places which presented more likelihood of growth." As for the parishes, he felt that those in cities and larger towns were greatly strengthened. More vigorous Church School programs and new parish houses were responsible for—or reflected—much of this progress. In concluding his summary of ten years' development, he charged his Churchmen to keep the Diocese in a vigorous condition by continuing to

CAMP MIKELL
Toccoa, Georgia
DIOCESE OF ATLANTA

Comprising 487 acres, purchased in 1941. Up until this time, Camp Mikell had operated since 1933 at Toccoa Falls Institute

Swimming Pool (built in 1958), with Claiborne Cottage in the background (this dormitory also built in 1958)

CAMP MIKELL
Toccoa, Georgia
DIOCESE OF ATLANTA

DORMITORY-CABIN
Built 1960

MIKELL CHAPEL
Built 1946

GEORGIA EPISCOPAL
CONFERENCE CENTER
Camden County

CHAPEL OF OUR SAVIOUR
Built 1960

GEORGIA EPISCOPAL
CONFERENCE CENTER
Camden County

DORMITORY
Built 1960

strengthen parishes, by working harder than ever with missions, and by giving more than ever to all of the Church's work.

Perhaps if the Bishop had realized what lay ahead for Americans in the next decade, he might have placed even more emphasis on his final charge to the Council of 1929. For the worst depression in the country's history was germinating, and in its wake the Episcopal Church in Georgia would suffer with the rest of the nation.

In 1930, before the full force of the depression was felt, Bishop Mikell noted with regret that some communicants in his Diocese were using "hard times" as "an excuse . . . [rather] than a reason for reduced benevolence." While it was true in some measure and in some localities, he admitted, that there were bad business conditions, nevertheless he did not think the times bad enough to justify excuses by some people for reducing pledges and contributions. The Executive Board ignored this phase of Diocesan problems in its report of the same year and praised the Diocese generally for a "very gratifying financial condition. Every cent for which the Diocese has obligated itself has been paid in full and there is not a single outstanding indebtedness."

The mission picture in 1930 looked better, judging by the Bishop's address and the report of the Committee on Evangelism. Further, the Council of that year adopted a new canon (No. 14) which allowed a new plan for organizing missions: when ten adult communicants in any community petitioned the Bishop for an organized mission, the Bishop could grant this request. An unorganized mission might be established when any ten adults of which at least three were communicants filed a petition. While such regulations might bring many additional missions into being, the Church leaders felt that the now successfully operating convocation system would give sufficient supervision to missions that none would "die on the vine."

"The most interesting event in our Church" during the previous year, stated the Bishop, "has been the use of the revised and enriched Prayer Book." He described some of the advantages, especially the latitude now allowed priests in the way of substitutions and abbreviations. But, warned Bishop Mikell, "if giving the individual clergyman greater liberty, it demands of him a corresponding loyalty." He listed some practices which this loyalty would demand: "No clergyman has the right to introduce into the public services a ceremonial to which the majority of his congregation strenuously object. The Church Service is not the exclusive property of the clergyman to do with as he will, it is for him to use for the edification of his people. . . . It is impossible, of course, for a clergyman to conduct a Service which will please everybody, but it ought to be possible to conduct a Service which will not displease a large majority of the Parishioners and alienate them from the Church. . . ."

In 1931 the Depression became a reality. The Finance Committee of the Diocese made a painful report to that year's Council in which reference was made to "the many embarrassments in not being able to meet the obligations of the Diocese promptly," including payment of part of the Bishop's salary. Some local situations were "acute." The Finance Committee had been asked to make reductions in assessments, and, in some cases, remissions. Not authorized to answer such requests, the committee had passed them directly to the Council. It recommended two budgets, one with the usual expenditures, and one with reductions affecting the Bishop's finances—the premium on his life insurance and his $1,200 travel expense were to be dropped. Thus the Council was faced with three prospects: (1) continuing on the same financial basis and exhorting parishes and missions to pay their full amounts, or (2) asking them to reduce their own budgets, or (3) adopting a budget which gave inadequate support to Bishop Mikell.

The last-named course, with some modification, prevailed. During the Council sessions it was voted that the premium on the Bishop's life insurance (amounting to $1,000) would be dropped from Diocesan expenditures. A laymen's committee then offered an amendment to the budget which would also drop the item of $750 for group insurance premiums for the clergy. This amendment carried. As finally approved, the budget for 1931 provided for expenditures totaling $9,902.50, as compared with $11,659.50 for the previous year. Other reductions included $75 from the printing expense, $475 from Convention expense, and $100 from the Bishop's pension. The Bishop's travel expense was reduced to $1,000.

In 1932 the Diocese celebrated its twenty-fifth anniversary. Despite the distressing financial conditions of the times, Bishop Mikell congratulated the Diocese upon the occasion. Addressing the Council in session at St. Luke's Parish in Atlanta, the Bishop expressed pride as he reviewed the quarter-century increase of parishes to seventeen, communicants to 7,879, and the clergy to forty-two. He welcomed several new clergymen to various posts: the Rev. John H. Morgan, rector of St. Paul's in Macon; the Rev. Mortimer W. Glover, rector of Christ Church, Macon; the Rev. John Moore Walker, rector of the Council's host church, St. Luke's; the Rev. Randolph R. Moore, priest-in-charge of St. Paul's in Atlanta and Archdeacon of the Negro work of the Diocese; the Rev. Charles E. Wood, St. James', Marietta; the newly ordained Randolph R. Claiborne, Jr., St. James', Macon, with charge also at St. Andrew's, Fort Valley; and the Rev. B. Scott Eppes, in charge of several North Georgia missions.

Perhaps if the Depression had not been so evident, Bishop Mikell might have given more time to his summary of the twenty-five years. But in view of the situation, he early shifted his remarks to the subject of finances. In addition to encouraging delinquent parishes and missions to meet their obligations in the best possible manner, Bishop Mikell urged Diocesan attention to the Church's endowment, which was, he remarked somewhat plaintively, "one of the smallest endowment of any Diocese of the Church." During twenty-five years it had increased not at all from the original $16,000 which was the new Diocese's share in the division of joint funds. The Bishop asked, as a worthwhile way of marking the anniversary, that the Diocese "celebrate our 25th birthday [in] a determined effort to increase [the endowment] and remove the burden of the support of the Episcopate from the Parishes and Missions."

Then Bishop Mikell invited the Council to reduce his own salary in order to avoid cutting the missionary budget. While he was out of the room during consideration of this offer, the

Treasurer presented the Finance Committee's budget for the coming year. This budget continued the Bishop's salary without reductions. When Bishop Mikell returned to the chamber, he learned that the Council not only had rejected his offer, but had determined to continue missionary work also without reductions.

Two special reports in the Council of 1932 give further evidence of financial hardships. The Appleton Church Home reported that their problems were especially serious, owing to the closing of the bank in which their funds were deposited. Had it not been for an anonymous donor, the Home would not have been able to pay its bills for the year.

Several parishes were delinquent on their assessments, and the Credentials Committee reported to the Council that in accordance with Diocesan canons, delegates from these parishes could not be seated. However, a minority report from this committee was introduced as follows: "That all parishes and missions having Delegates present be admitted to Council and their Delegates seated regardless of whether assessments have been paid in full." Apparently sympathetic with the plight of these parishes, and perhaps anticipating what might come up in the next several Councils, the assembly adopted the precedent-shattering minority report.

The overall precarious nature of Diocesan finances in this era is revealed in the report of expenditures and income for the year 1932, as reported in the 1933 *Journal*:

BANK BALANCE, January 29, 1932		$64.59
RECEIPTS:		
Diocesan assessments	$6,599.25	
From Permanent Fund	800.00	
Rebate from Pension Fund	348.09	
TOTAL RECEIPTS		7,747.34
TOTAL IN ACCOUNT		7,811.93
DISBURSEMENTS:		
Salary of Bishop	$5,450.00	
Expense of Bishop	749.97	
Pension of Bishop	564.88	
Interest	148.41	
On account Printing *Journal*	300.00	
Misc. expense	134.42	

Travel expense	31.75
Treasurer's salary	125.00
Secretary and assistants	270.00
Council expenses	24.80
Payment on notes	50.00
TOTAL DISBURSEMENTS	$7,756.23
BANK BALANCE, January 1933	$55.70

Bishop Mikell told the Council of 1933 that because of greatly reduced pledges from the parishes the Diocesan missionary budget had been cut so drastically that the principal missionary work "consists now of barely keeping open the Mission stations and aiding the smaller Parishes." Another budget reduction had occurred when the printing of the *Diocesan Record* was temporarily suspended.

An encouraging note in the midst of this financial anxiety was sounded when on June 18, 1933, ground was broken in Atlanta for a new Cathedral building. This action resulted from a period of activity dating back to 1927, when the Council of that year adopted a resolution "Regarding Site and Erection of New Cathedral." Noting that the old Cathedral was "situated close to the commercial center of a rapidly growing city," the resolution asked that the Church "give way to the march of progress and seek a location more appropriate and more inspiring. . . ." Such a location was finally found at the intersection of Peachtree Road and Andrews Drive in fashionable Northside Atlanta, the present site of the Cathedral. An agreement to purchase the property for $45,000 was entered into by the Cathedral Board of Trustees; $3,000 was paid in cash and the balance due in five years.

On September 10, 1933, Bishop Mikell consecrated the new Cathedral building, designating it the "Pro-Cathedral," since the structure was a "Cathedral building so appointed but not yet in full status and full function." During the morning services prior to the dedication exercises, Bishop Mikell baptized his grandchild, Henrietta Mikell Jones, in the new building's first baptismal service. One objection to the moving of St. Philip's had been that there would be a considerable loss of previously enrolled membership. However, this loss was offset in large part

by an influx of new members. In 1934 the Cathedral reported
599 communicants, only 15 less than the 614 reported for 1932.
Apparently the number of visitors increased beyond expectation, for the new building soon found itself taxed to capacity
nearly every Sunday, and on special occasions many persons were
turned away.

Another development in the year 1933 was also pleasing to
the Bishop. This concerned the plans for a summer camp for
young people. Bishop Mikell announced that he had made
preliminary negotiations with the Toccoa Falls Institute to lease
their facilities for two weeks in the coming June so that such a
camp could be held. If, as he hoped, more than fifty campers
registered, the retreat could be managed for only $15 individual
cost. The Diocese seemed receptive to the idea. Not only was
the camp endorsed by the Council of 1933, but enthusiasm was
generated in the parishes to the degree that the first session was
successfully held at Toccoa, with the Rev. Mortimer Glover
serving as Director and the Rev. R. R. Claiborne, Jr., as Assistant Director.

Despite the financial anxieties of the era, the Committee on
the State of the Church took time in 1935 to raise an age-old
complaint: the parishes were not submitting proper reports.
They were incomplete and often too tardy for the committee to
make its own report on time or full enough. "Apparently," the
committee stated in exasperation, "a considerable number of the
clergy and treasurers consider the making of these reports of no
importance." Nine parishes waited until the meeting of the
Council to make any reports at all, and one of these was given
orally (!). Even some of the seemingly complete reports which
were filed on time contained glaring errors, such as the parish
which announced "48 last year, added 3, lost 8, present number
31." Apparently this time-honored complaint would remain just
that. Only a few years later, at the Council meeting of 1939, the
Committee on the State of the Church disgustedly announced
that because of delayed and incomplete reports they were not
going to make a report at all.

Two of the Diocese's most loyal stalwarts were lost by death
during the mid-Thirties, one a clergyman, the other a member of

the laity. The minister was the Rev. Thomas Duck, who died in Decatur on November 13, 1935. As the many references to this long-serving rector and missionary in previous pages have indicated, Thomas Duck had served the Diocese in many places and was the oldest clergyman in point of service to the Diocese. The layman was Col. Zadok D. Harrison, who died in Atlanta the same year. His service extended as far back as 1877, when he had become a member of the Diocesan Council. In 1880 he was named to the Standing Committee and remained on that important group first with the Diocese of Georgia and then the Diocese of Atlanta until his retirement a few years before his death. In 1924 Sewanee conferred upon him the honorary degree of Doctor of Civil Law in honor of the service he had and was rendering as a member of the University's Board of Trustees since 1880. He was a vestryman of St. Philip's for five years and a vestryman and senior warden of St. Luke's for forty-three years.

Although the devastating effects of the Depression would be keenly felt in many areas for some time to come, things had so brightened for the Diocese of Atlanta by 1937 that a cheerful tone was apparent in the reports, addresses, and discussions at the Council meeting of that year, held in Trinity Church, Columbus. Bishop Mikell made the aura of "financial promise" the principal topic of his address to the assembled Episcopalians. He noted that the financial condition of the Diocese was more secure than at any time during the decade. He was proud that with the help of several laymen (especially Diocesan Treasurer H. M. Heckman and L. W. Conger of the Conger Printing Company) the *Diocesan Record* had resumed publication; its monthly appearances were enhanced by the interest and skill of its managing editors, the Rev. David Cady Wright and Mr. Heckman. Except for the sum of $3,000 still owed on the Bishop's house and a note for $750, the Diocese was no longer in debt.

But Bishop Mikell sounded a warning note for his Churchmen to ponder amidst the rising tide of optimism. Calling their attention to reports that in the larger cities an estimated ten millions of dollars had been spent New Year's Eve "on noise and dancing and jazz," the Bishop said, "Let us beware in our boasting of 'Good times are here again.'. . . Man's good fortune comes from God, and should not be boasted about but reverently appreciated." Episcopalians should remember the Twenties he urged, and avoid the moral lapses which the prosperity of that era brought.

But the Bishop himself had some boasting to do, this time in reference to the annual summer camp for young people, now named Camp Mikell. The one held in 1937 was "most successful," he stated, with more than one hundred from the church's youth present. He had himself served as Chaplain, with the Rev. Randolph R. Claiborne, Jr., of Macon helping as Director.

On a more somber note, Bishop Mikell commented on an event of international importance: "Sober and thoughtful Christians can be thankful . . . for an event of world interest in the closing days of last year, when responsible leaders in the Church and State told the king of the greatest empire of the world that he could not set an example of moral irresponsibility, and remain on his throne. We can be very thankful to the Primate of our Mother Church of England for the part he played in that crisis in his nation's history. . . ."

In one city in Georgia there was sadness in 1937. In April Gainesville was struck by a tornado which ripped through the town leaving destruction and havoc in its wake. Bishop Mikell visited Gainesville on April 8 and found that Grace Church there had been "utterly destroyed" and the rectory "badly damaged." Fortunately, the rector and his family escaped bodily injury. Searchers in the church wreckage were pleased to find the Chalice unharmed; the cup had been used barely an hour before the winds struck. Observers arriving on the scene spotted the Altar Cloth dangling high in the branches of a nearby tree. The Bishop later told the Council that a Diocesan appeal had brought contributions in the amount of $2,428.57 which were to be used for the rebuilding of Grace Church. Already, he reported, enough additional money had been raised in the congregation and among Gainesville friends to begin reconstruction of the church. The cornerstone of the new Grace Church was laid by Bishop Mikell on March 28, 1937, and the new building consecrated the following September. The senior warden, Mr. E. Norman Howard, "created an old world atmosphere in a brand new Church" by making several hand-carved decorations for the Sanctuary, including a rood screen of oak featuring intertwining grape leaves.

The Diocese's interest in the young students at the Fort Valley Normal and Industrial School underwent a shift in direction during this period. The recently established Board of Regents of the University System of Georgia took steps to make the Fort Valley School a Negro college of the University System; and this was made possible by agreement with the school's Board of Trustees. In order to provide religious training and counsel for Episcopal students at the college, in 1939 the American Church Institute of the Protestant Episcopal Church, with the cooperation of the Diocese of Atlanta, established the Fort Valley College Center. During the same year the Rev. Walter H. Marshall ended a twenty-year cure at the Fort Valley School, and the Rev. Lloyd M. Alexander was assigned to the Center.

In summarizing his first twenty years as the Diocesan, Bishop Mikell told the Council in 1938 that he had confirmed 7,024 persons in this period. But the statistics were not comforting, he warned. Overall, the Diocese then numbered only 8,195 communicants. This meant that over 4,000 members had become "lapsed communicants." While such a situation might be tragic under any circumstances, Bishop Mikell thought it "dangerous" in view of the times: "We cannot afford to let the Church grow weak today, for it has to withstand more fierce attacks from its enemies than at any time since the centuries of early persecution." By "enemies," he was referring to the European dictators who had swept their countries' churches aside.

By the end of the decade the Depression was being referred to in the past tense. In the Diocese of Atlanta steps were being taken to revive the convocations system as a missionary means, since the expense of the plan had caused its suspension during the lean years. The budget for the year 1940 had increased to $9,915, and a glance at its items indicate the economic upswing of the new era:

Bishop's salary $6,000.00
Bishop's traveling expense 1,000.00
Printing of the *Diocesan Record* 1,000.00

Bishop's Pension Fund 540.00
Secretary of Council and asst. 210.00
Printing of *Journal* 250.00
Expense of Council 15.00
Missionary Council expense 50.00
Traveling of Board and committees 25.00
Expenses of Deputies to General Convention . .   500.00
Presiding Bishop's expense 100.00
Expense Treasurer of the Diocese 225.00
                                          ————————
                                          $9,915.00

Late in 1939 Bishop Mikell announced that an anonymous donor had given $5,000 towards the securing of a permanent site for Camp Mikell, which was still operating in the Toccoa Institute School. A similar amount was still needed before the camp could be suitably located in a place of its own. Also indicative of the changed economic times was the Bishop's call in 1940 for an additional $7,500 for building or enlarging projects at three other locations in the Diocese. Churches were needed in Thomaston and Elberton at costs of $2,000 and $5,000 respectively. In the Kirkwood section of Atlanta St. Timothy's needed $500 to enlarge its small church building.

Several years were to pass before these and other needed sums could be completely obtained. But the new prosperity at the beginning of the decade showed the Diocese anxious and willing to resume full scale operations, to expand and improve its parishes, and to wage a more vigorous missionary campaign. Bishop Mikell announced in 1941 that "we are happy to have the report . . . that the budget of the Executive Board of the Diocese for 1940 has been met in full and that we paid in full our expectancy to the National Council of $4,500."

In his address to the 1941 Diocesan Council, Bishop Mikell was able to announce the partial realization of a long-time dream—the purchase of a permanent site and equipment for the Diocesan Camp. 487 acres had been obtained in the mountains of northeast Georgia, near Toccoa. Bishop Mikell stated, "We have been able to contribute enough to build and partially equip Camp Mikell," and he said that this could not have been done "without the splendid work of the Rev. Scott Eppes [vicar of

St. Matthias' Church, Toccoa, Grace Church, Clarkesville, and Calvary Church, Mt. Airy] who has practically built Camp Mikell." The necessary buildings were constructed: a combination dining hall and recreational hall, with kitchen (the gift of Miss Georgia Wilkins of Trinity Church, Columbus), separate dormitories for girls and boys, and an infirmary (the gift of Mrs. William A. Smith of St. Luke's Church, Atlanta.) Later, a beautiful Chapel was given to Camp Mikell by Mrs. Robert P. Shapard and R. P. Shapard, Jr., of St. George's Church, Griffin. Consecrated by Bishop Walker on September 2, 1946, this Chapel was named in memory of Bishop Mikell and constituted the first permanent building at Camp Mikell.

Yet two disasters early in the 1940's would again challenge the Episcopal Church in the Diocese of Atlanta. The first was American entry into World War II. Despite a certain continued prosperity resulting from the business boom, the increase in federal taxes and frequent calls for loans and donations to support the war effort would drain some of the Church's sources for giving; and, of course, many of the Diocese's young men would answer their country's call and enter the armed services.

More directly tragic to the Diocese of Atlanta, however, was the death of its Bishop, Henry Judah Mikell, on February 20, 1942. The last entry in the Bishop's Diary for 1942 is dated February 9th. Under this date he noted that he was forced to miss hearing an English clergyman in Atlanta because he went to Emory Hospital for "observation." The illness which sent him to the hospital took his life eleven days later. Impressive memorial services for the Diocese's second Bishop were held on April 28 at the beginning of the thirty-fifth Annual Council held in St. Peter's Church, Rome. The memorial words were given by the Rt. Rev. Frank A. Juhan, Bishop of Florida. Bishop Juhan's short but moving tribute praised Bishop Mikell as a "master:" "His messages were unfailingly masterpieces of logic and of concise and striking truth. . . . [He was] both master and masterpiece in manners. . . . He was a master in ministry. He was always conferring the gifts of God's Holy Spirit on those with whom he came in contact. His ministry was a clear and convincing commentary of his manners and his messages;

and that was because he was always giving the gifts of his Master's life. . . . We must thank God, for that He shared with us for so long a time this masterpiece."

In their resolution of tribute to the late Bishop, the Woman's Auxiliary characterized him as a "gallant leader" and a "dear friend." He was "the personification of his high office, dignified, gentle, poised, modest, highly cultured, with unfailing wit, reserved to the point of shyness, and with a whimsical sense of humor and much tact." They summarized his impressive record of honors and special achievements since becoming Bishop, especially these: Chancellor of the University of the South; Chairman of the Board of Trustees of the George Peabody College for Teachers, Nashville, Tennessee; Trustee of DuBose Memorial Training School, Monteagle, Tennessee; Chairman of the Hymnal Revision Commission of the General Convention; member of the Liturgical Commission also of the General Convention; and twice delegate to the Lambeth Conference in London.

Henry Judah Mikell became head of the Diocese of Atlanta during one World War and died during another. For twenty-five years he served his Diocese well, once again proving the value of longevity coupled with brilliant leadership. His death occurred barely over a hundred years since the first Episcopal Bishop in Georgia was chosen. Thus, Episcopalians in northern and western Georgia had known but four Bishops during 102 years: Bishops Elliott, Beckwith, Nelson, and Mikell. Fortunate indeed were the Georgia Churchmen whose parishes and missions had had such wise leadership during the first century of their development.

CHAPTER
✻ · XIV · ✻

ARRIVAL OF A "GOLDEN ERA"
1942-1957

THE TASK of securing a new Bishop was the first problem facing the Diocese of Atlanta in 1942. At the Annual Council in April, following a memorial service for Bishop Mikell, the Rt. Rev. Frank A. Juhan, Bishop of Florida and President of the Province, was named Chairman of the Council, and the Rev. F. H. Harding of St. Stephen's, Milledgeville, Secretary. A resolution was adopted for a memorial to Bishop Mikell "to be erected and maintained at the site or as a part of the proposed new Cathedral of St. Philip." The Standing Committee reported to the Council on the matters which it had handled in its canonical capacity as Ecclesiastical Authority following the death of the Bishop. After a number of other reports and resolutions, the Council entered into the nominations for Bishop. Four clergymen were nominated: the Rev. John Moore Walker, D.D.; the Rev. Theodore St. Clair Will, D.D.; the Rev. David Cady Wright, Jr.; and the Very Rev. Elwood L. Haines.

Dr. Walker, rector of St. Luke's in Atlanta, was then President of the Standing Committee, Deputy to the General Convention, and a member of the Board of Officers of the Diocesan Corporation. He was ordained in 1914 and began his work in the Diocese in 1931. Dr. Will was also ordained in 1914, but did not begin his work in the Diocese until 1938. Rector of All Saints' in Atlanta, he was a member of the Executive Board and a Deputy to the General Convention. The third Georgia clergyman nominated was the Rev. David Cady Wright, Jr., rector of

Emmanuel Church in Athens; ordained in 1931, he was admitted to the Diocese the same year. He was Secretary of the Standing Committee, member of the Executive Board, and a Trustee of the Appleton Church Home. The fourth nominee, the Very Rev. Elwood L. Haines, was the Dean of Christ Church Cathedral in Louisville, Kentucky.

After nominations were closed, the ballots were collected and counted. By previous agreement, regular business of the Council was conducted during the period of counting. It was well that this decision was made, for twelve ballots would be necessary before a candidate would receive a majority in both houses. The first ballot reported as follows: Dr. Walker, 9 by Clergy, 10 2/3 by Laity; Dr. Will, 6 and 6 1/3; Dean Haines, 8 and 4 2/3; and Mr. Wright, 4 and 3 1/3. For the next nine ballots there were fluctuations to and away from the several candidates, but none sufficient to bring the needed majority. Finally, Dr. Will and Mr. Wright asked that their names be withdrawn in favor of Dr. Walker. Therefore on the eleventh ballot Dr. Walker received 17 votes of the Clergy to Dean Haines' 10, but only 12 of the Lay votes to 11 2/3 for his opponent. Bishop Juhan ruled that another ballot would be necessary since Dr. Walker lacked a one-third vote of having the necessary majority in the Laity. The tellers reported after the twelfth ballot that Dr. Walker had been elected by majorities of 11 in Clergy and 5 1/3 in Laity. Upon motion of Dr. Will the vote was made unanimous in favor of John Moore Walker, the third Bishop of the Diocese of Atlanta.

The new Bishop assumed control of a Diocese then some thirty-five years old. At the time of his consecration on September 29, 1942, the Diocese consisted of twenty parishes, twenty-one organized missions, five unorganized missions, and three dormant stations:

PARISHES

Athens	Emmanuel	The Rev. David C. Wright, Jr.
Atlanta	All Saints'	The Rev. Theodore S. Will
Atlanta	Epiphany	(no rector listed)
Atlanta	Holy Comforter	(none listed)
Atlanta	Incarnation	The Rev. Theodore V. Morrison

Atlanta	Our Saviour	The Rev. Samuel C. W. Fleming
Atlanta	St. Luke's	(none listed)
Atlanta	St. Paul's	The Rev. Henry J. C. Bowden
Atlanta	St. Philip's (Cathedral)	The Very Rev. Raimundo de Ovies, Dean
Cedartown	St. James'	The Rev. J. B. Hunt, Jr.
Columbus	St. Christopher's	The Rev. Aubrey A. Hewitt
Columbus	Trinity	The Rev. Harry G. Walker
Decatur	Holy Trinity	The Rev. Charles Holding
Griffin	St. George's	The Rev. L. W. Blackwelder
Macon	Christ Church	The Rev. Raymond E. Feussle
Macon	St. James'	The Rev. A. S. J. Matthews
Macon	St. Paul's	The Rev. John Vander Horst
Marietta	St. James'	The Rev. James Savoy
Milledgeville	St. Stephen's	The Rev. F. H. Harding
Rome	St. Peter's	The Rev. James L. Duncan

Organized Missions

Atlanta	St. Timothy's	The Rev. Roy Pettway
Atlanta	Holy Innocents'	The Rev. T. S. Will
Carrollton	St. Margaret's	The Rev. J. B. Hunt, Jr.
Cartersville	Ascension	The Rev. Roy Pettway
Clarkesville	Grace	(none listed)
College Park	St. John's	(none listed)
Dalton	St. Mark's	The Rev. James Duncan, Rome
Elberton	St. Alban's	The Rev. David C. Wright, Athens
Ft. Valley	St. Andrew's	The Rev. J. F. G. Hopper
Gainesville	Grace	The Rev. E. H. Harrison
Greensboro	Redeemer	The Rev. D. C. Wright
Griffin	St. Stephen's	The Rev. J. H. Brown, Ft. Valley
LaGrange	Good Shepherd	(none listed)
LaGrange	St. Elizabeth's	The Rev. F. H. U. Edwards
LaGrange	St. Mark's	(none listed)
Macon	Mission of Christ Church	The Rev. R. E. Fuessle
Mt. Airy	Calvary	C. Cornwall (Lay Reader)
Talbotton	Zion	(none listed)
Thomaston	St. Thomas'	The Rev. A. S. Mathews
Toccoa	St. Matthias'	C. Cornwall (Lay Reader)
Washington	Mediator	(none listed)

Unorganized Missions

LaGrange	Holy Comforter	(none listed)
Manchester	St. Paul's	(none listed)
Sparta	Ascension	The Rev. F. H. Harding

Tallulah Falls   St. James'   (none listed)
Warm Springs   Foundation   (none listed)
                 Chapel

DORMANT STATIONS

Athens   St. Mary's
Helen   Transfiguration
Norcross   St. John's

After consecration in late September, the new Bishop plunged vigorously and immediately into his new work. From October 1 through December 31 his busy schedule in the Diocese included a variety of functions. The amount of such activity in so short a period indicates not only the burden borne by Bishops of the Protestant Episcopal Church, but Bishop Walker's own approach to the Diocese he knew and loved so well. Some indication of this dedicated approach is found in a later Bishop's description of John Moore Walker: "His intellect was keen and he loved his books, but with his love for people and his concern for the welfare of all God's children, with his patience and his understanding, he looked deep inside a man. He looked until he found some latent strength and let God use him to help build upon it."

Except for the brief services of the visiting Bishop of Rangoon, the Rt. Rev. George A. West, the parishes and missions of the Diocese of Atlanta had not had since the death of Bishop Mikell those visitations of the Bishop which are so necessary for the sustenance and continued growth of the Episcopal Church. Bishop Walker during the three remaining months of 1942 held confirmation services at St. Philip's Cathedral (Oct. 11), St. Paul's in Macon (Oct. 18), St. Matthias' in Toccoa (Oct. 20), Incarnation in Atlanta (Oct. 25), St. Timothy's in Atlanta (Nov. 1), St. Christopher's in Columbus (Nov. 8), the Bishop's Chapel (Nov. 10, 25, Dec. 25), St. Stephen's in Milledgeville (Nov. 15), Our Saviour in Atlanta (Nov. 22), St. Paul's in Atlanta (Nov. 26), St. James' in Marietta (Nov. 29), Grace in Gainesville (Dec. 6), St. James' in Cedartown (Dec. 13), All Saints' in Atlanta (Dec. 15, 20), and Epiphany in Atlanta (Dec. 27).

The Bishop officiated at Divine Services on thirteen occasions during the same period, often in connection with the visits

St. Margaret's, Carrollton
Organized 1893 • Present Church built 1953

Church of the Incarnation, Atlanta
Organized 1882 • Built 1958

SOME OF
THE NEW CHURCHES
in the
DIOCESE OF ATLANTA

HOLY INNOCENTS', Sandy Springs
Organized (in Atlanta) 1896 • Moved to Sandy Springs 1954
Present Church built 1958

CHURCH OF THE GOOD SHEPHERD, Covington
Organized 1950 • Church built 1951

St. Matthew's, Macon
Organized 1947 • Church built 1959

St. John's, College Park
Organized 1906 • Built 1957

SOME OF
THE NEW CHURCHES
in the
DIOCESE OF ATLANTA

St. Barnabas', Trion
Organized 1954 • Church built 1958

St. Bartholomew's, Atlanta
Organized 1954 • Church built 1957

enumerated above. He celebrated Holy Communion four times, one of which was at the home of "an earnest Churchman" who was confined because of illness. Bishop Walker solemnized the marriages of six couples, and performed one baptism, that of his grandson Blake Newton Tyler III in Virginia.

Of especial significance to his new office were the many Church organizations and boards which required the Bishop's immediate attention. Before 1942 ended Bishop Walker had met with the following: Executive Board of the Diocese (Sept. 29), Standing Committee of the Diocese (Sept. 29), Board of Officers of the Corporation (Sept. 29 and Nov. 15), the Daughters of the King (Oct. 17 and Nov. 24), Young People's Service League in convention (Oct. 1-3), District Meeting of the Woman's Auxiliary (Oct. 7), Diocesan Youth Commission (Dec. 2), Cathedral Board of Trustees (Dec. 10), and Executive Board of the Appleton Church Home (Dec. 17 and 22). In addition, the Bishop held formal sessions with rector and vestry at Trinity in Columbus (Nov. 7) and St. Paul's in Atlanta (Nov. 9).

Also during his first three months, Bishop Walker was present on two occasions of special interest. On October 11 he participated in the Fiftieth Anniversary celebration of the founding of Holy Trinity Church in Decatur; coincidentally, Holy Trinity's rector, the Rev. Charles Holding, marked his twenty-fifth anniversary of Ordination. On November 7, Bishop Walker visited with Episcopal officers and enlisted men at Fort Benning.

The Fort Benning trip was a war-time visit, for by the end of 1942 the United States had been at war with the Axis Powers for a year. Official reports at the thirty-sixth Annual Meeting, held in Athens in May of 1943, indicated that like other American denominations, the Episcopal Church was feeling the war's effect. Carl Scheussler of Trinity Parish in Columbus and a candidate for Holy Orders was reported killed in action; the Standing Committee announced that an air field in the Solomon Islands was to be named in his honor. Two postulants, John T. Speaks and Bruce LeFebre, were listed as serving in the Marine Corps and the Army Air Corps respectively. Bishop Walker exhorted the Athens convention to keep clear the

Church's two objectives, "apparently incompatible" as they may be: (1) the war must be fought to a finish, for victory was critically important, and "I have no apology to make when I say that we are following the will of God in fighting this battle." (2) The second objective might be even harder to reach —but it was equally important: that the war be fought without hatred. "It must never be said of the Churchmen of our generation that they stood up and preached hatred as a means of winning the war."

The Committee on the State of the Church reported in 1943 that the Diocese was commendably active in working at service camps. "The Rector and Assistant Rector of Trinity Church, Columbus, are doing an admirable work in cooperation with the Army Chaplains at Fort Benning. The Rector of St. Paul's, Macon, celebrates the Holy Communion every Sunday at Cochran Flying Field. The Macon Rectors also have been conducting services at Camp Wheeler when no Episcopal Chaplain has been stationed there." Throughout the war period Bishop Walker kept up a personal correspondence with many of the members of his Diocese who were in uniform, obtaining addresses from lists furnished by various rectors. In the year 1944 the Diocese of Atlanta gave $1,310.19 to the Army and Navy Commission of the National Church; and during the same year, received $6,450.00 for the Army and Navy Commission work in the Diocese. This work was under the direction of the Rev. Harry G. Walker of Columbus.

During the war an Atlanta church celebrated its twentieth anniversary. The Church of Our Saviour, on Highland Avenue, had enjoyed substantial growth since its establishment as a mission in 1924. Two aspects of this church's history deserve especial note. From the beginning, its priests and its congregation preferred the more formal ceremonies of worship, and the Church of Our Saviour in Atlanta soon became known "as one of the most notable Anglo-Catholic parishes of the Church in the United States." From the standpoint of parochial finances, in 1949 Our Saviour abandoned use of the Every Member Canvass and other membership pledge solicitations. In the following decade, parish income quadrupled.

In his first address to the Diocese during the Athens meeting in 1943, Bishop Walker concluded with this remark: "For both races, white and colored alike, there is the challenge of the Master himself, 'seek ye first the kingdom of Heaven and His righteousness.' " During the convention the Bishop appointed a special committee "to study racial relationships within the Diocese" and to make recommendations concerning the "duty and opportunity of the Church in that regard." This committee reported in 1944 that all available statistics revealed a total of 477 Negro communicants throughout the Diocese. Only Atlanta and Columbus had parishes, and only three missions for colored people existed: Fort Valley, Griffin, and LaGrange. The over-all picture, they felt, was definitely "not a rosy one," and the committee made some recommendations: "First, that the work we are doing is pitifully small and should be augmented as rapidly as possible." Secondly, there was a specific suggestion that Macon "which has a large negro population and no Church work of any kind for negroes," should be the starting point for the establishment of new missions. The report pointed out that Bishop Walker intended very soon to appoint an Archdeacon for Negro work; and also that the Bi-Racial Commission of the National Church had employed "a consecrated intelligent Christian," the Rev. Bravid W. Harris, as its Field Secretary, and that Mr. Harris would soon visit Georgia to assist in planning this phase of Diocesan expansion. However, the committee warned, no amount of outside help would be able to overcome alone what was probably the most serious deterrent to such expansion—the problem of leadership. "Until we can find and train suitable negro priests and lay workers, we can never accomplish anything very much . . . nationally as well as here in the Diocese." Such training would take time, and would mean a delay; but it would be a "penalty for the neglect of the years we have wasted when we should have been developing the necessary manpower to do this important job."

The report of this committee concluded with these remarks: "We know that the Church has a great deal to offer the negro, and the negro a great deal to give the Church. Without the Church he will ultimately become Roman Catholic, as many of them are doing already, or content himself with Churches which in many cases are close to Voodooism. If there is a solution to the negro problem . . . that solution lies largely in the genius of the Episcopal Church. Our historical position, the beauty of our liturgy and the forward looking liberal attitude of our leadership all give the Church a real opportunity of appealing to and providing for the needs of our negro population."

One "real opportunity" for extending Church work among Negroes existed in Macon. In 1947 this situation was explored by the Rev. J. Henry Brown, minister-in-charge of the Fort Valley College Center. Mr. Brown met with a number of Negro communicants in Macon and became convinced that a mission organized there with the known communicants as a nucleus would quickly attract others desiring to become Episcopalians. Within a year, afternoon services were being conducted twice monthly by Mr. Brown at Christ Church. On May 8, 1950, St. Matthew's Mission was legally incorporated in Bibb County, and a campaign was launched to secure funds for a church building. Although Mr. Brown died suddenly in 1951, lay readers of St. Matthew's and local clergymen in Macon continued to improve the mission's membership, finances, and facilities. Within a few months the Rev. Hugie Walker of Griffin had been named minister-in-charge, and he began commuting to St. Matthew's.

At the 1946 Council meeting at St. Paul's in Macon, the delegates took up a matter which had been "hanging fire" in the National Church for a decade. In 1937 the General Convention had invited the Presbyterian Church in the United States of America to join in a "declaration of purpose to reach organic unity." Both churches had ratified this measure; but, nothing further had been accomplished since then. The 1946 Council of the Diocese of Atlanta passed a resolution stating its "firm conviction" that the next General Convention "should take some definite step toward the goal of organic unity with the Presbyterian Church." The resolution further asked the Bishop to appoint a Diocesan committee of six, "three Presbyters and three laymen" to serve as a local group to study proposals for union and to coordinate with the National Church's Commission on Approaches to Unity. Upon passage of the resolution,

Bishop Walker appointed the following Committee on Approaches to Unity: the Rev. Messrs. Raymond E. Fuessle, Joseph T. Walker, J. Milton Richardson, and Messrs. Edwin Sterne, William C. Turpin, Jr., and Dr. H. E. Finley. Although this committee was listed in the Diocesan *Journal* for 1947, the group gave no report to the Council at that meeting, and by the following year there was no mention in the *Journal* of the Committee on Approaches to Unity.

John Moore Walker assumed the helm of his Diocese during a critical wartime period when manpower was short, money was being drained off for national uses, and hearts were heavy with war's inevitable tragedies. It is to the credit of Bishop Walker that he brought his Church into a postwar era which, by the late 1950's, would see the Diocese of Atlanta come of age in an era of unprecedented expansion.

A simple comparison of statistics reveals the growth of the Church during his decade of leadership. The Diocesan records for 1946 (representing data for 1945) show the situation at the end of World War II. Figures for 1951 indicate the remarkable increases up to the time of the Bishop's death:

		1946		*1951*
Baptized persons		11,984		16,587
Confirmed persons		9,615		12,469
Church Schools		27		34
Officers and teachers	358		516	
Pupils	2,629		3,889	
Members of Bible classes	222		781	
GRAND TOTAL IN CHURCH SCHOOLS:		3,209		5,186
Parishes	21		21	
Aided parishes	4		5	
Organized missions	15		21	
Unorganized missions	1		—	
GRAND TOTAL PARISHES & MISSIONS:		41		47

FINANCIAL STATISTICS

	1946	1951
Receipts	$ 355,720.71	$ 615,745.69
Receipts from organizations	16,608.51	26,835.86
Current expenses	168,126.86	275,293.47
Property values	2,078,309.00	3,485,476.65*

Insurance	1,247,100.00	2,227,444.00
Indebtedness	36,911.09	129,751.70
Parochial endowments	101,389.76	176,767.49†
Diocesan invested funds	166,266.51	212,605.43

*—Not including values of Bishop's house, Appleton Church Home, and Camp Mikell.

†—Includes parochial invested funds.

As these impressive figures indicate, the five post-war years saw a large over-all increase in the number of baptized and confirmed persons in the Diocese, as well as a tremendous growth of interest in Church School activities. Although the total number of parishes did not change (21), two of them were new by 1951: St. John's, College Park, which had been elevated from the status of aided parish; and Good Shepherd, Covington, which had not been listed in 1946. (The two churches no longer named among regular parishes were Holy Comforter, Atlanta, which had become an aided parish; and St. Christopher's, Columbus, by 1951 an organized mission.) One former organized mission had become an aided parish; this was St. Matthias' in Toccoa.

Good Shepherd's sudden growth in Covington was one of the most phenomenal in the entire history of the Church in Georgia. On April 23, 1950, a small group of Episcopalians (less than a dozen) met in Covington at the invitation of Mrs. R. A. Tribble, celebrated Holy Communion (administered by the Rev. Roy Pettway of Our Saviour in Atlanta), and then discussed the community's need for an Episcopal Church. A petition to the Diocese for organized mission status was enthusiastically and unanimously signed that night; and plans were made for immediate continuation of Episcopal services in Covington. Father Pettway came on alternate Sundays. In between, services were conducted by Lay Readers, notably Mr. Ned Freeman of Conyers, who read Lessons from his Braille Bible and led prayers from memory.

Two months later (June 11), Dean Raimundo de Ovies conducted services in the old Phi Gamma Hall on the Emory-at-Oxford campus for the newly named Church of the Good Shepherd. Mr. Dewey Gable, a Seminary student, lived in Covington during the Summer of 1950 and conducted services. In the Fall, the Rev. L. F. Blackwelder of Griffin came out of retirement to take temporary charge of Good Shepherd. The generosity of a vestryman, Mr. L. J. Moore, brought Mr. Gable back for the following summer. The inspiration of Mr. Moore's beneficence brought like demonstrations from the growing congregation, and construction was begun on a Church building in Covington. Then these Episcopalians petitioned the Diocese for recognition as a parish! Upon assurance from Mr. Moore that he would personally guarantee all parochial expenses until Good Shepherd could become self-sustaining, the Diocesan Council in May, 1951, admitted this remarkable new church to full standing as a parish.

Two other elevations in status came for two formerly unorganized missions, All Saints' at Warner Robins, and Mediator, Washington, both of which became organized missions. The other new organized missions were St. Martin-in-the-Fields, Atlanta; Calvary, Cornelia; St. Andrew's, Hartwell; St. Matthew's, Macon; and St. Michael and All Angels, Stone Mountain.

The organized mission of All Saints' at Warner Robins was originally founded just after World War II. A small group of Episcopalians secured the assistance of a nearby Presbyterian Church, which provided its building for Episcopal services. The rector of St. Andrew's in Fort Valley was the first priest-in-charge of All Saints'. After a succession of priests-in-charge, the Rev. Gerhard D. Linz was named in June, 1956, as the mission's first full-time vicar.

On September 29, 1950, some two dozen communicants of the Stone Mountain area assembled at the Woman's Club there for a Communion service conducted by the Rev. Harry Tisdale of Holy Trinity, Decatur, assisted by Mr. Austin Ford, then a student in Seminary. The day was the Feast of St. Michael and All Angels, and therefore the group chose that name for their mission designation. Various Lay Readers and visiting ministers conducted services in Stone Mountain until Sepember of 1952, when the Rev. Edward S. Aldworth, a retired army chaplain, was named priest-in-charge; and on Thanksgiving Day of 1953

Col. Aldworth moved his congregation into their new Church building at the corner of Memorial Drive and Park Circle in Stone Mountain.

In addressing the Diocesan Council in May, 1951, Bishop Walker, after challenging the delegates to set their sights on various long-range purposes, made specific recommendations for immediate goals. Among these were: (1) that every aided parish and mission in the Diocese strive for full self-support; (2) that each parish, aided parish and mission in the Diocese make an earnest effort to accept and pay its full Church Program Fund quota each year; and (3) "Without reservation, I endorse the plan embodied in the formation of the Diocesan Foundation, Inc., which has just been authorized by this Council. This will be a permanent institution whose function it will be to acquire funds from interested and willing donors. It will be administered by a Board of Trustees. To the extent that funds are made available, enterprises having to do with the greater usefulness of the Episcopal Church in the Diocese of Atlanta will be financed."

Bishop Walker concluded his address with these stirring words, "When the program here outlined becomes actual, our generation of the Church in this Diocese will have gone a long way in fulfilling its obligations. I solemnly call upon each individual communicant that he seek first the Kingdom of God with faith, with hard work, and with unselfish co-operation. Then in the providence of God and with His blessing, the Diocese of Atlanta will have in some measure cultivated that small portion of the Lord's vineyard which has been committed unto it."

Bishop Walker died on July 16, 1951, leaving the Diocese of Atlanta without a Bishop for the third time in its history. Once again the Standing Committee of the Diocese moved into the breach to help maintain the administrative detail so necessary in the Church organization. The Committee notified the Diocese that a special meeting of the Diocesan Council would take place at Trinity Church in Columbus on October 9 of that year for the purpose of electing a successor to Bishop Walker; and it invited Bishop Edwin A. Penick of the Diocese of North Carolina to preside at the Council.

The most important order of business at the Council meeting was the election of a new Bishop. Three prominent clergymen were nominated: the Very Rev. John Buckman Walthour, Dean of the Cathedral of St. Philip in Atlanta; the Rev. J. Milton Richardson, Rector of St. Luke's Church, Atlanta; and the Very Rev. Frederick John Warnecke, Dean of Trinity Cathedral, Newark, New Jersey. Voting proceded by orders, with each clergyman entitled to one vote, each parish one vote, each aided parish 2/3 of a vote, and each mission 1/3 of a vote. It was announced that "there must be a concurrent majority" to be elected, with not less than nineteen clerical and seventeen lay votes, the latter from the parishes, aided parishes, and missions.

The first two ballots were as follows:

	1st		2nd	
	Clergy	Lay	Clergy	Lay
Mr. Richardson	13	9 2/3	12	9 2/3
Dean Walthour	10	9 1/3	11	10 1/3
Dean Warnecke	13	12 2/3	13	12

Through four additional ballots these tallies did not change more than one or two votes. Then a lay delegate to the Council, Mr. Rutherford Ellis, moved that additional speeches be allowed. This proposal was adopted, whereupon Mr. Ellis spoke for Dean Warnecke, Mr. William A. McClain for Dean Walthour, and Mr. Edgar A. Neely, Jr., for the Rev. Mr. Richardson. The result of the seventh ballot showed exactly the same votes for the three candidates except that a one-third lay ballot shifted from Dean Walthour to Dean Warnecke. After an eighth ballot produced no single majority, Bishop Penick led the Council in prayer.

The fourteenth ballot occurred about 9:00 p.m. and showed no majority. At this time lay delegate Horace E. Weems proposed that if the next ballot had the same result, the Council should recess so that the members could "convene in two conferences one for the Clergy and the other for the Lay members to last for 30 minutes to consider the situation and if possible to find a way to its solution." The motion carried, the fifteenth ballot was as unproductive as its predecessors, and the two conferences were duly held.

Out of the group meetings there came a parliamentary solution to the apparent impasse. By motion after the recess, the Council became a meeting of the Committee of the Whole, with Bishop Penick serving as Chairman. Then another successful motion provided that "a secret ballot be taken as individuals upon the two men who had been nominated from Atlanta to determine their choice for Bishop of these two from within the Diocese and that then another ballot be taken between the choice of the conference and the outside nominee." The upshot of the Committee of the Whole was that the members chose Dean Walthour over Mr. Richardson by a vote of 83 to 40, and Dean Walthour over Dean Warnecke by 69 to 52. Thereupon the meeting reverted to its regular status, Mr. Richardson withdrew his name, and the sixteenth balloting showed Dean Walthour with majorities of three in the Clergy and two and one-third in the other column. By motion of Mr. Richardson, the election of the Very Rev. John Buckman Walthour as the fourth Bishop of Atlanta was declared unanimous.

The minutes of this special Council meeting contain a small but significant statement following the record of Dean Walthour's nomination for the Episcopate: "Health certificates were presented to Council signed by his doctors certifying to Dean Walthour's health." Less than a year after his consecration (January 9, 1952), Bishop Walthour was taken from a promising and auspicious work; he died on October 29, 1952, at the age of forty-eight.

Bishop Walthour's remarks to the forty-fifth Annual Council at Christ Church in Macon reflect his positive approach to the challenge which lay before him, and suggest the promise of his new work which was to be so suddenly cut off. After reminding the delegates of the greatness of Bishop Walker's achievements, the new Bishop stated that while he knew that he could not take his predecessor's place, he hoped "to make some place of my own in your hearts." He would wear the Bishop's pectoral cross "as a sign that I take up the burdens and the cares" which the former Bishops of the Diocese of Atlanta had laid down. "So long as God shall give me the strength to fulfill the duties of this office, I shall endeavor to follow in the footsteps of those men. . . ."

Then the new Prelate described his travels about the Diocese and cited in plainspoken language some conclusions derived from these visits. His "gravest concern" which seemed to call loudest for immediate attention was for "the work of the Church in the smaller cities and towns of the Diocese." Many of these places had no resident Episcopal clergyman, some had infrequent visits from a minister, while in others the Church was not even known. For too long, Bishop Walthour charged, "we have permitted many of our own communicants, as well as our Christian brethren, to think of this branch of the Holy Catholic Church as an exclusive club or as a post-graduate Church. We have permitted other people to think you had to be voted into membership in the Episcopal Church." Continuing in this vein, the Bishop repeated things he had been told—that his was a Church interested only in "socially acceptable folks"; that "the Episcopal Church is interested in the quality folk and not in the quantity of folk in the world." If such criticism of the Church were true, the Bishop said, "we should be no Church at all. We would be rather a society for self-admiration." In an effort to encourage his Diocese to combat this attitude and the ignorance about the Church which existed here and there, and to expand the missionary activity, Bishop Walthour issued this challenge: "The good things of the Church are given to us as trustees, and they are not truly possessed until we share them freely with all men everywhere. No man can call himself truly a Christian who is not eager to impart his faith to other men; and no man can call himself a loyal Churchman unless he is eager to help his Church share in delivering the Christian faith to all men everywhere."

Associated with this problem was another development which the Bishop had noted in his visitations, one which brought him greater comfort. "Clergy, laymen, women, the young adults of the Diocese are all awaking to the need for a revitalizing of their personal religion." This, he said, was the necessary start toward revitalizing the missionary activity. He had found many "laymen who are no longer ashamed to speak of Christ and their religion; of laywomen who are no longer ashamed to be seen going about doing good in the name of Christ." Especially pleasing was the news that young people were asking to be assigned roles in the expansion of the Church, many as lay readers who could work among "thousands of people in the Diocese of Atlanta who have no real Church affiliation." On this point, Bishop Walthour urged the Council to "provide for the encouragement, stimulation, and the effective use of this newly found field on the part of our lay people."

Other developments within the Diocese seemed encouraging. St. Mark's of LaGrange had become a parish by action of the present Council. Two missions of long standing whose status had waxed and waned for many years were now so revitalized that a resident minister was being provided for in one of the towns to serve both of them; these were Mediator in Washington and Redeemer in Greensboro, to be served by the Rev. John Paul Jones who would reside in Washington. Another resident clergyman, the Rev. Donald G. Mitchell, Jr., was being placed in Dalton for St. Mark's, while St. Margaret's in Carrollton expected to have one shortly. "Full financial responsibility" for a new rectory was being assumed by Toccoa's St. Matthias' Church; a much needed parish house was being constructed by Ascension in Cartersville; and All Saints' at Warner Robins was able to utilize the services of an Episcopal clergyman on duty with the Air Force there. Bishop Walthour directed the special attention of all the delegates to the work recently performed by Trinity Church in Columbus which had "delighted the heart of the Diocesan" by arranging to support a new mission in Manchester with "a considerable amount of money for the next five years."

A particular phase of the Church's expansion in the Diocese was next discussed by Bishop Walthour. This concerned the recruitment of clergy. "My brethren, we need a native clergy." He mentioned the number of men native to the Diocese then in seminary training, as well as those who were Postulants and Candidates for Holy Orders. He announced a new plan whereby the seminarians were to be assigned to missions and parishes during summers for "a little clinical experience." In such work, "they will be given the opportunity to develop the leadership that we so desperately need." The full utilization of its own potential clergy must be supported by the Diocese if the needs of its expansion were to be met. But such support would require the spending of money. Somewhat ruefully, Bishop Walthour remarked, "I was told not to speak of money tonight, but you cannot speak of work without speaking of money." Missionaries could not be expected to labor at the same rate of pay as Atlanta yard men were receiving—yet that was happening in some places. "Excuse me for mentioning money."

The new Bishop directed the delegates specifically to certain objectives, or "opportunities" for the future. In first place, in line with his previous remarks, he asked for "expansion in those places where the Church is not represented, or is inadequately represented." Secondly, he wanted to see a "trained and full time Diocesan Director of Religious Education," whose duties were not to be restricted to children's work in Sunday Schools. The third request was for arrangements to provide for the religious needs of students in the state's institutions of higher education. Fourth, he asked the Diocese to provide "city missioners—men who are trained in the field of Christian social relations, men with clinical experience;" such men, the Bishop argued, were needed to care for the aged in institutions, for alcoholics, for criminals in prisons, and for "those who would break with criminal tendencies."

The Council moved swiftly to implement Bishop Walthour's recommendations. Upon the conclusion of his address, a committee was created to study the address and to report back to the delegates; committee members were the Rev. A. Ronald Merrix, the Rev. W. Russell Daniel, and Messrs. H. Wayne Patterson, H. M. Heckman, and John Rabbe. This group reported at 9:00 a.m. the next day. Opening with appreciative enthusiasm for Bishop Walthour's "bringing before us so forcefully . . . a direct challenge," the Committee presented five resolutions to the Council. These resolutions were unanimously adopted. Since they represent the impact of the new Bishop's program upon the Diocese's clergy and leading laymen, and because an untimely death was to prevent further direct evidence of such large-scale enthusiasm for Bishop Walthour's potential accomplishments, the resolutions are given here in their entirety:

I. RESOLVED, that the Bishop be asked to appoint a Committee on Spiritual Renewal and Advance whose task shall be, in consultation with the clergy, laymen, women and young people of the Diocese, and in co-ordination with existing committees and groups, to prepare a program of at least three years duration, looking toward the deepening of our spiritual life, the extending of our Christian witness, and growth in Church membership.

II. RESOLVED, that this Council request its Finance Committee to increase the budget in 1953 to provide adequately for a sound expansion of the Church's work in smaller cities and towns of the Diocese.

III. RESOLVED, that this Council commends the action of missions in the Diocese which have become self-supporting, and earnestly requests that other missions take steps towards the same end as quickly as possible, thus releasing funds for expansion elsewhere.

IV. RESOLVED, that this Council instruct its Department of Promotion to prepare Diocesanwide publicity, giving information of the financial needs of the Diocese, and arrange for practical aids to parishes and missions, to make this fall the most thorough and successful visitation of every family and individual, at the time of the Every Member Canvass.

V. RESOLVED, that this Council, supporting the Bishop's concern, for the provision of qualified workers on college campuses in the Diocese, request the Bishop to initiate cooperative studies in conjunction with the Diocese of Georgia, in the hope that such workers may be secured with support from both dioceses.

Shortly afterwards, Bishop Walthour appointed the Rev. A. Ronald Merrix of St. James' Parish, Macon, to be Chairman of the Committee on Spiritual Renewal and Advance, as called for in the first resolution. According to the Chairman's report at the next Council, "a week before Bishop Walthour's death, he sat for an hour in my office discussing plans for the next steps in our diocesan program of Spiritual Renewal and Advance." Previously the Bishop had taken these steps in implementing this important phase of his program: (1) since this committee would mean most if it functioned on local levels, Bishop Walthour had named every clergyman and every confirmed person in the Diocese to membership on the committee; (2) each parish and mission was given specific instructions to encourage small group meetings to consider this activity; (3) suggestions were obtained from delegates to the mid-summer conference of the Woman's Auxiliary which were mimeographed and distributed among the churches; (4) in July the Bishop met with the heads of all Diocesan departments to secure their cooperation in this work; (5) all suggestions on procedure were combined into a questions-and-answers booklet which was sent to all parishes and missions with instructions to have the material discussed by each vestry and in groups of not more than eight members each; (6) the Cathedral clergy were asked by the Bishop to compile "an outline of instruction for Confirmation" which was to be utilized over a period of three months; (7) preliminary plans were made for a series of preaching missions within the Diocese; (8) during the laymen's conference in September, the group method was again used to discuss all material then available, to summarize it so as to include further suggestions arising out of the conference, all of the material then to be distributed via the *Diocesan Record* throughout the Diocese; (9) the Bishop had specially prepared some "Prayer Cards" which he distributed to the Clergy during their mid-September Retreat, with the wish that they be used daily; and (10) other plans had been initiated for a Pre-Lenten clergy retreat.

Mr. Merrix told the Council in 1953 that Bishop Walthour intended to appoint an Advisory Committee to coordinate the Diocesan-wide activities on Spiritual Renewal and Advance, but that his death in October had prevented this further step. It seemed fitting that the Council should take some steps to continue the work which was so earnestly begun by Bishop Walthour; and therefore Mr. Merrix asked the Council to request the Standing Committee of the Diocese to create such an Advisory Council. A resolution to this effect was passed unanimously. The Standing Committee postponed action, but agreed to acquaint the new Bishop with all the details and to assist him in promoting the plan.

The Standing Committee set the date of January 13, 1953 for a Special Council to meet in Emmanuel Church, Athens, for the purpose of electing a new Bishop. For the second time in a year Bishop Edwin A. Penick of the Diocese of North Carolina was invited to serve as Chairman. The following clergymen were nominated: the Rev. James W. Kennedy, D.D.; the Rt. Rev. Louis C. Melcher, Missionary Bishop of Brazil; the Rt. Rev.

Randolph R. Claiborne, Jr., Suffragan Bishop of Alabama; the
Very Rev. Alfred Hardman, Dean of the Cathedral of St. Philip;
and the Very Rev. J. Milton Richardson, Dean of Christ Church
Cathedral, Houston, Texas. Upon announcement from the Chair
that the election must be a concurrent majority of both houses,
with at least nineteen from the clergy and seventeen from the
laity, the Council proceeded to the balloting. The first ballot
was as follows:

Bishop Claiborne	(Clergy) 8	(Laity)	10 2/3
Dean Hardman	12		5
Dean Richardson	8		5 2/3
Bishop Melcher	7		7
Dr. Kennedy	1		2 2/3

On the next two ballots, minor shifts showed a slight trend
toward Bishop Claiborne and Dean Hardman. By the fourth
ballot, however, Bishop Claiborne had captured the lay vote
with 18 2/3, and the fifth ballot was as follows:

Bishop Claiborne	21	23 1/3
Dean Hardman	14	7 2/3
Dean Richardson	0	0
Bishop Melcher	1	1 1/3
Dr. Kennedy	0	1/3

Bishop Claiborne was named the choice of the Council, and the
Rev. Harry Tisdale of Holy Trinity, Decatur, moved that the
delegates pledge their support and loyalty to their new Bishop if
he should wish to accept the election. The motion carried by an
enthusiastic standing vote.

Randolph Royall Claiborne, Jr., had been consecrated Suffragan Bishop of Alabama on June 29, 1949. Following acceptance of the election, and installation as the Fifth Bishop of
Atlanta on May 5, 1953, Bishop Claiborne moved into his
new duties with perhaps greater ease than any of his predecessors. The smoothness of his transition resulted primarily from
these factors: He was familiar with the area of the Diocese, and
very well conversant with its ecclesiastical arrangement. He had
served in Georgia as rector of St. James', Macon, and vicar
of St. Andrews', Fort Valley; and he knew much of Episcopal

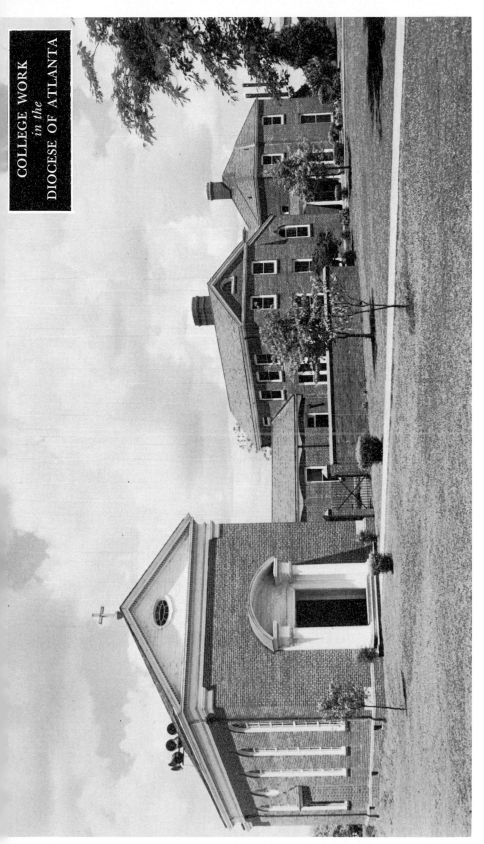

COLLEGE WORK
in the
DIOCESE OF ATLANTA

FORT VALLEY COLLEGE CENTER, Fort Valley
Organized 1940 at Fort Valley State College, Fort Valley

COLLEGE WORK
in the
DIOCESE OF ATLANTA

HODGSON HOUSE

COLLEGE WORK
in the
DIOCESE OF ATLANTA

STUDENT LOUNGE IN COLLEGE CENTER, Atlanta

The Lounge occupies entire third floor of All Saints' Parish House. This Center serves primarily the college community of the Georgia Institute of Technology and Agnes Scott College. This Center was built in 1957.

COLLEGE WORK
in the
DIOCESE OF ATLANTA

Canterbury House, Atlanta
College Community of Atlanta University, Clark College, Morehouse

responsibilities not only because he had his own experience as a Suffragan Bishop, but also because he had in his lifetime known intimately all of his predecessors in the Diocese. As he told the forty-sixth Council at Rome in 1953, "every Bishop of Atlanta has been my friend." Bishop Nelson had visited often in the Claiborne home during the Georgia ministry of Randolph Claiborne, Sr. Bishop Mikell "was an inspiration during the days of my youth" and later. Bishop Walker was the examining chaplain who certified him for ordination. And Bishop Walthour "became my friend during the year in which we both took Holy Orders." The tragic circumstances surrounding the short Episcopate of Bishop Walthour meant that Bishop Claiborne would begin his work in the immediate shadow of not one but two Bishops whose impress had been noticeable. Furthermore, the era of the 1950's, the decade when the Diocese of Atlanta would reach its Golden Anniversary, was to see a period of tremendous growth.

In his first remarks to Council, Bishop Claiborne called Bishop Walker's program for the Diocese an "invigorating" plan of action which "seemed to provide a blueprint for future development for many years." The "irrepressible enthusiasm," the "zealous ardor," and the "tireless energy" of Bishop Walthour "welded the Diocese into such a driving force of single-visioned purpose" that much of Bishop Walker's program of action seemed to be reached already. As for his own role in continuing such work, Bishop Claiborne told the Council delegates that he would emphasize two of the objectives which he felt were yet unfilled: (1) that "every aided-parish and mission in this Diocese strive for full self-support;" and (2) that "each parish, aided-parish, and mission in the Diocese make an earnest effort to accept and pay its full Church Program Fund quota each year."

On the challenge which an era of unprecedented growth would present, Bishop Claiborne expressed a complete awareness of the situation: "The growth in the Diocese of Atlanta has been phenomenal. Our National Council quota for 1953 is nearly seven times the quota ten years ago." He explained this by the large and impressive growth in numbers of communicants and in "financial expenditures for local purposes." When such quotas were raised, Bishop Claiborne saw a need both for thankful prayer and resolutions of courage.

During the first few months of his Episcopate Bishop Claiborne was greatly pressed to meet the accumulated administrative and ecclesiastical needs of the Diocese; and consequently had little time to formulate and implement his own plans. Within the year, however, the new Bishop prepared and began to initiate a comprehensive program which reflected a sagacious approach suitable to the requirements of an age of expansion. Speaking to the Annual Council of 1954 in Holy Trinity Church, Decatur, Bishop Claiborne recommended that canonical changes be made to establish a new system of convocations which would better grapple with the problems of Church expansion. He showed the delegates a map of the proposed plan; the Diocese was divided into Northern, Eastern, and Southern convocations, with the lines of division running out of central Atlanta. "Thus," he remarked, "this type of pie-shaped convocational division will make possible use of the interest, personal resources for leadership and organizational and administrative strength of one of our three largest parishes in each convocation." As his map indicated, the Northern Convocation included the Cathedral of St. Philip, and extended westward just south of Carrollton and north-eastward between Toccoa and Hartwell. The boundary between the Southern and Eastern convocations extended between St. Luke's and All Saints' in Atlanta in a south-easterly direction just east of Griffin and Macon. The Bishop suggested that a Dean of each convocation could direct its affairs properly, and that eventually the Diocese might decide to name Archdeacons for this supervision.

The Bishop's tri-convocational plan featured a regional approach, and, upon adoption by the Council, proved to be a very workable operation. The substantial expansion of churches in the Diocese of Atlanta which took place during the next few years was enhanced and in many cases initiated out of this new convocational program.

Another factor played an important role in the progress of the mid-Fifties; and this too stemmed from proposals of Bishop

Claiborne. At the 1954 Council he asked for reorganization of the Executive Board of the Diocese, with especial reference to membership and functions. The Council adopted a new canon which provided that membership on the Executive Board, in addition to the Diocesan officers and the President of the Standing Committee, include three clergymen and three laymen from each of the convocations, to be initially elected by the Council for three-year, two-year, and one-year terms and thereafter for three-year terms. In advocating this change, the Bishop told the Council that the arrangement of staggered terms and rotating memberships for elected members "would insure the discovery of new leadership that might never be found with the Bishop acting as sole nominator." Further, "if the powers of the Council are given to the Executive Board between Council meetings, it will be possible for action to be taken with real democratic backing of representative authority."

Concerning the functions of the reorganized Executive Board, Bishop Claiborne outlined the following departmental plan which was adopted:

DEPARTMENT OF FINANCE
1. Committee of the Budget
2. Diocesan Foundation
3. Trustee Funds Committeee
4. Pension Fund Committee

DEPARTMENT OF CHRISTIAN EDUCATION
1. College Division
2. Youth Division
3. Church School Division
4. Camp Mikell Board
5. Adult Division
   a. Laymen's Work
   b. Woman's Auxiliary
6. Pre-school

DEPARTMENT OF CHRISTIAN SOCIAL RELATIONS
1. Ecumenical Relations
2. Race Relations
3. Mentally Ill
4. Physically Handicapped
5. Homeless Children (Appleton Church Home)
6. Church Periodical Club

7. Supply Boxes
8. Armed Forces Committee

DEPARTMENT OF PROMOTION

1. *Diocesan Record*
2. Bishop's Advance Fund
3. Builders for Christ
4. University of the South

DEPARTMENT OF MISSIONS

The Bishop proposed that the Executive Board should meet at least quarterly, at which time written reports should be presented by departments. "Some division of some department" would handle every item of Board business. Each member of the Board could expect to be assigned to at least one department; and departments were given the privilege of "choosing additional members subject to the approval of the Executive Board."

One of the important divisions in this departmental plan is the Bishop's Advance Fund. During the first year of his jurisdiction Bishop Claiborne determined to establish a revolving loan fund which would meet urgent needs in the Diocese. To accomplish this he issued a general call in the Diocese for donations to a "Bishop's Advance Fund," and he utilized existing funds collected for Bishop Walker's Diocesan Foundation. At the beginning of his address to the Council of 1954 he expressed gratitude for "the wonderfully successful Bishop's Advance Fund Campaign."

During the next several years this fund continued to swell. Money obtained for the Advance Fund was designated personally by the Bishop to advance the dual causes of missions and youth work, but he announced that it would be administered by him on the advice of the Trustees of the Diocesan Foundation. When, for example, a mission had exhausted all commercial sources for building funds but still needed money for successful completion of its plans, it could secure a loan from the Bishop's Advance Fund; this loan was to be repaid in installments. Meanwhile, the Bishop could assist another struggling mission at a crucial moment. Thus, at a time when a new convocational system and a reorganized Executive Board would promote new and expanded missions to a greater degree than at any previous era in the history of the Diocese, a special source of money could be loaned to help needy new congregations past the point which had often proved nearly insurmountable in the past.

About one-third of the Bishop's Advance Fund during these years was utilized to implement one of the most important areas of progress under Bishop Claiborne's leadership: Youth Work. The continued development of Camp Mikell is a case in point.

In 1934 the camping program was enlarged to take care of children from the ages of eight to eighteen, and camps were scheduled for Midget Girls, Midget Boys, Junior Girls and Boys, Intermediate Girls and Boys, and Senior Girls and Boys. In 1955 the Council was informed by the Board of Governors of Camp Mikell that the previous season had been "one of the best camping years in anyone's memory." The camp use grew so rapidly, including sessions for adults, that by 1957 the Board of Governors was able to report to the Council that "900 persons were in attendance" during the year and "the financial operation was in the black." An increasing realization of the importance of Camp Mikell in the field of Christian Education led the Council of 1957 to direct the Board of Governors of Camp Mikell to make long-range plans for future development. A redevelopment program, which included new permanent buildings and a swimming pool, was therefore adopted so that objectives could be carried out in an effective manner.

In this connection, it should be noted that a camping period for Negro children of the Episcopal Church is conducted each summer at Camp John Hope, near Fort Valley, under the direction of the Rev. Odell G. Harris. This camp is the joint responsibility of the Diocese of Atlanta and the Diocese of Georgia, and the two Bishops make an annual visit to the camp.

A second important area of work in the Diocese which capitalized upon the availability of the Bishop's Advance Fund, as well as a renewed interest in this activity, was the Division of College Work. The Diocesan Council in 1954 adopted a resolution authorizing this division to "proceed with such an over-all planning as it deems necessary to provide an adequate ministry, sufficient to meet the needs of college youth," and directed that specific recommendations be presented to the

1955 Council. In compliance with this directive, the Rev. Milton L. Wood, Jr., Chairman of the Division of College Work, presented to the 1955 Council recommendations for the development of college work in five major areas:

(1) The Atlanta University Center, comprising six colleges, the program to be parish-centered with the cooperation of St. Paul's Church, Atlanta; (2) Georgia Tech, Georgia State, and Agnes Scott, with the work centered at All Saints' Church, Atlanta; (3) Emory University, to be a cooperative program on the campus of Emory, supporting the existing program of the University and using their on-campus facilities for the Canterbury group; (4) University of Georgia in Athens, to have a Student Center adjacent to the campus but with a parish-centered program with the students being drawn into the full life of Emmanuel Church: (5) the Macon area with Wesleyan and Mercer, to be continued with St. Paul's Church as its center, but with all the parishes of Macon jointly responsibile for the program.

This report further recommended that for colleges in which there were fewer Episcopalians, such as Brenau in Gainesville, Shorter in Rome, Oglethorpe in Atlanta, LaGrange in LaGrange, and State College for Women in Milledgeville, the local Churches sponsor Canterbury Club programs and the local rectors be encouraged to work with students individually in their own parishes.

Following upon these proposals, the first major college work program of the Diocese of Atlanta got underway in 1956. All Saints' Church built a new parish house in which one floor was set aside as a College Center for Georgia Tech and Agnes Scott, and the Rev. W. Robert Mill, Assistant at All Saints' Church, became the College Chaplain. Mr. Mill also supervised the Canterbury Club at Georgia State College of Business Administration, a non-dormitory college in downtown Atlanta whose commuting Episcopal students continued to be active with their respective parishes.

College work at the University of Georgia came under the direction of the Rev. Nathaniel S. Parker, Jr., Assistant at Emmanuel Church, Athens. By using the resources of the former

St. Mary's Mission in Athens and with a loan from the Bishop's Advance Fund, a house and lot on Lumpkin Street across from the campus of the University of Georgia was purchased as the Episcopal College Center. This Center became known as Hodgson House, in honor of Mr. and Mrs. E. R. Hodgson who for many years had nurtured college work at Emmanuel Church. The Diocese of Georgia, as well as the Division of College Work of the National Council, contributed to the work here as well as at All Saints', and the two parishes helped finance the work being done in their respective fields of interest.

During the same period St. Paul's Church in Atlanta was actively cooperating with the Diocesan Division of College Work, with an accelerated program for the six Negro institutions which comprised the Atlanta University Center, and plans were initiated to secure a full-time Chaplain for this work.

Since the establishment of the College Center at the Fort Valley College, an active college work program has been carried on there under the Chaplaincy of the Rev. Odell G. Harris. An organized mission, St. Luke's, comprised of the faculty and students of the College Center, contributes generously to the support of the Center as well as to the Diocesan program. In addition to this self-support, the College Center is maintained by funds received from the Diocese of Atlanta and the American Church Institute for Negroes.

Construction of new buildings and improvements in existing facilities among the various parishes and missions accompanied the progress in youth activities during this period. From 1954 through 1957 seventeen new Churches were built, twelve parish houses were constructed or improved, and fourteen rectories were erected or renovated. The versatile use of loan funds to assist this physical growth is exemplified in a report made for the year 1957:

From the Revolving Loan Fund loans have been made with the advice of the Trustees of the Diocesan Foundation for the following purposes:
    St. Bartholomew's, Atlanta—New Church
    Holy Cross, Decatur—New Church
    Zion, Talbotton—Renovation
    St. Martin's, Atlanta—New Church

House for Archdeacon of Metropolitan Atlanta
Property on which to build new Mission in Metropolitan Atlanta
Holy Innocents', Atlanta—Land
St. John's, West Point—New Church
St. Margaret's, Carrollton—Rectory
St. Jude's, Smyrna—Land
Grace-Calvary, Cornelia—Parish House

As a further source for gifts to expansion projects in the
Diocese, Bishop Claiborne in 1954 inaugurated the "Bishop's
Dollar." Every communicant in the Diocese was given an opportunity to contribute $1.00 (or more) toward this fund and
year by year the amount has grown so that substantial gifts may
be made by the Bishop toward new building projects of mission
churches, Camp Mikell, and College Centers.

In 1957, his fifth year of Diocesan leadership, Bishop Claiborne could find considerable justification for terming the 1950's
a Golden Decade in his Church's history. The comparisons below
show this growth from 1950 through 1957 during a period of
three Bishops:

	1950	1957
PERSONNEL DATA		
Baptisms (for the year)	591	868
Confirmations (year)	841	1,251
Congregations		
Baptised	14,850	24,353
Confirmed	11,800	18,136
Communicants	11,476	16,988
Church Schools		
Officers and teachers	446	1,039
Members of Bible classes	602	847
Pupils	3,442	6,983
Clergy (including Bishop)	47	67
Ordinations		
Deacons	3	5
Priests	5	2
Candidates for Holy Orders	2	11
Postulants for Holy Orders	9	17
FINANCIAL DATA (a sampling)		
Property Values (excluding Ap- pleton Church Home, Camp Mikell and Bishop's residence)	$2,891,319.25	$6,931,146.39

Insurance (fire and tornado)　1,771,449.00　　5,329,585.36
Parochial endowment and
invested funds _____　　253,199.36　　872,761.76

During the seven-year period the number of self-supporting parishes increased to twenty-six and aided parishes to nine. The five parishes which were largest in 1950 held this leadership through 1957. The table below indicates their increases:

	Communicants		Members & Staff Bible Classes & Church Schools	
	1950	1957	1950	1957
St. Luke's, Atlanta	1,710	2,071	615	775
Cathedral of St. Philip, Atlanta	1,656	3,000	573	1,615
All Saints', Atlanta	1,169	1,334	340	556
Holy Trinity, Decatur	770	1,003	543	768
Trinity, Columbus	710	986	382	474

Closely associated with all this increase of Church work in the Diocese and benefitting greatly from the new convocation system after 1953, was a steady expansion of missions and parishes, especially in Greater Atlanta. This activity was accelerated in 1955 with the appointment of the Rev. John L. Womack of Louisiana as Archdeacon for Metropolitan Atlanta.

The experience of St. Martin-in-the-Fields is typical of the urban Church growth. Episcopalians in the area which included Brookhaven, Oglethorpe, Chamblee, Doraville, and Dunwoody near Atlanta were anxious for a church of their own, and several communicants began an appeal to the Diocese which eventually resulted in the establishment of a mission. The first congregational meetings were held at Oglethorpe University in 1951, and during the same year the Oglethorpe Mission (as it was at first called) petitioned the Diocese for recognition as an organized unit. In seeking a permanent name for their Church, the communicants determined to utilize some designation which had an association with James Oglethorpe, for whom Oglethorpe University was named. When investigation revealed that Oglethorpe was baptized in London's St. Martin-in-the-Fields, that name was chosen for the new mission. On May 9, 1951, at Oglethorpe University, the first service took place. The college remained the site for services and meetings until late in 1954, when the new church building for St. Martin-in-the-Fields on Ashford-Dunwoody Road was opened with a Christmas-Eve service. The rector of Holy Trinity Church in Decatur supervised the mission until June, 1952, when the mission obtained a resident vicar, the Rev. A. L. Burgreen. The membership grew rapidly, and on January 26, 1956, with more than 500 communicants, St. Martin-in-the-Fields was granted full parish status.

A similar and somewhat more rapid advancement came for two other Atlanta area missions, St. Bartholomew's and St. Anne's. Founded by parishioners of Holy Trinity, Decatur, and Epiphany, Atlanta, in 1954, with the Rev. Harry Tisdale as priest-in-charge, St. Bartholomew's Mission in the Northeast Atlanta and North DeKalb region had its own building on LaVista Road and a resident vicar (the Rev. Austin M. Ford) within a year, and became a parish in 1957. St. Anne's Mission had operated for some time prior to 1956 ("with no Canonical connection with the Diocese and no legal status") to serve the Northwest Atlanta area. In January, 1956, St. Anne's was recognized by the Diocese as an organized mission. Shortly after Easter of that year, the Rev. E. Dudley Colhoun, Jr., of Virginia, took up his duties as resident vicar of St. Anne's; services at this time were being conducted in the Lovett School. St. Anne's grew so rapidly that in January, 1957, this very new church was admitted to parish status.

The classification of aided parish existed primarily so that the Diocese could launch a mission into preliminary parish status to test the ability of local people to support the new church without putting it completely on its own. Apparently in the 1950's most such new establishments passed this testing period; and the scheme as a whole was proved sufficiently so that its use would continue for some time.

Aided parishes during the era 1950-1957 were these:

Atlanta, Holy Comforter	Dalton, St. Mark's
Atlanta, St. Timothy's	Elberton, St. Alban's
Carrollton, St. Margaret's	Toccoa, St. Matthias'
Cartersville, Ascension	Warner Robins, All Saints'
Cedartown, St. James'	

One of the most unusual elevations in status was that which came for St. Margaret's in Carrollton. Although the mission had been founded in 1892, the congregation never had regular services on Sunday mornings until 1949, when Bishop Walker appointed Atlanta layman D. W. Durden as Lay Reader to conduct weekly morning services in Carrollton. This appointment followed a period of revitalization at St. Margaret's; by 1952 a resident priest, the Rev. Dewey Gable, Jr., was assigned to the mission. On All Saints' Day, 1953, the first services were held in a new church building. During the following year St. Margaret's was advanced to the status of aided parish.

1955 was an excellent year for the Diocese's domestic missionary efforts. In that year alone, new organized missions were launched at five locations: Decatur, Madison, Monroe, Newnan, and Trion. The new mission at Trion represented the interests of several groups of Episcopalians desiring to serve communicants and to expand the Church in that area of North Georgia including Summerville, Trion, and LaFayette. After several meetings and services in these three towns during 1954, and with the support of the rectors and Lay Readers of St. Peter's in Rome and St. Mark's in Dalton, the Mission of St. Barnabas was established at Trion early in 1955. Ground-breaking for a church building occurred on Palm Sunday, 1957.

Altogether, throughout the era 1950-1957, twenty-one churches were organized missions at one time or another:

Alpharetta-Roswell, St. David's (est. 1957)
Clarkesville-Cornelia, Grace-Calvary (separate until 1956)
Columbus, St. Christopher's (from parish status in 1954)
Decatur, Holy Cross (est. 1955)
Ft. Benning, St. Michael's (est. 1952)
Ft. Valley, College Center
Greensboro, Redeemer
Griffin, St. Stephen's
Hartwell, St. Andrew's
LaGrange, St. Elizabeth's
Macon, St. Matthew's
Madison, St. Michael-and-All-Angels' (est. 1955)
Monroe, St. Alban's (est. 1955)
Newnan, St. Paul's (est. 1955)
Smyrna, St. Jude's (est. 1956)

Stone Mountain, St. Michael-and-All-Angels' (est. 1951)
Talbotton, Zion
Thomaston, St. Thomas' (est. 1952)
Trion, St. Barnabas' (est. 1955)
Washington, Mediator
West Point, St. John's (est. 1954)

The first organized mission listed above, St. David's of Alpharetta-Roswell, represented successful fruition of probably the most recent missionary work in the Diocese. Established in September, 1956, following a few meetings the previous month, St. David's operated under the care of the Rev. Joseph T. Walker.

The last-named organized mission on this list, St. John's at West Point, represented a long-dormant station which had been revived. For thirty years after the Chapel of the Christ Church Mission in West Point was destroyed by tornado in 1920, efforts to re-establish the mission were of no avail. Then, on March 8, 1953, a little group of Episcopalians met for Evening Prayer. The service was conducted by the Rev. J. F. G. Hopper, rector of St. Mark's Parish in LaGrange. The enthusiasm generated from this small beginning resulted in recognition of the St. John's Organized Mission barely four months later by Bishop Claiborne and Diocesan mission authorities. On August 7, 1955, the Rev. Mr. Hopper conducted ground-breaking services for St. John's; and on June 17, 1956, the new church building was dedicated.

St. Paul's Mission in Newnan was another long-dormant station lately restored to vigor. Originally a mission had been established in Newnan in the late nineteenth century, but by 1914 interest had so waned that the Diocese sold the Church building. Forty years later, in February, 1954, a group of Newnan communicants under the leadership of Charles Mottola and James Hardin were able to obtain Diocesan recognition for a revived St. Paul's and the Rev. M. Dewey Gable, Jr., of St. Margaret's in Carrollton, was named priest-in-charge. Official status as an organized mission was granted to St. Paul's in 1955.

The very young St. Jude's Mission at Smyrna derived its name from the parish which helped bring it into being. Several members of St. James' in Marietta who lived in Smyrna were leaders in a movement by that church to begin the new mission in January, 1956. Because the original St. Jude was a brother of

St. James, the Smyrna Episcopalians decided to name their Church St. Jude's. The first service was held on February 5, 1956, at the Girl Scout house, with the Rev. Carl Nelson celebrating Holy Communion; seventy communicants participated. By the end of 1957 land had been secured near Belmont Hills for a Church building.

A new mission which offered services for communicants in the southern part of DeKalb County was Holy Cross, founded in 1954 by Holy Trinity in Decatur, under the active sponsorship of that parish's chapter of the Brotherhood of St. Andrew. While devoted South DeKalb Countians were fashioning an altar and kneeling rails—the latter made from lumber a century old— vestrymen John M. Royall, Glen W. Watson, Ben M. Eubanks, Robert L. Towles, Jr., Aubrey R. Morris, H. G. Almand, Jr., Arthur S. Grant, and J. K. Roberts were meeting with Holy Trinity's rector, the Rev. Harry Tisdale, to complete plans for organization of the new mission. On June 20 the first service of the Holy Cross Mission took place at the Southwest DeKalb High School. Within six months the members were meeting in a church of their own, located on McAfee Road, which had been renovated from a surplus war building obtained from the Lawson General Hospital.

Two of the Diocese's mission efforts were combined during this era. The long-time station of Calvary at Mt. Airy was transferred to Cornelia in 1950. Among most Episcopal churches in Georgia, however, the situation was one of increased productivity, continued expansion, new building projects, and greater opportunity—like, for example, St. John's in College Park and Ascension in Cartersville. On October 14, 1956, exactly fifty years from the time that Bishop Nelson originally had laid the cornerstone for a church building in College Park (which became hopelessly overcrowded by mid-century), the first service was held in St. John's new church building. Parishioners there seemed convinced that the most expansive part of their history lay ahead.

So too must have felt Episcopalians in Cartersville. Since 1954 the Church of the Ascension had remodeled the rectory for teaching use with a reorganized Sunday School, established an active Men's Club, built communicant strength promisingly, erected a new vicarage, and obtained the services of a resident vicar, the Rev. William D. Winn. In view of such progress, the Diocese elevated Ascension's status from organized mission to that of aided parish.

Hundreds of Churchmen crowded into the Hall of Bishops at the Cathedral of St. Philip on a December evening in 1957 to celebrate the Golden Anniversary of the Diocese of Atlanta. Speakers and printed program commented on the achievements of fifty years of Diocesan history and the glories of more than two centuries of the Church in Georgia. Thousands of television listeners heard the vast throng pronounce a grateful Prayer of Thanksgiving "for the blessings which have come to the people of the Diocese of Atlanta during a half century of Christian Witness lived in the framework of American freedom." Blessings were invoked "for the vision of the founders of our Church in Georgia," and "for the wisdom and courage of our leaders. . . ."

Well might these Episcopalians praise their predecessors. From the days of Dr. Bray and Bartholomew Zouberbuhler, the Church enjoyed a steady growth in Georgia through the brilliant leadership of Stephen Elliott, John Watrous Beckwith, Cleland Kinloch Nelson, Frederick Focke Reese, and Middleton Stuart Barnwell in the Diocese of Georgia; and Nelson, Henry Judah Mikell, John Moore Walker, and John Buchman Walthour in the Diocese of Atlanta. Under Albert Rhett Stuart and Randolph Royall Claiborne, Jr., Georgia's two Dioceses in 1957 enjoy a happy prospect of continued inspired leadership in an expansive era.

APPENDIX I

• ⚜ •

DIOCESE OF ATLANTA—1957-1960

THE THREE years that have elapsed between the Fiftieth Anniversary Festival Service in December of 1957 and the publication of this *History* have seen a continuation of the missionary expansion within the Diocese of Atlanta that is characteristic of the post-war years. To spur us on to ever greater efforts in this field in our next fifty years of life as a Diocese, we had the honor and pleasure of a visit from the Presiding Bishop, the Right Reverend Henry Knox Sherrill, who spoke at the dinner held during the Diocesan Council in January of 1958.

At this same Council St. Mark's Church in Dalton achieved Parish status and then called its Vicar, the Rev. Donald G. Mitchell, to become its first Rector. Also at that Council St. Mary's Church in East Point was admitted as an Organized Mission and a Mission Station was created in the neighboring Forest Park. Another Station, also, as in East Point, dedicated to St. Mary, was established at Montezuma.

At the Diocesan Council held in January of 1959 St. Timothy's Church, Atlanta, was recognized as a self-supporting Parish, St. Augustine's, Forest Park, passed from Mission Station to Organized Mission, and St. Thomas' Church in Columbus was admitted as an Organized Mission. At the 1960 Council St. Thomas' became a Parish and its first Vicar, the Rev. M. Dewey Gable, became its first Rector. One of the early actions of the Vestry of St. Thomas' Parish was to find and buy a tract of land which, it is hoped, will some day be the site of another new church building in the city of Columbus.

Two long-established Missions were admitted as Parishes at that same Council: The Church of the Ascension in Cartersville (the Rev. W. Douglas Winn, Rector), and St. Alban's Church in Elberton (the Rev. William A. Yon, Rector). In the meantime, at the 1959 Council Bishop Claiborne announced that he had transferred the location of the dormant Mission Station of St. James' Church, Tallulah Falls, to Clayton, also in Rabun County, and that he had established a Mission Station at Perry (St. Christopher-at-the-Crossroads). The Council held in the following year advanced this latter to the status of Organized Mission, and recognized St. Francis' Church in Macon as an Organized

Mission. During 1960 St. Bede's Church was organized in the Chamblee-Tucker section to serve a part of the area formerly included in St. Bartholomew's Parish, under the joint sponsorship of St. Luke's and St. Bartholomew's Churches.

An unprecedented number of new buildings has been erected in these years. Nearly every Parish and Mission in Atlanta and its environs, and a large number of those in other cities and towns in the Diocese, have found it necessary to add to the size and number of their buildings.

One such building, completed very shortly before the publication of this *History,* is the new Church of the Holy Comforter. Founded as a Mission of St. Philip's in 1893, Holy Comforter is now located in East Atlanta, where it moved when dislodged from its old site on Pulliam Street by the development of the Atlanta Expressway System.

Of the very greatest Diocesan-wide interest is the fact that at long last building has begun for the Cathedral in Atlanta. Ground was broken on Thanksgiving Day, 1959; and at this writing the great structure is being raised on the impressive site at Peachtree Road and Andrews Drive. The new building will be visible from many parts of the city, and will stand as a splendid witness to the Church and her work in the city and Diocese. The building is expected to cost nearly two million dollars. The nave will be 123 feet long and 55 feet high, and the great center tower will reach 125 feet from the floor of the nave. Subscriptions to the building have been requested only from the members of St. Philip's Parish, although various churches and individuals in the Diocese have made voluntary contributions.

The following is a list of new church buildings that have been constructed in the past three years. In 1958: Incarnation, Atlanta; Holy Innocents', Sandy Springs; St. Francis', Macon; St. Barnabas', Trion; St. David's, Roswell; in 1959: St. Alban's, Monroe; St. Matthew's, Macon; St. Thomas', Columbus; St. Michael and All Angels, Madison; in 1960: Holy Comforter, Atlanta; St. Augustine's, Forest Park; St. Paul's, Newnan; and the Cathedral, Atlanta.

Parish Houses have been built in Washington (Mediator), Decatur (Holy Trinity), Atlanta (St. Luke's and St. Anne's), Cedartown (St. James'), Gainesville (Grace), Greensboro (Redeemer), Toccoa (St. Matthias'), Cartersville (Ascension), and Sandy Springs (Holy Innocents'). Rectories have been built or purchased in Macon (St. James'), Monroe (St. Alban's), Marietta (St. James'), Elberton (St. Alban's), West Point (St. John's), Sandy Springs (Holy Innocents'), Columbus (St. Thomas'), Atlanta (Epiphany, Cathedral, St. Timothy's, St. Martin-in-the-Fields), in Atlanta a Chaplain's house near Atlanta University, and a house for the Diocesan Consultant in Christian Education.

It is apparent from an account of the activities of the Diocese since

1953 that Bishop Claiborne has opened the eyes of Churchmen to the fact that the Church's ministry to college students in these crucial days is urgent. The program of college work which he began to develop strongly when he came to Atlanta has been expanded since 1957. A full-time Chaplain for Atlanta University, the largest center for negro education in the world, was secured in 1958. The Rev. Warren H. Scott came to this new work from St. Philip's Church, New York City. A house was bought for him out of funds loaned from the Bishop's Advance Fund. This house was used not only as the Chaplain's residence but also as a College Center in which the students could meet for discussion and pleasure. In the Spring of 1960 a property near the college campuses, containing two houses, was bought as a more adequate College Center. This purchase was made possible by a gift from an interested layman and a further loan from the Bishop's Advance Fund. The buildings, at 791 Fair Street, S. W., were completely renovated and contain a Chapel, lounge, kitchen, and recreation rooms.

At the present time the Diocesan Division of College Work is trying to carry out the directive of the 1960 Council which was to "make every effort to assure the placement of a Chaplain" for full-time work on the campus of Emory University, with responsibility for work at Georgia State College. In the meantime, the work at Emory is the responsibility of the Rev. William H. Littleton of St. Luke's Church, and that at Georgia State College is being carried on by the Rev. James L. Johnson. When full-time work begins at Emory, the five year program of the Division of College Work presented to the Diocesan Council in 1955 will have been carried out.

In the Fall of 1961 an important effort of the Episcopal Church in secular education will be accomplished. This will be the completion of the expansion program of Lovett Episcopal Day School to include in its curriculum all four high school grades. Lovett School is the only accredited day school operating under the auspices of the Church in this Diocese. It has a student body of approximately 1,100 pupils, divided equally between primary and high school grades.

In 1926 Mrs. William C. Lovett founded the school, and under her guidance it progressed and expanded. In 1954, when the school included all grades from kindergarten through the seventh grade, the Cathedral (which had by then begun a parish school of its own) was asked to assume the operation of Lovett. Under the new ownership a Board of Trustees was elected, made up of seven members of the Cathedral Parish, seven from other Episcopal Churches, and seven who are not members of the Episcopal Church. The Dean of the Cathedral is the Chairman of the Board.

An eighty-three acre tract of land on the Chattahoochee River has been bought and the first units of the new buildings will be in use by the time this book is published. The whole project will cost about

$1,800,000.00. At the present time the School is filled and has a large waiting list of persons who wish to enroll their children. The Headmaster is Dr. Vernon B. Kellett.

During the past three years a swimming pool and five new dormitory cabins have been built at Camp Mikell. The pool cost about $20,000. $10,000 was contributed by the Churchwomen of the Diocese; a smaller amount was contributed by the Churchmen's organization. In the Spring of 1960 a deep well was dug at the Camp, and a 10,000 gallon water tank was installed. So has been solved the old and vexing problem of an adequate water supply.

St. Luke's Church, Atlanta, made a gift to pay for one of the new cabins, and individuals have contributed generously to the redevelopment program of the Camp. To date, the total cost of the new developments at Camp Mikell has been $97,395.62. The Camp becomes increasingly popular with each new year and most of the Summer conferences have waiting lists.

The final development of the Diocesan Christian Education program of these past few years has been the securing of a Diocesan Consultant in Christian Education. The Rev. Dr. E. Eager Wood came to Atlanta in the Summer of 1960. His office is at the Cathedral. It is expected that he will develop ways to improve the standards and practice of religious education in the Diocese, and no doubt his services will be especially valued by Missions and Parishes too small to employ their own Directors of Religious Education.

As can be seen from the above, the energies and resources of the Diocese in recent years have been largely taken up by building programs and by developing some long-neglected opportunities in Christian Education. Advance in other ways has not been entirely wanting, however. Most significantly, the Diocese has moved to meet the increasing need for the Church's ministry in the city of Atlanta, which now has a metropolitan population of more than one million people; this naturally presents many demands and many opportunities to the Church.

In 1958 the Rev. Stephen W. Ackerman became the Church's full-time Chaplain to Atlanta institutions. With a special responsibility for Church people, he visits such public facilities as jails, prisons, detention homes, work farms, and hospitals. He also ministers to Episcopalians in private hospitals who have come to Atlanta from some other city, and he is frequently asked by local rectors to visit and assist persons who are members of their Churches. Once each week he Celebrates the Holy Communion in the Goddard Chapel at Grady Memorial Hospital. On Sundays he officiates at a service at Fort McPherson, where he is Chaplain to the Episcopal community; and later in the day he conducts a service at the Georgia Training School for Girls.

At the Fifty-third Annual Council of the Diocese, meeting in All

Saints' Church, Atlanta, in January, 1960, Bishop Claiborne expressed the gratitude of all Churchmen for God's blessings upon our work in this decade. He noted that in the past ten years the Church Program Budget has increased by three and a half times to $219,235.35; the number of clergy has gone from thirty-four to fifty-four; and while the population of that part of the State which falls within the Diocese has increased eighteen per cent, the number of Communicants has increased sixty-five per cent. Our total membership now numbers 27,202. These statistics make it obvious that the Church is moving forward in the Diocese of Atlanta both in Evangelism and in gaining the increased financial support of its members.

The many crises that the Diocese has seen in the past ten years could have led to opposite results. But under Bishop Claiborne's bold and efficient leadership the Church has gone forward, witnessing to her Lord, maintaining in a materialistic and frightened world the power of faith, of reason, and of love.

AUSTIN FORD
for the Anniversary Book Committee

BISHOPS OF THE DIOCESE OF ATLANTA

Cleland Kinloch Nelson	1907-1917
Henry Judah Mikell	1917-1942
John Moore Walker	1942-1951
John Buckman Walthour	1952
Randolph Royall Claiborne Jr.	1953-

CHANCELLORS OF THE DIOCESE OF ATLANTA

Robert C. Alston	1907-1933
Edgar E. Pomeroy	1934-1946
William C. Turpin	1947-
Deputy Chancellor: Edwin L. Sterne	1955-

PRESIDENTS OF THE WOMAN'S AUXILIARY OF THE DIOCESE OF ATLANTA

Mrs. Nellie Peters Black	1907-1910
Mrs. Emma LeConte Furman	1910-1913
Mrs. C. L. Pettigrew	1914-1919
Mrs. Ulric Atkinson	1920-1922
Miss Lucinda Snooks	1922-1926
Mrs. Henry Davis	1926-1929
Miss Theodosia Tinsley	1929-1931
Mrs. A. H. Sterne	1932-1934
Mrs. T. L. Ross (Mrs. Marshall Ellis)	1935-1936

Miss Mary E. King 1937-1939
Mrs. John F. Heard 1940-1943
Mrs. Alvin E. Foster 1943-1946
Mrs. Lloyd McEachern 1946-1949
Mrs. Irwin T. Hyatt 1949-1952
Mrs. Lester N. Quattlebaum 1952-1955
Mrs. William C. New 1955-1958
Mrs. Seaton G. Bailey* 1958-

*On May 13, 1959, the name of the Woman's Auxiliary was changed to that of "Episcopal Churchwomen."

APPENDIX II

• ✵ •

DIOCESE OF GEORGIA—1957-1960

D URING the period 1957-1960, under the capable and indefatigable leadership of the Diocesan, Albert Rhett Stuart, the Diocese of Georgia continued its steady growth. In total church membership its increase was not significant, but in other categories the growth was much more evident. In the year 1959 there were 786 confirmations and persons received—the largest number of any year during the history of the Diocese.

The physical properties of the parishes and missions continued to be developed and augmented. At the 1960 Diocesan Convention, Bishop Stuart announced that during the previous year there had been constructed, purchased or received by donation, two church buildings, three rectories, four vicarages, four parish houses and three sites for new missions.

The admission to parish status of St. John's Church, Moultrie, in 1958 was offset by the reversion of one of two Negro churches in the Diocese—St. Athanasius—to mission status, so that the number of parishes in the Diocese remained at 21. In the same year, however, three new organized missions were admitted to the convention: Church of the Holy Spirit, Dawson; All Saints' Church, Savannah Beach; and Church of the Holy Cross, Thomson. In 1959 St. George's Church, Windsor Forest, Savannah, was recognized as an organized mission, as was St. Augustine's, Augusta, in 1960. The number of organized missions, thus, increased from 34 at the beginning of 1958 to 38 at the time of the 1960 Diocesan Convention.

During this period there was a large turn-over in the clergy ranks. In the years 1958 and 1959 14 clergy were lost to the Diocese by transfer and death, while only ten new clergy were being added—resulting in a net reduction in the total active clergy to 45 at the beginning of 1960.

The outstanding physical accomplishment during this period was the construction of a new Camp and Conference Center on a 140-acre tract at Honey Creek, Camden County, replacing old Camp Reese on St. Simon's Island. Old Camp Reese opened its doors in 1932 and

301

closed them in 1954, at which time the buildings were becoming out-moded and the original privacy of the Camp was being lost as a result of continued residential construction adjoining the Camp. The plans for the new Center had been approved in principal at the first session of the 136th Annual Convention held in May, 1958, at St. Mark's Church, Brunswick, and Christ Church, Frederica. A special session of the Convention was held at St. Paul's Church, Augusta, in December, for the purpose of determining ways and means of raising the necessary funds. Of the $235,000 estimated cost to complete the first phase of the Center, it was resolved by the Convention, after considerable dis-cussion, to raise $150,000 of such sum from the parishes and missions by, in effect, doubling the assessment of each for a period of five years. The 1959 Convention authorized an additional year in which to pay the required assessment. The Center, consisting of modern-designed buildings constructed primarily of glass and concrete block, was com-pleted in early 1960 and dedicated at an impressive ceremony on April 30th. A beautiful new chapel with glass reredos overlooking the marsh was dedicated on the same date to the memory of Bishop Barnwell, who had died in May, 1957. The summer of 1960 witnessed a full schedule of camps and conferences for the first time in many years. During the period ending with the closing of old Camp Reese, youth conferences of limited duration had been held at Kolomoki State Park and Abraham Baldwin College.

Another significant achievement during this period was the adoption of a new constitution and canons. Pursuant to action taken at the 1957 Convention a committee had been appointed to undertake the task of "bringing up to date," editing and clarifying the existing con-stitution and canons. Their proposals were submitted to the Conven-tion of 1959 at the Church of the Good Shepherd, Augusta. They were adopted with minor changes at the 1960 Convention at St. Paul's Church, Albany. An attempt to institute proportionate representation, with several plans having been submitted, failed. A proposal to lay to rest the accepted construction of the word "laymen" as excluding women, with reference to qualifications for delegates to the Conven-tion, was effected by providing that such delegates must be "male communicants." This proposal was adopted after a lengthy and spir-ited discussion.

An interesting development in the Diocese was the opening of a Diocesan Book Store for the sale of religious books and medals, altar supplies and Sunday School material. This innovation had its begin-ning at the Church of the Good Shepherd in Augusta in 1956 as a Parish Book Store. The 1960 Convention acted to accept ownership of the enterprise as a Diocesan undertaking, subject to working out satisfactory arrangements with the Vestry of the Church of the Good Shepherd.

The small increase in church membership during this period has been alluded to above. After experiencing a steady enlargement in the Diocesan rolls for several years, the membership dipped from 14,948 in 1957 to 14,597 in 1958. However, in 1959 the upward trend was resumed with the total reaching 15,388. A possible explanation for this drop was the adoption of a new formula for determining assessments and quotas at the 1958 Convention. Heretofore the formula had been based solely on the amount of money expended by each parish and mission for its own operation. The 1958 formula added as a new factor the communicant strength of each parish and mission. This action undoubtedly resulted in a more realistic counting of the number of communicants in some of the parishes and missions where finances remained a problem, since a reduction in the number of communicants reported had the effect of reducing the amount of a parish's quota and assessment.

Another noteworthy development in 1958 was the reorganization of the diocesan monthly newspaper, "The Church in Georgia." Beginning in September, 1958, the paper was published with a new format and style and with greater coverage than in the past. The paper was sent to each church family in the Diocese.

Other significant events occurring during this period were the creation in 1959 of a Department of Evangelism in the Executive Council; the success of a Diocesan-wide Advent Bible study program under the leadership of the Bishop; and the announcement that the Order of St. Helena would open a branch house in Augusta, perhaps in 1961, on land donated by an Augusta layman.

In his addresses to the various conventions during these years, Bishop Stuart continued to be concerned about the lack of understanding of stewardship in the Church, the small number of vocations to the priesthood and the various problems and challenges presented to the Church and its members by the segregation issues of the day. At the 1960 Convention, Bishop Stuart noted that missionary giving had fallen short of the expected goal. Because of insufficient pledges, the Executive Council had been forced to cut the budget for 1960, including a reduction of the quota asked of the Diocese by the National Council. Fortunately, the Bishop reported, this reduction was restored due to generous gifts of members of Christ Church and St. John's Church, Savannah, who responded to an emergency appeal by their clergy. Despite the yearly increases in the convention budget, the actual giving of the Diocese continued to lag. In his address, the Bishop suggested that a parish give for the mission of the church the same amount as it expended for itself. If each congregation expressed its stewardship in accordance with the injunctions of Jesus Christ, Bishop Stuart predicted that the Diocese could do away with assessments and quotas. To achieve this end, he suggested the creation of a

Department of Stewardship, which might eventually lead to a full-time Director of Stewardship.

During 1959 and 1960 a team from the General Division of Research and Field Study of the National Council conducted a survey of the Diocese and made its report to the Clergy and subsequently to lay representatives of each congregation at the Conference Center in September. Although optimistic about the future impact of the Episcopal Church in the Diocese and its continued growth, the report indicated that the Church in the Diocese had fallen short of its potential in the past. On a relative basis the progress in recent years was encouraging, but for the Church to fulfill its real mission, the report sounded the cry for increased evangelism and intelligent and effective planning for the future.

SAMUEL C. WALLER
for the Anniversary Book Committee

BISHOPS OF THE DIOCESE OF GEORGIA

Stephen Elliott 1841-1866
John Watrous Beckwith 1868-1890
Cleland Kinloch Nelson 1892-1907
Frederick Focke Reese 1908-1936
Middleton Stuart Barnwell 1936-1954
Albert Rhett Stuart 1954-

CHANCELLORS OF THE DIOCESE OF GEORGIA

Mr. C. A. Read, Atlanta (Served one year—1898)
Mr. Frank H. Miller, Augusta
Mr. William K. Miller, Augusta
Mr. W. Walter Douglas, Savannah
Mr. B. Barnwell Cubbege, Savannah (present Chancellor)

PRESIDENTS OF THE WOMAN'S AUXILIARY, DIOCESE OF GEORGIA

(Now known as the Episcopal Churchwomen of the
Diocese of Georgia)

Miss Annie C. Johnson . . . . Savannah
Mrs. Frank H. Miller . . . . Augusta
Mrs. H. C. White . . . . Athens
Mrs. Nellie Peters Black . . . . Atlanta
Mrs. Frederick F. Reese . . . . Savannah
Mrs. William H. Elliott . . . . Savannah
Mrs. J. K. McIver . . . . Savannah
Mrs. A. H. Hull . . . . Savannah

Mrs. A. C. Haskell . . . . Augusta
Mrs. W. N. Pratt . . . . Savannah
Mrs. James Davenport . . . . Americus
Mrs. F. B. Screven . . . . Savannah
Mrs. W. B. White . . . . Augusta
Mrs. J. Hunter Hopkins . . . . Brunswick
Mrs. Roy E. Breen . . . . Jesup
Mrs. Gawin Corbin . . . . Savannah
Mrs. Henry C. Cullum . . . . Augusta
Mrs. Lottie J. Crowther . . . . Thomasville
Mrs. George C. Heyward . . . . Savannah
Mrs. D. Lee Krauss . . . . Saint Simons Island

GLOSSARY

• ✤ •

AIDED PARISH—Designation of a congregation that has achieved much but not all of the goal of self-support.

ANGLICAN COMMUNION, THE—A body of independent Churches throughout the world that are daughter Churches of the Church of England.

BISHOP—A person who has been consecrated to the Episcopate. Bishops are the lineal successors of the Apostles, and a person is not judged a lawful Bishop in this Church unless he has been consecrated by the form in the Book of Common Prayer, or has been consecrated by some other form by Bishops who are themselves in Apostolic Succession. A *Bishop Coadjutor* is an assistant Bishop who at the same time has authority over some designated work within the Diocese, as, e. g., College Work. He has the right to succeed the Diocesan in office. A *Bishop Suffragan* is a Bishop who assists a Diocesan Bishop in such ways as he is directed, but who does not have the right to succeed the Diocesan in office. A *Missionary Bishop* is the Bishop of a Missionary District of the Church. He is elected by the House of Bishops. A Suffragan Bishop and a Missionary Bishop may be elected Bishop or Bishop Coadjutor in any Diocese.

BISHOPRIC—Sometimes used as a synonym for Diocese, but more usual as referring to the rank or office of a Bishop. That which is conferred upon a Diocesan Bishop. "A priest of piety and ability is the sort of man who may expect a bishopric."

CANDIDATE—A man who has completed a designated time as a Postulant and, with the approval of those who have had the charge of his training during his Postulancy, is awaiting Ordination to the Diaconate.

CANON—A priest on the staff of a Cathedral. Originally so named because such a priest held his office by right, and ruled some part of the Cathedral's work—as, e.g., The Canon Precentor who rules the music; the Canon Almoner, in charge of social service. In the American Church the title is used of assistants in a Cathedral parish who do not have tenure of office or oversight of any particular work.

CANONS—From the Latin for "rule." The laws of the Church.

CANTERBURY CLUB—The usual name adopted by groups of Episcopal students in colleges.

CATHEDRAL—From "chair" or "seat." The Bishop's Church in a Diocese. Here he has his official seat. Ancient Cathedrals do not have parishes attached to them and function as centers of worship and administration for the Diocese and city. Only three Cathedrals of this type exist in the United States—New York, Washington, and Los Angeles.

CHANCELLOR—The Diocesan lawyer. He advises the Bishop and other governing authorities upon legal and canonical matters.

CHURCH OF ENGLAND, THE—The Established Church of the English nation. The origins of Christianity in England are lost in antiquity. It has a continuous history since the third century. The See of Canterbury was founded by Augustine in 596. Declared itself independent of Papal interference in 1533, but did not break its continuity with its Catholic past. See Established Church.

CHAPTER—The Dean and Canons of a Cathedral. In the Diocese of Atlanta includes also the Cathedral parish vestry.

CLERGY—A group of clergymen.

CLERGYMAN—An ordained minister. Because of its derivation from the Latin for "priest" the term is resented by many Protestants; hence often designates an Anglican or Roman Catholic.

COMMUNICANT—A person who has been Baptized and Confirmed and maintains an active connection with some Parish or Mission.

CONSTITUTION—A document which sets forth the essential structure and fundamental beliefs of the Church.

CONVENTION—See Council.

COUNCIL—The official legislative assembly of the Diocese of Atlanta. It is composed of the Bishop and clergy, and of elected representatives from every Parish and Mission. The name "Council" is unusual, and was probably suggested by the ecumenical councils of the ancient Church. In most Dioceses it is called a Convention.

CURE—A pastoral unit under the charge of a clergyman. The rector of a parish has the "cure of souls" and consequently is the curate. The term "curate" used of an assistant to a rector is an abbreviation of "assistant-curate."

DEACON—The first of three Sacred Orders of the ministry.

DEAN—The chief administrator of the Cathedral. He functions under the Bishop. In most American cathedrals, he is also the rector of the Cathedral parish. In England the title "Provost" is used instead of "Dean" when the two functions are combined in this way, but the title is rare in America. The word "Dean" comes

from Latin for "ten"; it is so applied because a Dean was originally in charge of a chapter of ten Canons.

DIOCESE—A geographical area which is under the charge of a Bishop.

EPISCOPATE—The highest order of the Church's ministry. It is used of
Bishops in the same way that "Priesthood" is used of priests.

ESTABLISHED CHURCH—A Church (e. g., the Church of England) which
is officially the Church of a given nation. An Established
Church is expected to provide a conscience for the nation and
to exercise a ministry toward all citizens. Established Churches
are sometimes supported by public funds although the Church
of England today receives no public support.

GENERAL CONVENTION—The official governing body of the Episcopal
Church. It meets every three years. It is composed of two houses,
the Bishops and the Deputies. Deputies are lay and clerical
representatives elected from each Diocese.

GLEBE—In colonial times, and in modern England, a parcel of real
estate set aside for the use of the rector of a parish.

GUILD—As used in connection with the Church, a group of people organized to do some special kind of local work—as an Altar Guild
or a sewing guild.

HOLY ORDERS—The three orders of the ministry—the Diaconate, the
Priesthood, and the Episcopate. That which an Ordained person receives. "He was admitted to Holy Orders"; "He is a man
in Deacon's Orders."

HOUSE OF BISHOPS—Composed of all Bishops. Meets separately from the
House of Deputies in years when General Convention is not in
session. Usually issues a Pastoral Letter to be read in all parish
churches.

LAITY—From Greek for "people." Those members of the Church who
are not in Holy Orders.

LAYMAN—A member of the laity.

LAY READER—A layman who assists at a Celebration of the Holy Communion by reading the Epistle (liturgically, a "sub-deacon"),
who may read Morning Prayer; or read sermons prepared by an
Ordained person. Must be licensed by the Bishop.

MEMBER—A person who has been Baptized.

MINISTER—A person in Holy Orders.

MISSION—A congregation that is considerably supported by the Diocese
or some parish. The Bishop is the rector of a Mission. The mission clergy serve as his representatives.

NATIONAL COUNCIL—The executive arm of the General Convention.
Carries out directives of the Convention during the intervening
time that Convention is not in session. Headquarters are in New
York. The Presiding Bishop is President.

ORDINATION—The service of admission to Holy Orders. The term "Consecration" is usually used of Ordination to the Episcopate.

PARISH—A self-supporting congregation which carries out all its obligations without aid from the Diocese.

PARISH HOUSE—A place provided in most parishes which is used for the Church School, meetings, suppers, informal gatherings.

PERPETUAL DEACON—A Deacon who does not expect to be advanced to the Priesthood. The Perpetual Diaconate is a recent revival in the American Church, but was usual in the early centuries of Christianity.

POSTULANT—A man who has been accepted by the Bishop for preparation for the ministry.

PRESIDING BISHOP—Elected by the House of Bishops from among its members. Holds office until death or retirement. Executive head of the National Council. Represents the Church on public occasions. Has no authority within the Dioceses.

PRIEST—The second Order of the Ministry. The office of the priest is rejected by most Protestants because of its connection with the offering of sacrifice. The fact that this Order has been retained by Churches of the Anglican Communion indicates the importance they place on the Holy Communion. There are several words used of persons occupying this Order. The word "priest" seems to be used interchangeably in the Bible and the Prayer Book with the term "Presbyter." The term "priest" may indicate the over-all work, though it refers especially to the exercise of liturgical functions—see Rubrics in Prayer Book. The word "pastor" in Anglican churches is usually reserved for a Bishop, who is chief Pastor or "Pastor Pastorum," but in his ministry to individuals and families a priest acts as a pastor and is properly referred to in this connection as a "pastor." "Preacher" is never properly used except in regard to preaching. A priest may be a good preacher, or the preacher on a certain occasion, but he should not be referred to otherwise as a "preacher." "He was the preacher at the eleven o'clock service" is right. "He is our preacher" and "The preacher came to call" are wrong. "Parson" may be used of the rector of a parish; "Minister" is a collective term and may be used of a Deacon, Priest, or Bishop. In speaking of Ordination to the Priesthood it is not accurate to say, "Ordained a Rector" or "a Clergyman," but "Ordained a Priest." See "rector"; "clergyman"; "minister."

PROVINCE—The geographical subdivisions of a national Church. The Episcopal Church is divided into eight Provinces; the Diocese of Atlanta is in the Fourth Province, usually known as the Province of Sewanee. See Synod.

RECTOR—A priest in a parish who has charge and responsibility, with tenure of office.

RECTORY—The house in which the rector of a parish lives. A vicar lives in a vicarage. A dean lives in a deanery.

SYNOD—The Convention of the Province which meets annually except in the year when General Convention meets. Has little authority in the American Church, but held to be valuable for educational, consultative, and co-operative purposes.

VESTRY—The governing board of a Parish or Mission. So named from the original custom of holding meetings in the room where the clergy vest for services.

VICAR—In America usually the minister in charge of a Mission Church. From "vicarious," meaning that he acts on behalf of the Bishop, who is rector.

VICARAGE—See Rectory.

WARDENS—The Senior and Junior Wardens, with the Rector, are the chief officials of the Vestry.

INDEX

• ❧ •

Abbreviations used: app., in appendix; m., missionary; m.c., missionary in charge; r., rector; v., vicar.

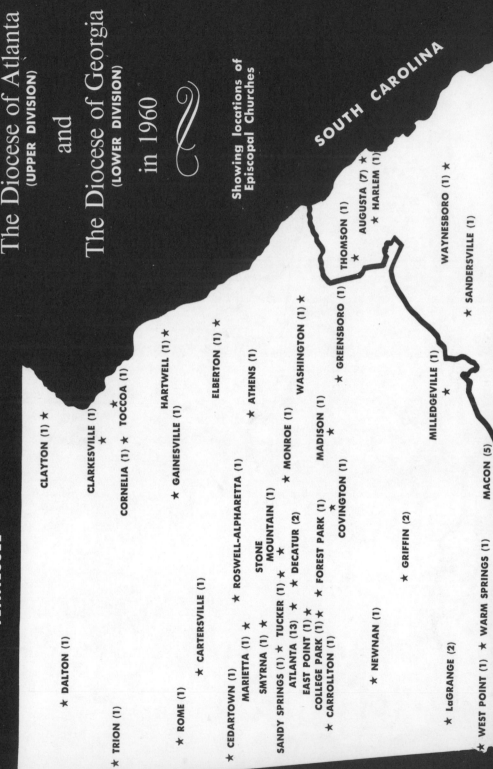

The Diocese of Atlanta
(UPPER DIVISION)
and
The Diocese of Georgia
(LOWER DIVISION)
in 1960

Showing locations of
Episcopal Churches

TENNESSEE

SOUTH CAROLINA

★ DALTON (1)

★ TRION (1)

CLAYTON (1) ★

CLARKESVILLE (1)
★

CORNELIA (1) ★ TOCCOA (1)
★

HARTWELL (1) ★

★ GAINESVILLE (1)

★ ROME (1)

★ CARTERSVILLE (1)

ELBERTON (1) ★

★ ATHENS (1)

WASHINGTON (1) ★

★ CEDARTOWN (1)

★ ROSWELL-ALPHARETTA (1)

STONE
MOUNTAIN (1)
★

★ MONROE (1)

MADISON (1)
★

★ GREENSBORO (1)

THOMSON (1)
★

AUGUSTA (7) ★

★ HARLEM (1)

WAYNESBORO (1) ★

★ SANDERSVILLE (1)

MARIETTA (1) ★

SMYRNA (1) ★

SANDY SPRINGS (1) ★ TUCKER (1) ★

ATLANTA (13) ★

EAST POINT (1) ★

COLLEGE PARK (1) ★

★ CARROLLTON (1)

★ DECATUR (2)

★ FOREST PARK (1)

COVINGTON (1)
★

★ GRIFFIN (2)

MILLEDGEVILLE (1)
★

MACON (5)
★

★ NEWNAN (1)

★ LaGRANGE (2)

★ WEST POINT (1) ★ WARM SPRINGS (1)